MW00781139

FEMALE LEADERSHIP IN THE AMERICAN JEWISH COMMUNITY

Bessie Gotsfeld and the Mizrachi Women's Organization of America

Baila Round Shargel

Studies in Judaism

University Press of America,® Inc.
Lanham · Boulder · New York · Toronto · Plymouth, UK

Copyright © 2007 by
University Press of America,® Inc.
4501 Forbes Boulevard
Suite 200
Lanham, Maryland 20706
UPA Acquisitions Department (301) 459-3366

Estover Road
Plymouth PL6 7PY
United Kingdom

Library of Congress Control Number: 2007922248
ISBN-13: 978-0-7618-3699-6 (paperback : alk. paper)
ISBN-10: 0-7618-3699-3 (paperback : alk. paper)

Studies in Judaism

TABLE OF CONTENTS

Preface and Acknowledgments

After the publication of my book, *Lost Love: the Untold Story of Henrietta Szold*, I accepted many invitations to address women's groups. One was Amit Women, which invited me to a meeting of its National Board in New York City in 1998. That occasion set a pattern for the six years of my life. Leona M. Goldfeld, scheduled to introduce me, begged my leave to discuss her aunt, Bessie Gotsfeld, the founder of Amit. As she spoke, my mood changed from irritation (at being upstaged), to interest (Why hadn't I known about this woman?), to fascination with an intriguing subject. I could hardly wait to conclude my own presentation, so that I could investigate the life of a woman whose story was as riveting, whose contributions to Jewish life as remarkable, as Szold's.

Bolstering the decision to write this biography was an extensive collection of files at the Amit National Office in New York, dating from the inception of the Mizrachi Women's Organization of America in the late 1920s to the present. The archives contain letters, memoranda, notes to members, and issues of several journals published by the organization (after 1973 known as American Mizrachi Women and since 1982 designated Amit.) Further investigation of the contents, with the aid of Naomi Abrahami, then an office assistant, yielded a treasure trove of Bessie Gotsfeld's personal letters. Marvin Leff, Amit's Executive Director, now retired, was especially helpful. He found other letters, directed their copying, and abetted my research trip to Israel in 2000.

I soon learned that the Amit Archives are actually located in two places, New York and Israel. In May and June, 2000 I examined the latter papers when Shoshana Dolgin -Be'er, the Amit historian, kept the bulk of them in her Jerusalem home. Ardie Geldman, former head of Amit in Israel, kindly offered access to files in the Jerusalem office. Recently, the Jerusalem files were transferred to the Bar Ilan University Archives. After I left Israel Ms. Dolgin-Be'er sent me others that have been placed in the collection. To forestall confusion for future researchers, I have designated all data from Israel AABI, and those in New York AANY.

During the same visit, I investigated two sets of papers in the Central Zionist Archives in Jerusalem. One was the Henrietta Szold Papers. While I was there, the librarians were beginning a new system of designating them. At their suggestion, I cite documents where I found them. Batya Leshem offered help in investigating the contents of a second CZA collection, designated Youth Aliyah. The Max and Ruth Hagler Archives at the Mosad Harav Kook in Jerusalem also housed information vital to this study. For finding data pertinent to my research I owe a debt of thanks to Daniel Rubinoff and Dina Schiff. Smaller collections pertinent to my research were found at the Jewish History Center in New York. They include the Archives of the American Jewish Historical Society and Hadassah Archives, the latter under the competent direction of Susan Woodward.

I owe a debt of gratitude to librarians and archivists at all of these institutions who guided me to the necessary papers as well as the people who agreed to be interviewed. Leona Goldfield, Joel Shiftan, Leon and Raisel Rauchwerger, and the late Eliezer Goldman were especially generous with their time and their useful information. "Bessie," a pamphlet written by Goldfeld, is a splendid outline of Bessie Gotsfeld's life and labors. Judith Iseman and Debbie Lyman, successive Amit administrators, also helped the project along. Credit is due Barbara Goldberg of Amit and Maureen Kindilien and Anthony Taylor at Manhattanville College, who facilitated the transfer of Bessie Gotsfeld's photograph to the book cover. Equally deserving of kudos is Caroline Fike, responsible for the transition from manuscript to book.

Special thanks are due Shoshanah Dolgin-Be'er, who, along with her husband Naftali Be'er, graciously hosted me in their Jerusalem home. They provided food and shelter for the body, information for the mind, and sustenance for the soul. Annette Crohn was also helpful on that score. That essential journey to Israel would not have been possible without the financial support of the Hadassah International Research Institute on Jewish Women at Brandeis University. Thanks also to Brandeis's and IRIJW's Sylvia Barack Fishman, Shulamit Reinharz, Joyce Antler, and Susan Kahn, whose devotion to Jewish women's history has become a model for all who labor in that field.

Adopting common nomenclature before 1948, Gotsfeld referred to the land where she settled as Palestine, Eretz Israel, or Erez Yirsroel. My references to the same place follow suit. In the Mizrachi vocabulary the term "Religious Zionism" was coterminous with the movement's philosophy and practice. When I follow their usage, I do not intend to imply that all Jews who cherished Jewish ethnicity and traditional Judaism were partisans of any political party or denominational group.

As usual, my family has been my mainstay. Nahum Shargel has been with me every step of the way, from conceptualization to copyediting. Our children, Dina, Raphael, and Rebecca, bore my six year obsession with Bessie Gotsfeld with light teasing and tender support.

Baila Round Shargel
Harrison, New York
October, 2006

Introduction
Female Leadership in American Zionism

American Women in Zionism

In the early 20th century women struggling for recognition as equal participants in Jewish communal life encountered serious obstacles. Because many men harbored an irrational if unconscious fear of female power, conventional standards for women called for passive submission to their husbands' wishes and demands. Woman's domain, convention stipulated, was the home, and those intrepid females who ventured into the public arena felt called upon to curtail their activities and even reduce their visibility. Jewish women concerned with public affairs were expected to sit quietly in meetings while men deliberated, and then to prepare and serve refreshments. Their other role was fundraising for projects men deemed worthwhile.

The situation, however, was fluid. Female advocates of Zionism formed new Zionist organizations independent of men. Hadassah, the large centrist group, was first. Founded in 1912, it supported health care and social services, mostly for and children, in the Yishuv (Zionist settlement in Palestine before 1948). The new ZOA was formed in 1918 from existing Zionist organizations, with the exception that all groups would disband and then reorganize on a regional basis. Hadassah, however, refused to give up the ghost and continued to pursue its own program. Labor Zionism, too, remained separate. Until 1925 the women of Poale-Zeire Zion chapters were, on paper, part of the general membership. Then they too broke away and formed Pioneer Women, an independent national organization. In the same year younger Orthodox women who belonged to auxiliaries known as *Achios Mizrachi* also opted for sovereignty and founded Mizrachi Women's Organization of America (hereafter MWOA). Like Hadassah and Pioneer Women, it was a national organization with local chapters.

In time one woman came to exemplify each group: Hadassah's Henrietta Szold, Pioneer Women's Golda Meir, and Mizrachi Women's Bessie Gotsfeld. Of the three only Szold was a native American, but by the accident of a single year; her parents migrated from Hungary to Baltimore a year before her birth. Goldie Mabowitz was eight when she arrived in Milwaukee from Russia and Beilkha Goldstein was 17 when her father brought his family from Poland to New York.

After they settled permanently in Palestine all three women sustained close ties with the American matrix, remaining organizational advocates in America after emigration. Common American values and know-how informed their conduct in

Palestine[1] but there were also conspicuous dissimilarities. Of the three Goldie was the most assimilated into the Yishuv, partly on account of the earlier age at which she emigrated. The young wife deliberately rejected America when she convinced Morris Myerson, her new husband, to depart Denver for the pioneering life in Palestine. From time to time she returned to America, first to assume an office in Pioneer Women, the women's organization that embraced Labor Zionism. She lectured all over the country in 1928-9 and 1932-4, advocating the cause of Labor Palestine in general and American Poale Zion-Zeire Zion in particular. Nevertheless, she did not found the woman's group. When Meyerson came to America in the late '20s, it was to shore up Pioneer Women, already five years old.

Back in Palestine Meyerson (Golda Meir after her husband's death) effectively abandoned the women's movement. It was left to Ada (Fishman) Maimon, sister of Rabbi Yehudah Fishman-Maimon (the latter to assume importance in the Gotsfeld story) to lead the women workers movement in Palestine. Maimon helped organize the *Moezet HaPoalot* (Working Women's Council of the Histadrut). Like Golda Meir, she served on the Central Council of Mapai, but always as a representative of the women of the Yishuv and the State of Israel. Meir, on the other hand, set her sights on greater things, first the Histadrut and then the young state.

All the American woman's Zionist movements were founded by a consortium of women, but in each case a single charismatic leader spurred them on. In the case of Pioneer Women, that woman was Sophie Udin. In 1924 Udin received a letter from Rahel Yanait (later Ben-Zvi), director of a girls' agricultural school and tree- nursery near Jerusalem who expressed deep distress there was no money to dig a cistern. Udin published the letter in *Der Tog*, a Yiddish newspaper, and asked for funds to save the nursery. Then she called together six friends, all wives of Poale Zion members to help with the project. After their efforts bore fruit, the women continued to meet, and encouraged like-minded friends to join. When the group reached thirty women, they created an organization with the objective of aiding women's *kvutzot* in Palestine. The New York group grew and became the nucleus of a national organization. The Woman's Organization for the Pioneer Women of Palestine, founded in 1924, would be known as Pioneer Women after 1939. Udin, a trained librarian, served as president in the early years, but performed her greatest service in setting up the library system in Palestine-Israel. She didn't settle there until late in life.

Henrietta Szold arrived in Palestine in 1920 as a representative of the American Zionist Medical Unit (later renamed Hadassah Medical Organization.) Szold had founded Hadassah some eight years before and set it on its feet before her departure. Many subsequent visits to America helped build up the organization, but shortly before Hadassah achieved full independence from the ZOA,[2] she withdrew from leadership. In 1927 she became a member of the *Va'ad Leumi*, the national governing body of the Jewish community in Palestine, and thereafter her life was inextricably bound to Yishuv and Jewish Agency officialdom.

Like Golda Meir, Bessie Goldstein Gotsfeld journeyed to Palestine with the intention of permanent settlement. Like Henrietta Szold and Sophie Udin, she came with a Zionist mission. Unlike the others, however, she identified totally with a women's organization. There was no separation between Bessie Gotsfeld the woman, Bessie Gotsfeld the Zionist, and Bessie Gotsfeld, "Palestine representative of Mizrachi Women of America" (hereafter MWOA), her official title. Her life's story is the story of MWOA between its inception in 1925 and her death in 1962.

The Mizrachi Organization

MWOA was an affiliate of the Mizrachi Organization, founded in 1905 when the Fifth Zionist Congress passed a resolution to educate the young in the spirit of nationalism, not religion. At this point Rabbi Isaac Jacob Reines called a Zionist Orthodox Conference. There Mizrachi was born; the name, an amalgam of two Hebrew words, *Mercaz* (center) and *Ruhani* (spiritual), also denotes the place where the spiritual center would be established, the *Mizrah* (east).

Mizrachists remained staunch Zionists, willing to cooperate with secular Jews in rebuilding the land, and embracing Hebrew as a spoken language. They insisted, however, upon separation in other cultural matters. Years before the Balfour Declaration of 1917, the factionalization of Zionism had already begun, with education the oil that fueled the engine. Mizrachi leaders understood that the best way to promote a religious perspective among the youth, thereby guaranteeing a future for their movement, was to create an autonomous school system. Whether they lived in cities, in smallholder villages or in the new *moshavot* and *kvutzot* (cooperative and collective villages), young parents had to select schools for their children. The choice of an educational track for one's children indicated allegiance to a certain philosophy of Zionism. Under the British mandate, Mizrachi's school system, like the general school system (and later, Labor's setup), operated under the direction of the *Va'ad Leumi*. In Mizrachi schools, Torah subjects took up 60% of the curriculum and secular subjects but 40%. For the general schools, the reverse was true. The smaller Labor network, formed in the 1920s, allotted only 30% of its curriculum to Jewish studies; instructors were more likely to dwell upon A.D. Gordon's "religion of labor" than traditional Judaism. When the state of Israel was declared, the secular sectors combined. Ever since, there have been two autonomous Zionist school systems (*mamlakhti* and *mamlakhti-dati*), both dependent for funds upon the central Jewish government. The Agudat Yisrael network, ultra-Orthodox and anti-Zionist, did not operate under the auspices of the Va'ad Leumi and later, the State. For political reasons however each Israeli government has contributed to its upkeep. The current ascendancy of Rabbi Ovadia Yosef's Shas party, which maintains a separate school system, demonstrates the enduring significance of education in modern Israel.[3]

In the early days of the Yishuv, secondary education for children of the Orthodox was largely confined to boys. Jerusalem, of course, boasted many *yeshivot*. In various parts of the country there were also vocational schools run along Orthodox lines. In 1909 the Mizrachi took over the Takhkemoni School, a modern high school for boys in Jaffa, possibly in response to the successful co-ed secular Herzliah High School. The language of instruction there, as in Herzliah, was Hebrew, and students learned world history, math and science. Jewish subjects were taught in a traditional rather than a critical vein. The only Mizrachi-sponsored female educational institution was a Teachers' Seminary.

To Bessie Gotsfeld, an earnest supporter of Mizrachi, it was clear that there was a great gap in the religious instructional system of the Yishuv. Why should boys and not girls, she asked, reap the benefits of a secondary education that was both traditional and modern? Since men contributed to education for Orthodox boys, why shouldn't women support secondary education for Orthodox girls?

The Literature of Leadership

How did this slight, foreign-born, and sickly woman position a woman's Orthodox organization in the American Zionist mainstream? Consultation with the literature of leadership is a useful tool in understanding Bessie Gotsfeld's role as founder of MWOA and facilitator of its work during the middle years of the twentieth century. Social psychologists have analyzed the personal traits of representative female leaders. In 1948 R.M. Stogdill summarized findings in the academic analysis of leadership. Female leaders under investigation, he noted, demonstrated intelligence, alertness, insight, responsibility, initiative, persistence, self-confidence, and sociability.[4] Nearly three decades later he added cooperativeness, tolerance, and influence.[5]

Since Stogdill's early work, researchers have added additional factors. Michener, DeLamater, and Schwartz define leadership as a process that takes place in groups in which one member influences and controls the behavior of the other members toward some common goal. They focus on the leader's ability to plan, organize and control the activities of the group.[6] Along the same lines H. Astin and C. Leland and Jay A. Conger discuss leadership in terms of empowerment and collective action.[7] To the literature of personality has been added the question of situation. Some analysts promote the contingency theory of leadership. They maintain that the emergence of a particular leader at a given time and in a given place flows at as much from the situation at hand as from the qualities of the individual.[8]

We will see how Bessie Gotsfeld's personality traits, life experience, and religious convictions together with the peculiar circumstances of the 1920s and 30s triggered the founding of MWOA and advanced its religious, ethnic, and feminist principles. We will examine the process by which her leadership empowered Orthodox women in America and helped a generation of young people become productive members of the New Yishuv even as they preserved their religious faith and practice. Finally, we will compare her leadership qualities with those of Henrietta Szold.

1

Born for Leadership

That official documents and organizational publications always referred to her as Bessie Gotsfeld was exceptional. In the early and middle years of the twentieth century, Jewish organizations took pains to comply with American custom, and a "Mrs." preceding a husband's full name was *de rigeur* in its lists, memoranda, and publications. Only never-married women, divorcées, and some widows went on record under their own given names. Mizrachi Women of America was no exception. Perusing documents of the 1920s, '30s, and 40s, I found it difficult, for example, to ascertain the first name of Mrs. Abraham Shapiro, who figured prominently in the organization's early history. To learn that it was the unusual Jrena I had to consult more recent publications that reviewed the past. The rule did not obtain for Bessie Gotsfeld. Everyone associated with Mizrachi Women recognized Mendel Gotsfeld, her supportive husband, but his wife was always designated by *her* given name, not *his*. In contacts with Hebrew-speakers in the Holy Land she went by her Hebrew name, Batya.

On the surface, there was nothing extraordinary about Bessie Goldstein Gotsfeld. In her youth she was quietly pretty, endowed with a shiny corona of red-gold hair, but no one would have called her a beauty. Her high school education, though more advanced than that of most women in her circle, was unexceptional for a Galician-born girl of her station. She was no orator; her speaking voice was pleasant rather than forceful, her delivery cogent rather than grandiloquent. Though not averse to passionate appeals, she preferred gentle persuasion to belligerent harangue. Yet, confident in her own abilities and convinced of the rightness of the cause that she espoused, she exemplified a new type of female Jewish leadership.

Childhood and Youth

Przemsyl, a mid-sized city, was one of the more favorable sites of Jewish life in the nineteenth century. Located in the Rzeszow Province of southeastern Poland, it was part of Galicia, which had been absorbed by Austria in 1772. Przemsyl was renowned for its clean streets, wide boulevards and magnificent Catholic churches. Luckily for its Jews, in the mid nineteenth century, it adopted the tolerant

outlook of Emperor Franz Joseph. As a consequence, its Jewish population grew from about 5700 in 1870 to 16,000 in 1910.[1]

Beilkha Goldstein, born in that city in October 1888, was the eldest child of Leibush Goldstein. Her father was a Galician Hasid, reputedly a follower of Rabbi Moses Friedman, a descendent of the Hasidic master Dov Baer, the Maggid of Mezhirech.[2] Leibish dwelled comfortably in several worlds. Though drawn to charismatic Hasidic leaders, he was also open to traditional Talmudic learning as well as the Hebrew renaissance and proto-Zionism.

Leibush Goldstein participated actively and successfully in the commercial life of his city. With the aid of his energetic wife Raisel, he managed two substantial enterprises, a general store and a wholesale timber business. Raisel frequently traveled to the forests with her husband in an open wagon, leaving competent servants in charge of the six children, three boys and three girls. The couple would return on Fridays, in time for her to prepare a special *cholent* (Sabbath bean-based stew). On Saturdays the large house was open to neighbors and travelers alike, all welcomed with savory dishes and learned conversation. Raisel reserved Sunday mornings for the children. Gathering them around her, she regaled them with Biblical, midrashic, and medieval tales that circulated among women.[3]

Beilkha enjoyed a blessed childhood: adoring parents and grandparents, siblings who looked up to her, school friends who admired her, good books, and the glories of nature. Each summer, paternal grandparents and a few servants would accompany the Goldstein children to a country house. Beilkha would lie on her back for hours, gazing at the gnarled oaks, the colorful leaves and flowers, the birds, and the blue sky. From immersion in nature flowed a distinct aesthetic that would govern her personal style and the conduct of her work.

The new century brought tragedy to the Goldstein family. Raisel died, apparently quite suddenly. Although Leibush would soon find a new wife, the family dynamic was unalterably changed. Without delay, twelve-year old Beilkha assumed a protective role, standing at her mother's grave, broken-hearted but dry-eyed, a small sibling's hand in each of her own. Hard upon the sheltered childhood followed full-blown adulthood. No longer a carefree pubescent girl, Beilkha found a serious friend in the person of a cousin a few years her senior. On long walks Nissen Goldstein, a keen observer of contemporary life, introduced her to new trends in the Jewish world, notably Jewish renewal and Zionism.[4]

Burgeoning intellectual curiosity accompanied fast-growing emotional maturity. To the younger children she was mother, to the widowed father, companion. By the time of Leibush's remarriage in 1900 or 1901, less than a year after Raisel's death, the bonds were indestructible. She dressed her siblings in their best clothes and marched them to the train to greet Leibush and his new wife with hugs and smiles. Nevertheless she would remain the children's second mother and her father's close confederate. Before the age of antibiotics, infections carried away so many young women that quick remarriage of men with children to care for was customary. Still, Adela Piltz Goldstein must have been a woman of tact and perseverance and a very loving stepmother. There is no record that any child resented her assumption of their mother's place. Between Adela and Beilkha especially grew an intimacy so comfortable that, after the family's transfer to America, even intimates did not one realize that affection and respect rather than biological kinship cemented their relationship.[5]

It was not uncommon for forward-thinking Orthodox Galician Jews to enroll daughters in government schools. Goldstein was happy to avail his three daughters — Beilkha, Sarah, and Zipporah— the opportunity to better themselves. Beilkha, called Berta in school, completed a secondary course of instruction in the local gymnasium. The girls read Polish writers such as Mickiewicz as well as the German classics. Science and literature were Beilkha's favorite subjects. Long after graduation, she retained the ability to read German and, even on occasion, lecture and write letters in that language.

Indicative of Beilkha's scholastic ability was her selection as valedictorian of her class, a singular honor for a Jewish girl. Blond braids cascading down a pink batiste dress, "Berta" at graduation was the picture of innocence. Outward appearance notwithstanding, the young woman, hardened by family circumstance, was already anticipating a new life.[6]

Leibush Goldstein did not attend her graduation. At the time he was in the United States, where he had repaired shortly after his second marriage. A turn-of-the-century worldwide depression had damaged his businesses and he wanted to scout out economic opportunity in America. A clothing factor, he traveled all over the United States. One spring found him in San Francisco in need of new kitchen utensils for the upcoming Passover festival. While shopping, he met another man on the same errand; the two lonely Jews decided to cook, eat and celebrate the festival together. In the course of a single week, Leibush established a warm friendship with his new companion, Shimshon Gotsfeld. The two men exchanged addresses and promised to remain in touch.

Marriage

After five years away from his family, Leibush, now called Leon, was sufficiently settled in New York to send for his wife and children. There Beilkha-Berta became Bessie. Of the six siblings, only two, Samuel and Sarah, retained their original designations, acceptable in a country that still valued Biblical references. The other four acquired names common in America at the time: Bessie, Tillie, Irving, and Max.

The family had been in America only three months when a visitor appeared at the Goldstein home on the Lower East Side. He identified himself as Mendel Gotsfeld, son of the man with whom Leon had shared his California Passover. Mendel explained that his father had sent him to Hungary for religious instruction and thence to New York. Like so many European Jewish families, the Gotsfelds had moved from place to place, though their travels ranged over an exceptionally wide span. Born in Romania (probably Transylvania), Shimshon Gotsfeld had married in Palestine and settled in Petah Tikvah in the early 1880s. Most East European Jews who tried to reclaim the Jewish homeland during the First Aliyah encountered such unfavorable conditions that they had to depart. The Gotsfelds were no exception; they soon left Palestine, stopping in Cairo long enough for the wife to give birth to Mendel. The family, which also included a daughter, set off for Australia. Settled in Melbourne, Shimshon became a clothing factor, frequently traveling to India and California. Even while traveling, he managed to retain religious punctiliousness. He considered the *kashrut* supervision in Melbourne inadequate and wouldn't eat the meat of animals slaughtered there; consequently the family dined on vegetables and fish. When he and Leon had celebrated Passover in San Francisco together, his ability to prepare savory though meatless Seder meals had impressed his new friend. [7]

Mendel, equally staunch in religious practice, also mastered the art of meatless cookery. Another talent was his linguistic ability. Education in an English-speaking country had bequeathed a deep appreciation of the King's English, a love of theatre in general and Shakespeare in particular, and a talent for dramatic reading. Leon welcomed Mendel into his home and may have asked him to teach English to his immigrant brood. Mendel befriended all the Goldstein children but fell in love with the eldest. Bessie spent so much time with Mendel that she soon spoke American English with a hint of the Australian. As Bessie lost her European accent, Mendel gained her heart. They married in 1909.

Their marriage of nearly forty years was exemplary; a nephew called it a lifelong love affair. It was saddened yet somehow strengthened by Bessie's childlessness; early on, a tubal pregnancy destroyed her reproductive capacity. Still, there would be many children in their lives, in Seattle, Brooklyn, and Palestine.[8]

Seattle

In 1911 Mendel and Bessie moved to Seattle and opened a retail clothing store. Bessie, manager of the office, acquired business skills, the technique of buying in particular, that would later prove invaluable. In the western city the Gotsfelds found a dynamic Sephardic Jewish community, continually revitalized by Russian Jewish émigrés escaping Tsarist oppression. Bessie did whatever she could to help all the immigrants, but was especially drawn to the Russian Zionists. Conversations with them revived cherished memories of discussions with her cousin Nissen back in Przemsyl.

Seattle's Orthodox community was small and close-knit. Bessie, always drawn to children, helped her friends care for them in time of need. When four year old Sam Genauer took ill, Bessie freed his mother to care for her other little ones by sitting at the child's bedside during an extended hospital stay. Such acts of kindness cemented lifelong friendships.[9] On Sabbaths in particular, the Gotsfelds welcomed guests with an open hand, in conscious or unconscious imitation of Raisel Goldstein's hospitality. One of the guests may have been Rabbi Wolf Gold, who traveled throughout the United States organizing Mizrachi chapters during and after the Great War. If he reached Seattle, then Bessie certainly met him there and helps explain the affinity of the two leaders.[10] Other Mizrachi stalwarts who traveled to Seattle conveyed the need for a Mizrachi women's auxiliary. Bessie approached her friend Libby Anches and suggested that they form one, with Anches as president and herself as vice president. Anches agreed and held the office for ten years, during which time she conducted meetings in Yiddish, Hebrew, and Russian.[11]

Return to New York

The west coast sojourn ended abruptly. In 1919 Bessie suffered terrifying episodes of diabetic shock. Leon Goldstein feared for the life of his eldest child and preferred New York doctors to unknown western practitioners. Actually, time was more crucial than place. Had Bessie suffered pancreatic dysfunction earlier in her young life — she was just thirty-one — she probably would have succumbed within a year. But physicians had recently found a way to keep a diabetic alive though a diet low in carbohydrates and sugar until the wonder drug insulin became available during the 1920s. Bessie heeded her physician's advice. Thereafter, no matter how busy her schedule, three times a day she would find a secluded spot and inject herself with insulin. Carefully she weighed out her food. For the rest of her life, she would zealously maintain the regimen of nutrition and medication prescribed for her.

To safeguard his daughter's physical well-being and financial security, Leon Goldstein persuaded Sarah's husband Sol to accept Mendel as a partner in his jewelry business. Bessie was more than happy to remain with her family. Peripatetic Mendel, who treasured his wife and fretted about her fragile health, willingly made the move. Though Mendel was not particularly astute in business, "Goldman and Gotsfeld" reaped a steady profit during the prosperous 1920s.

The years in Seattle and the return trip to New York had solidified Bessie's Zionism. In the western city she had encountered refugees from two Russian revolutions and a world war (1905, 1917, 1914-18). During their cross-country return train ride the Gotsfelds undoubtedly read about widespread post-war pogroms in the Ukraine, not far from her birthplace. When they reached New York, they found the large Jewish community abuzz with the promise of a Jewish State that the Balfour Declaration, issued a year and a half before, seemed to offer a persecuted people. A combination of these factors turned a conventional wife and auxiliary businesswoman into an ardent religious Zionist and a leader among women.

Settled once again in New York, Bessie found solace in the bosom of a large and warm extended family, now comfortably settled in Williamsburg, Brooklyn and rapidly growing. She was especially drawn to Belle Goldstein, who had married her brother Samuel, a lawyer, in her absence. Belle later described their first meeting.

> Eager anticipation mingled with awe - I had heard so much from each member of the family. As we waited at Grand Central, Bessie came down the ramp. With her happy smile she came toward me, and as she embraced me there was kindled the spark of sisterly love, which burned as a bright and steady flame throughout the years.[12]

The Goldsteins, Goldmans, and Gotsfelds – they called themselves "the G families"[13]— had by this time left the Lower East Side and, like so many in the rising East European immigrant cohort, moved into an area of second settlement. The families rented apartments in the same Williamsburg building, where structure betokened immigrant achievement of middle class status.[14] 186 Hooper Street was an elevator building with a fine lobby. It was also proudly Jewish; a large *sukkah* back of the building was open to all tenants.

Together the "G families" celebrated nearly every Sabbath and holiday main meal in one of the three apartments. Mendel, like his father a fine vegetarian cook, often prepared a special rice dish for the occasion. He was, in addition, a source of after-dinner enlightenment. After the closing blessings, he would regale the extended family with long passages from his beloved Shakespeare or the Hebrew prophets. Sometimes Bessie's sister Sarah would join him. For adults this was a source of enjoyment. The younger children were lulled by the sound if not the sense of the words.

The Gotsfeld's wedding had taken place on *lag b'omer*, a minor Jewish festival elevated to agricultural and historical prominence after the return to Zion. On subsequent anniversaries, Mendel would leave work early and take Bessie on an excursion, with a niece and/or nephew in tow. A visit to Bear Mountain made a lifelong impression on Eliezer Goldman, the oldest child. To commemorate American summer holidays, Mendel would prepare a picnic basket for the Gotsfeld and Goldman families to enjoy on a trip to the country. All the children loved the Gotsfeld apartment, where a treat was always ready and canaries sang in full voice.[15]

Bessie did not surrender to chronic illness, but resumed work in her husband's business as bookkeeper and salesclerk. With the return of vitality, she also realized a new talent. She was aware that the more established American Jews encouraged young immigrants to better themselves through the acquisition of technical skills. To aid younger coreligionists, they instituted programs of industrial education. Girls as well as boys benefited from their largesse. As early as 1880 they had established a vocational girls' school in New York. Seventeen years later came the Clara De Hirsh School for Girls featuring classes in sewing and domestic service. The Hebrew Technical School for Girls opened in 1916; it offered industrial and commercial classes.[16] Pursuing the same objectives but on a much smaller scale,

Bessie organized courses for young women in home economics.[17] Willy-nilly, this venture was prologue to her life's work.

That it materialized in the context of religious Zionism is primarily, though not solely, attributable to one man, Rabbi Meir Berlin (later Bar Ilan). Bessie and Mendel met him at her father's house,[18] where his learned discourses and Mizrachi advocacy reinforced previous discussions with her cousin in Przemsyl and Russian Zionists in Seattle.

The Achios Mizrachi

In 1919, when the Gotsfelds returned to New York, the American Mizrachi movement was only five years old. Female sympathizers with the movement, however, had raised funds for religious institutions in the Holy Land since the turn of the twentieth century. Conscious of this fact, Mizrachi leaders encouraged the women to form auxiliaries to support specific Mizrachi projects. Old-fashioned Orthodox women residing in the immigrant enclaves of New York were happy to comply. But the young woman chafed at the older women's old-fashioned notions. For the latter *zedakka* meant dropping pennies into *"pushkes"* (charity boxes) before lighting Sabbath candles, hardly the activity to excite a young wife's imagination. Some of them organized auxiliaries called *Achios Mizrachi*[19] and conducted fund raisers modeled on prevailing norms of American and American Jewish organizations: tea parties, auctions, bazaars. At first they followed the time-honored pattern of turning over the fruit of their labors to their husbands and fathers, implicitly granting them supreme power to determine the beneficiaries. It didn't take long, however, for murmurs of discontent to surface.

This had nothing to do with the patriarchal structure of religious Judaism. At the time few Jewish women, traditional or liberal, questioned their marginality on this level. It wouldn't have occurred to them, for example, to demand personal synagogue membership or voting rights on synagogue boards, or even serious immersion in Talmudic study. The *Achios Mizrachi* were comfortable with the halakhic mechanism that excluded them from the rigors of intensive prayer and study. At the same time, Jewish immigrant women were discovering new means of expression in America: assertion of independence in the social and economic aspects of society. The 1902 boycott of Kosher meat markets is a well-known example.[20] Because the Achios Mizrachi were God-fearing women, their religious passion required expression. To form an organization of their own was to channel religious energy into a conventional social structure, at the same time asserting female autonomy. Gotsfeld urged them to inform Mizrachi emissaries Rabbis Meir Berlin and Yehuda Leib Fishman that they would organize a Mizrachi women's movement on two conditions, "complete autonomy over their funds and jurisdiction of their projects in Palestine."[21]

The motivation, then, was more psychological than ideological: indignation over frequent slights on the part the all-male Mizrachi establishment. None of their efforts would completely eradicate the attitude; on the contrary, some men would continue to oppose the women's group on grounds that it absorbed capital better put to "more worthy causes."[22] Many years would pass before Mizrachi would come to terms with the fact that America was not Europe, where rabbis dictated policy in matters philanthropic. At this time — post World War I and in this place — New York City, the women of Mizrachi absorbed attitudes of their environment. They observed that the women of America, having proved their grit in the Great War and having won the right to vote, made decisions on their own. Led by Bessie Gotsfeld, they would select their own means of advancing religious Zionism in the Holy Land.

Preparation for Leadership

Bessie Gotsfeld's life to this point indicated the leadership qualities discussed by Stogdill and other social psychologists.[23] Her assumption of adult responsibilities after her mother's death testifies to early dependability and conscientiousness. Her success in school and quick grasp of idiomatic English are clear indications of alertness and intelligence. Within her Orthodox circle she established contact with women of all ages and was admired by many. And when she decided to devote her life to Zionism she took the initiative and followed her program with unabated resolution. Other personal factors assisted the assumption of leadership. Eldest children in large families, generally esteemed by younger siblings, often assume leadership positions in adulthood; Henrietta Szold, who had founded the large, centrist Hadassah in 1912, is a case in point. In Gotsfeld's case, the early death of her mother forced adult responsibility upon the pubescent girl. After marriage, her childlessness offered free time unavailable to most young wives.

Then there is the all-important factor of situation. The contingency theory of leadership maintains that the emergence of a particular leader at a given time and in a given place flows at as much from the situation at hand as from the qualities of any individual.[24] Awakening feminine consciousness in America offered an opportunity for female leadership. This factor also eased the formation of new female Zionist organizations– Pioneer Women on the left, and on the right Mizrachi Woman's Organization of America

The Modernization of American Orthodox Women

New York's Orthodox women were not, of course, flappers who bobbed their hair and wore skirts that grazed the knee. Nevertheless they were women of to their own time and place as well as heirs to two legacies: Jewish philanthropy and American custom. According to sociologist Sheila Rothman, at the turn of the last century American clubwomen took pride in their title of "virtuous women," who cherished expertise in home management. Members of societies that they organized would enter the homes of the less fortunate to show them how to manage an American kitchen and nurture their children. Between the 1920s and the 1950s they advanced to a second stage, "educated motherhood,...apply(ing) new scientific findings to the healthful ordering not only of the home, but of society." They campaigned for "higher public standards of health, education, morality, and even their own emancipation." William Toll draws on Rothman's analysis in his investigation of the acculturated, mostly Reform members of the National Council of Jewish Women (NCCJ).[25] Still, there were parallels between the fully Americanized NCJW and the acculturating Orthodox women in Bessie's circle.

Disruptions in Jewish life had followed the immigration of more than two million Jews from Eastern Europe to America. Every turn-of-the-century community had its share of unemployed men, penurious widows, and sick children. At first NCCJ women and others of German-Jewish ancestry dispensed charity. After they got on their feet, "virtuous women" among the immigrants irritated by their patronization, formed their own Ladies Benevolent Societies, The women dispensed advice about household management, stocking larders when the breadwinner was out of work, and caring for other women's children at times of bereavement.[26] From the general community and existing Jewish organizations, they learned new methods of fund-raising: card parties, bazaars, and strawberry festivals.

After World War I younger Orthodox women were primed to enter the second stage: "educated motherhood." More Americanized and better informed than their mothers, they hoped to apply science to philanthropic efforts. They lobbied for better conditions in the tenements and urged poor immigrants to keep their daughters in school and, if economically feasible, complete high school. At the same time they asserted their personal independence and the right to self-expression.

Some of these women looked beyond the immediate environment and embraced Zionism. They joined Hadassah or its rival organization, Keren Hayesod Women's League. Bessie Gotsfeld probably affiliated with the latter.[27] Those to whom socialism and Yiddishism were as compelling as Zionism founded Pioneer Women. Those to whom religion was no less important than Zionism formed the Mizrachi Women's Organization of America (MWOA).

Three Rabbis

To consider the Mizrachi movement during the National Home Period (1918 - 1948) is to summon memories of three rabbis: Wolf (Ze'ev) Gold (1889-1956), Meir Berlin (Bar-Ilan) (1880 - 1949), and Yehuda Leib Fishman (Maimon)

(1876 - 1962.) The men were European-born and exceptionally brilliant, educated in the finest Lithuanian yeshivas. All three embraced Zionism long before world Orthodoxy made its peace with the movement. All three settled in Palestine and represented Mizrachi to the world at large.

Rabbi Wolf Gold was handsome, personable, and an outstanding orator. Son of the Gaon Rabbi Yaakov Meir Krafchinsky of the Volozhin Yeshiva and a fine Torah scholar in his own right, he was one of the few traditional rabbis to earn a decent living as spiritual leader of a pre-World War I American congregation. When Rabbi Berlin reached these shores, Gold, a stripling of twenty-four, had already served congregations in Chicago, Scranton, and San Francisco and was newly appointed to the prestigious South Third Street Synagogue in Brooklyn. There, to indicate support of dual-track education, he enrolled his own young son in the new Yeshivah Torah Vadaat. Like Berlin, Gold traveled throughout the United States, forming new Mizrachi branches, shoring up others, and raising funds. Among American rabbis, he would prove the most vociferous supporter of the Mizrachi Women's Organization of America (MWOA). Gold settled in Palestine in 1924 and considered the Yishuv his home, although he returned to serve as the president of the Mizrachi Organization in America from 1931 to 1934.[28]

Unlike his rabbinic colleagues Gold and Berlin, Rabbi Yehudah Leib Ha-Cohen Fishman had to claw his way to the top. As incisive a scholar as the others, his roots were not in Lithuanian Talmudic centers but in a small Bessarabian village. He attended the First Zionist Congress and the three conferences (1902, 1903, and 1904) that positioned Mizrachi on the Zionist map. Zionism was Fishman's loadstone and life outside Eretz Israel a trial to be endured. He settled in Palestine in 1913, but the Turks deported him two years later, along with other Zionist leaders. In World War I America, he labored alongside Gold and Berlin, promoting religious Zionism and education. Unlike the others rabbis who lingered, he couldn't wait to leave and returned on the first ship that sailed to Palestine after the war. Of his departure Wolf Gold wrote "Anyone who didn't witness Rabbi Fishman's enthusiasm when he boarded the ship bound for Jaffa's shore has never seen true excitement."[29]

A prolific apologist for the movement, Fishman headed Mizrachi in Palestine and directed funds set up to develop Mizrachi settlements and Mizrachi-sponsored schools. Education was always of special concern, and he would represent Mizrachi on many educational committees in the Yishuv government and the State of Israel.

Primus inter pares was Rabbi Meir Berlin (later Bar Ilan), the late-born son of the "*Netziv*," Rabbi Naftali Zvi Yehudah Berlin, head of the Vohlozhin Yeshiva and an adherent of the proto-Zionist *Hovevei Zion* movement. Deep immersion in Jewish sources, family background, and personal proclivity brought young Meir to Zionism and he dedicated his entire life to the Mizrachi movement. In 1910 the thirty year old scholar moved to Berlin, a center of Zionist life, where he acquired Central European polish and familiarity with modern thought. At a time when Yiddish was the *lingua franca* of European Orthodoxy, Berlin edited the Hebrew weekly *Ha'Ivri*. When he reached the United States, he was already general secretary of World Mizrachi.

Like Gold, Berlin was a forceful speaker; like Fishman, he repeatedly underscored the sustaining function of education for Orthodox Judaism and religious Zionism. His activities extended into other spheres as well. The principal Mizrachi ideologue, he coined the movement's motto: *"Eretz Yisrael l'Am Yisrael al pi Torat Yisrael"* (The Land of Israel for the Nation of Israel, in accordance with the Law of Israel). He devoted eleven years in America to religious Orthodoxy, the Mizrachi movement, and Jewish social service. He was president of American Mizrachi as well as the Rabbi Isaac Elhanan Theological Seminary. He helped found the Central Relief Committee, established by Orthodox businessmen to aid suffering Jews in war-torn Eastern Europe during the Great War. When that group amalgamated with two others to form the American Jewish Joint Distribution Committee, he remained an active board member. In 1926 he returned to Palestine and settled there permanently. He soon entered the political world of the Yishuv, wheeling and dealing with other party leaders. Champion of World Mizrachi until his death in 1949, Berlin held posts in the World Zionist Organization and the Jewish Agency.[30]

When Bessie Gotsfeld encountered the three rabbis, she was deeply moved by their qualities: the vigor of young manhood, the charisma of Talmudic learning, deep faith in religious Zionism, and the determination to spread its message. Despite their commonalities, however, she observed, they maintained disparate perspectives on women. Shrewdly she exploited the differences in order to strengthen the position of women and promote female concerns within Religious Zionism.

A Critical Juncture

An event of December 1919 fortified Gotsfeld's resolve to form a national organization. Members of *Achios Mizrachi* in Williamsburg, Brooklyn raised more money as an independent group that they had as a mere auxiliary. Proud of their accomplishment, the women invited the distinguished Rabbi Yehuda Leib Fishman to address a gathering of 130 members. The rabbi congratulated them, and then naively requested the funds they had raised. The response was stony silence. To alleviate the awkward predicament, Bessie Gotsfeld rose to her feet, thanked the rabbi for his praise, and suggested a future meeting to discuss the dispersal of the collection.[31] Rabbi Fishman was furious; in all his European and Palestinian experience, he had never encountered such insubordination! But what appeared an offense to Fishman became the impetus for a breakthrough. His response awakened the realization that good work did not automatically lead to participation in decision-making. After a few more encounters with rabbis expecting total compliance, the Williamsburg women concluded that only numbers would convince the men to take them seriously. Led by Bessie Gotsfeld, they undertook to rally other Mizrachi auxiliaries into a national woman's organization. Gotsfeld had found a way to turn Zionist sentiment into Zionist action while, at the same time establish her position as a leader among women.

Leon Goldstein died in 1924. For Bessie this was "a shattering loss." Leon was more than a father to her; he was "her close companion and confidante".[32] For the second time in her young life she channeled grief into constructive activity. When she lost her mother at age twelve she had assumed adult responsibility in the family. The death of the second parent activated her personality and potential for broader concerns.

Along with Adela Goldstein, Gotsfeld reorganized the women of Williamsburg and Eastern Parkway into a larger group with a new name. On November 10, 1924, in the living room of the devoted member, a Mrs. Buchanan, parent and daughter created a pilot chapter, Mizrachi Sisters of Brooklyn, the English translation of *Achios Mizrachi*.[33] As in Seattle, Bessie preferred that someone else assume the title of president; in this case it was her stepmother. Her plans extended far beyond that single parlor.

The Mizrachi Women's Organization Of America

For years women had accompanied their husbands to Mizrachi national conventions. In 1925, when the Brooklyn women traveled to Cleveland to attend the Eleventh Convention, they bore their own agenda, "formulated and projected by Bessie Gotsfeld."[34] Meeting with other female leaders apart from their spouses, they formed a national organization and adopted a charter. That charter is unavailable to me, but the opening paragraphs of the 1928 charter indicate not only faithfulness to the Mizrachi ideal but a need for personal and group affirmation:

> The Mizrachi Women's Organization is the organization for Mizrachi women, contributing its full share towards the upbuilding of Palestine, under the banner of the Mizrachi, the orthodox group of the World Zionist Organization. The Mizrachi, having as its aim the perpetuation of the original content of our spiritual values in the land of our fathers, has a particular appeal to the Mother in Israel, who has always been in the first rank of the builders of Zion. (It) is therefore little wonder that the orthodox Jewish woman welcomes the Mizrachi as a medium of expressing her sentiments and serving the great cause of Palestine. The Orthodox Jewish woman, urged by the desire of self-expression and self-assertion in her work for Palestine, responds to the message of the Mizrachi, recognizing it as the spiritual bridge spanning the gulf between historical traditional Judaism and modern civilization. And so the Mizrachi has created a place for itself in the life of the modern Jewish woman.

Unsurprisingly most Mizrachi men were not at all concerned with female "self-expression and self-assertion;" to most foreign-born men of their generation, the very concept was incomprehensible. But they did fear loss of control over money collected for Mizrachi. Fortunately for the incipient organization, Rabbi Fishman had departed the country soon after the infamous Hanukkah meeting. Happily for Gotsfeld and her followers, Rabbis Meir Berlin and Wolf Gold offered their support. Adela Goldstein was elected national president, while Gotsfeld assumed the position of national secretary. The older woman would retain the position for many years. Nevertheless, everyone knew that the daughter rather than the mother, or indeed anyone else, set policy and developed tactics.

Gotsfeld's refusal to assume official office marked her as a model of female leadership. According to Florence L. Denmark, male leaders tend to dictate policy from above while female leaders typically encourage participation by others.[35] On the surface at least, Gotsfeld took pains to indicate that she was no dictator and only carried out the will of the organization.[36] Throughout her career Gotsfeld followed this early pattern. Her title would be unpretentious but her authority would remain sizeable.

On lesser matters Gotsfeld deferred to rabbis whom she respected. In original deliberations about the name, for example, she suggested "*Geulah*" (redemption), perhaps echoing Chief Rabbi Isaac Kook's messianic outlook. That name, however, was short-lived. The following year Rabbi Berlin, attending the Twelfth Convention in Washington, changed it to Mizrachi Women of America (MWOA).[37] His motives were, in all likelihood, political rather than ideological; it was important to place the Mizrachi seal and the Mizrachi name on the women's activities.

Finding a Project

The women had won autonomy, or so they believed. Now they needed an activity around which to rally the new national organization, accomplishing for them what the Hadassah Medical Organization was doing for the larger woman's Zionist organization. Again Bessie Gotsfeld came to the rescue by volunteering to discover a project in the Yishuv worthy of their efforts. She was the right woman to do this. In initial deliberations, her Zionist fervor and practical good sense had earned universal respect. Her childlessness and her husband's business success, moreover, made her more mobile than the women whom she represented. Furthermore, on some trips she would reap personal benefit en route from treatment at a European spa. While in Europe she could communicate with other religious Zionists. Fluent in Polish, German, and Yiddish and comfortable with all sorts of people, she could reach potential supporters: Orthodox women attracted to Zionism.

In 1926 Bessie Gotsfeld sailed to Europe on the S.S. President Arthur, then continued by smaller ship to the Holy Land. What she saw during a six-month stay encouraged her but at the same time, gave her pause. European Jews who had fled from the Turks during the war had returned and Jewish idealists added population to the Yishuv, though not as many as had been anticipated. Gradually, the land was being transformed from treelessness and waterlessness to livability. The desert did not yet bloom, as Zionist propaganda trumpeted, but the men and women of the Third Aliyah were sowing the ground. Hardy pioneers drained swamps and planted trees; controlling and ultimately eliminating malaria and trachoma, major scourges of the Middle East. Paved roads now connected settlements. Some of the early *moshavim, moshavot* and *kvutzot* were taking hold and stabilizing. Yet the American comforts to which Gotsfeld was accustomed were not yet available. Pinhas Routenberg's electrical grid was in place in only three cities— Haifa, Tel Aviv, and Tiberias — though a small British electrical company made electrical current available in selected Jerusalem neighborhoods. Automobiles and telephones were scarce; modern plumbing uncommon; central heating, even in chilly Jerusalem, non-existent.

Unsurprisingly Gotsfeld was drawn to that Holy City, where she found remnants of the Old Yishuv, Orthodox Jews who had dwelled there for generations, and recent immigrants from other parts of the Near East. In Gotsfeld's eyes, their deep faith was as engaging as their pre-industrial lifestyle was disheartening.
The plight of young girls was of special concern. With only an elementary school education, most fourteen year olds were confined to their parental homes until early marriage. They busied themselves with housework and childcare. A few worked as maids in the better parts of the city. An even smaller number found menial jobs in textile mills.

In New York Gotsfeld had heard Rabbis Fishman, Berlin, and Gold (who remained to head American Mizrachi when the others left) prod the Orthodox public to support yeshivas, the Tahkemoni School, and Jewish education in America. She herself had volunteered to teach household management to young girls. To raise the status of Jerusalem girls through a practical education seemed appropriate.

We can be sure that the energetic and pragmatically inclined woman investigated every type of Jewish school in the Yishuv. During the '20s and '30s elementary level instruction of girls from religious homes in Jerusalem was divided between Zionist and non-Zionist institutions. A recent dissertation on the education of Orthodox girls during the National Home period indicates that the schools were divided between Zionist-Mizrachi and non-Zionist Agudat Israel. Only one of the five under consideration extended beyond the elementary level and prepared girls for college; only one was co-ed.[38]

By 1926 the Mizrachi movement was firmly in charge of education for children from Zionist Orthodox religious homes; for six years it had been functioning as an autonomous sector within the Zionist educational system. Its leaders realized that nothing was more important to the growth and development of religious Zionism in the yishuv. Years later the Israeli historian Israel Kolatt reiterated their convictions and actions with these words: "The nucleus of Mizrachi in Palestine grew out of an

Orthodox school network."[39] Yet beyond sixth or eighth grade only one Mizrachi institution offered education for adolescent girls: the Mizrachi Teachers Seminary, opened in 1924.

Several factors dictated Gotsfeld's choice of vocational high school education for religious girls. One was the desire to promote religion in the Yishuv in a fresh, new way. A second was the craving for a program with appeal to her group: females, women helping girls. This was closely connected to her own abiding interest in young people, indicated by her personal concern for nieces and nephews and her having herself taught home economics to young girls. (Whether this implied sublimation of motherly instincts I leave to psychologists.) Gotsfeld's enduring fear of competition from other women's Zionist organizations was an additional incentive. Women's organizations conventionally aided programs that were extensions of their home responsibilities. Hadassah was already the recognized agency for health maintenance and care of the sick in the Yishuv, its nursing school the first in the Middle East. To concentrate on female education outside of the health field would carve out a niche not yet occupied by other American women's Zionist organizations.

Here the operative word is Zionism, for Gotsfeld's heartfelt commitment to Zionism inspired all her efforts. Her visit to Palestine had already convinced her that hands-on experience was a requirement for the new society that Zionism hoped to mould. Formal and informal instruction during the Jewish Home Period was oriented towards the practical rather than the academic. The Hebrew University had recently opened, but its student body was small. There were no female students at the Haifa Technion. Only a small elite prepared for the university anyway: modern European émigrés and graduates of elite schools such as the Rehavia Academy in Jerusalem, Tel Aviv's Herzliah, and *Bet Sefer Reali* in Haifa. Even for many of them, academic life seemed sterile and unproductive. In a pioneering society many people considered higher education a pleasant but dispensable luxury. Of course learning for its own sake was a deeply ingrained Jewish value, but at this time and in this place it reeked of anomalous ghetto existence. Gotsfeld's visit had already convinced her that hands-on experience was a requirement for the new society that Zionism hoped to mold.

She knew, furthermore, that vocational rather than academic education for girls was the rule in New York. Even those Jewish parents whose boys completed high school and considered college often forced their daughters to go to work after the ninth or tenth grade.[40] As late as the 1940s, when most Jewish adolescents of both sexes did receive high school diplomas, guidance counselors advised Brownsville girls to opt for a commercial course of study. [41]

In line with all of the above, Gotsfeld conformed to John Steinbeck's statement: "Need is the stimulus to concept, concept to action."[42] For this tenderhearted yet practical woman, one need outweighed all others, that of innocent and neglected adolescent girls. When she inquired about plans to raise their economic and social status, she learned that no existing institution satisfied that requirement. Consequently she promoted a concept that was innovative for its time and place: Orthodox female vocational ("technical" in the parlance of the day) secondary instruction.

To accomplish her objective she both embraced Mizrachi values and challenged them. She knew that education was a magnet for donations of Mizrachi men and women. She could argue that instruction that was practical as wall as religious would tie its beneficiaries to the New Yishuv and retain them for Orthodoxy. The challenge came from the gender issue. The Mizrachi organization ascribed negligible value to female education beyond basic literacy and numeracy and acquaintance with Jewish laws and customs. This partially explains its appeal to female Mizrachi supporters. An educational program intended to raise the status of girls understandably fascinated women suffering second-class status within a traditional society.

Gotsfeld's tender heart was matched by her tough mind; she knew the value of imparting the latest information to the organization that sent her. Soon after her return home, she set up a conference at which she presented her findings. There she won over two women whose aid during the ensuing years would prove indispensable. One was her sister-in-law Belle Goldstein, with whom she traveled to various cities, explaining her plan and forming new MWOA chapters. The other was Jrena Shapiro, who was not yet affiliated with MWOA when she attended the conference. Inspired by Gotsfeld's message, she immersed herself in organizational work.

In 1927 at MWOA'S third national convention Gotsfeld presented an official resolution: to establish and support a vocational school for Orthodox girls in Jerusalem. Her moving addresses, softly spoken, convinced members to accept her recommendation as the primary agenda of the new movement.

The fifth resolution passed at the MWOA national convention of 1928 indicates as much. The extant text reads:

> The following resolutions were formulated at the annual convention of the Mizrachi Women's Organization of America held in Boston, Mass., January 8, 9 and 10th, 1928, and adopted at a meeting of the officers and the New York members of the Executive Board of the Organization.

> **BE IT RESOLVED:**
> 1. That the Mizrachi Women's Organization of America express a vote of full confidence to the Mizrachi World Organization, with its seat in Jerusalem, Palestine.
> 2. That the Mizrachi Women's Organization of America express a vote of thanks to the 1927 administration of the Mizrachi Organization of America and to the 1927 officers and Executive

1. Born for Leadership   *17*

Committee of the Mizrachi Women's Organization of America for the arduous work in the past year.

3.That a vote of thanks be extended to the Boston Reception Committee of the Mizrachi Women's Organization for the hospitality accorded the women's delegation.

4.That the Mizrachi Women's Organization of America express their dissatisfaction with the fact that no representation was granted them by the convention on the Administrative and Executive Committees of the Mizrachi Organization of America.

5.a) That during the following year all Agudoth [chapters] concentrate their efforts on the building of the Technical Home and Communal Center for Girls in Jerusalem.

b) That the convention in session urges the officers and the executive committee to begin work on the Technical Home and Communal Center as soon as possible.

6.a) That a budget for the ensuing year be drawn up by the officers and executive board.

b) That each individual Aguda be allotted a quota according to the budget provision.

1. Agudoth engaged in individual projects in Palestine are to participate in the general budget with the minimum annual sum of one hundred ($100.) dollars until the completion of their respective undertakings.[43]

That the women's organization was still struggling for autonomy within the Mizrachi movement is evident in Resolution #4. That it needed an on-site representative to initiate the program, thereby securing autonomy and exclusivity within Mizrachi was a pressing need. Gotsfeld alone, the women agreed, had the temperament, the time, and the wherewithal to achieve these objectives.

2

Preparations

"All beginnings are difficult" is a rabbinic dictum that obtains in this case. Gotsfeld's second visit to the Holy Land took place in 1929, the year of major Arab rioting. Especially unsettling to Orthodox sensibilities was the massacre in Hebron of sixty yeshiva students. (All told, 133 Jews were killed during the 1929 riots, and 399 wounded.)[1] Gotsfeld was not in the country when the riots took place, but en route, taking a cure in Franzensbad, Czechoslovakia, at a spa frequented by middle-class Jews (among them Franz Kafka's father.)[2] A letter to Belle Goldstein, the first of many on record,[3] conveyed the rumor, fortunately incorrect, that Rabbi Wolf Gold's young son Moshe had been among the victims.[4]

In August, Gotsfeld attended the Sixteenth World Zionist Congress, held in Zurich, the only woman on the Mizrachi roster.[5] It was thrilling to hear speeches by three prominent Zionists: Hayim Nahman Bialik, the national poet; the orator Zvi Hirsch Masliansky, whom she knew from New York; and Vladimir Jabotinsky, the polymath and stormy petrel who demanded revenge for the Arab riots.

More important for Gotsfeld's particular assignment were meetings with Mizrachi women whose aid she solicited. Her most important contact was Anita Müller-Cohen, a wealthy Mizrachi devotee who lived in Germany.

Nevertheless, the question of advancing the project beyond the planning stage persisted until major change in the Gotsfeld family facilitated its execution. Mendel's father Shimshon Gotsfeld owned a number of properties in a Tel Aviv neighborhood. After the Great War he left Australia and settled with his wife and daughter Sarah in that city. With a base from which to operate, Bessie returned to Palestine as MWOA's official representative, authorized to purchase a suitable building in Jerusalem, obtain permits for construction, supervise the refurbishment, and equip the building. Jrena Shapiro, now an officer of MWOA, would join her there.

Upon arrival Gotsfeld found another teammate. Three years earlier she had created a Palestine Committee to publicize the projected "Technical Home" among American women who supported Mizrachi. Heading the Committee was Fradelle Haskell, a member of Brooklyn's Eastern Parkway. In the interim Haskell had settled in Haifa.[6] Until her death early in 1936 this confederate would guard MWOA interests, both within in the Yishuv and on forays to America.

Unanticipated Competition

Gotsfeld settled into her mother-in-law's Tel Aviv house, but traveled frequently to Jerusalem to lay the groundwork for the proposed "Technical Home and Communal Center for Girls" in that city. Preventing total concentration on her mission was a group of women who, though Orthodox and Zionist, cherished a different philosophy and program. Hapoel Hamizrachi, established in 1922, added socialist values to the Zionism-plus-religion mix. The following is an Israeli scholar's synopsis of its philosophy:

> The dominant trend (of three factions) interpreted Jewish tradition as a revolt against the conditions of *galut* (exile). *Galut* was comprehended not only as discrimination against Jewish individuals but also as an impediment to religious fulfillment. The content of this fulfillment was interpreted in socialist terms. Capitalist society was criticized according to religious criteria, thus establishing a link between religious observance and social ethics.[7]

At first, Hapoel Hamizrachi's progress was slow, owing to disputes with the secular Labor movement, Mizrachi veterans, and internal factions. Nevertheless, during the 1920s young people from the European *Brit Halutzin Datiim* or *Bahad* (Federation of Religious Pioneers) traveled to Palestine to create collective settlements. Some programs to prepare Orthodox youth for collective life assumed the names of important rabbis from the distant and recent past. The first permanent *kvuzah* (collective farm), atypically named after a German town, was Kibbutz Rodges, near Petah Tikvah. Founded in 1929 - 30 by German immigrants, it would figure in a later phase of Gotsfeld's work. Hapoel Hamizrachi also formed workers' sections in Tel Aviv, Jerusalem, Haifa, Petah Tikvah, Ramat Gan, and B'nai Brak. They patterned their agenda after undertakings of the general Labor movement: farm schools, medical benefits, and workers' dormitories.[8]

In the United States, Hapoel Hamizrachi was co-ed; no American Hapoel Hamizrachi woman's organization would exist until 1948.[9] In its absence some female supporters of the movement took on individual projects. When Gotsfeld revisited Palestine in 1929, she learned that a Boston group of female supporters was soliciting funds for a working girls dormitory and an agricultural school. In her absence some members confused MWOA with the American Hapoel Hamizrachi supporters. Instead of exploring vocational education for young girls, they helped fund the Boston projects. Gotsfeld and Shapiro worked tirelessly to steer the Committee onto their track, and not that of a Mrs. Karlsberg of Boston, who would remain Gotsfeld's nemesis for many years. This dispute introduced a trope into

Gotsfeld's program: Mizrachi women must not divide their loyalties and their contributions but devote all efforts to their own projects. For the rest of her life, Gotsfeld would fight for the hearts, minds, and funds of all American and European women who cherished Religious Zionism.

Late in 1929 Gotsfeld returned to America. During the course of the following year she conducted a battle in opposition to the Bostonians' proposed Agricultural School and on behalf of a vocational school, as the following document indicates:

EXECUTIVE BOARD MEETING, APRIL 17, 1930
BROOKLYN JEWISH CENTER, 667 EASTERN PARKWAY

This special meeting was called for the express purpose of discussion, and ultimately to reach a decision as to the form and content of the reply to be sent in response to the many communications received from the Committee of Two in Palestine.

Mrs. Gotsfeld read the letters written by Mrs. Karslberg in order to acquaint all those present of the activities of the Committee — of the land purchase made which is quite contrary to the instructions and advice given them prior to their departure - not to undertake any building proposition, but to buy a house.

Furthermore, Mrs. Karlsberg speaks about establishing an Agricultural School on the land purchased by them, which is not within the scope of the Mizrachi program. The lifelong aim and purpose of the Mizrachi Women's Organization is to establish a Technical Trade School for Girls in Jerusalem (Palestine scratched out) and not to undertake any other project until this is accomplished.

The decisions passed by the Committee precipitated much discussion with the result that the various following suggestions were made:

Mrs Lippa was of the opinion that from the contents of Mrs. Karslberg's letter, she gathers that there seemed to be friction between the two ladies on the Committee, each one no doubt pulling from different angles and because of the indiscretions of the members of this Committee, their work in Palestine cannot continue.

She is also of the opinion that the balance of the Committee consisting of Mrs. Gotsfeld and Mrs. Shapiro should leave for Palestine, in an effort to clarify matters and carry out the plan of the Organization.

Rabbi Gold, who was also present at this meeting, very carefully analyzed the situation and brought to the forefront the fact that they would be far from the ideal and goal set by the Mizrachi Organization if they were to finance the building of an Agricultural School as the Committee proposes in their communications. He suggested that we forfeit the deposit placed on the land by the Committee, if necessary. It would be a very small loss in comparison with the amount involved if we were to go ahead with the proposition

Mrs. Schnur suggested we cable our representatives to stop all work, in view of the fact that they are not carrying out the orders of the organization.

Mrs. M.I. Cohen made a motion that was passed unanimously, that a cable be sent today to the Committee, since such a move would be at variance to the ideals of the Organization.

However, before sending any cable, Mrs. Gotsfeld, whom we all recognize as one of the most ardent members of the group, and one who at all times has the ideals, the honor and the purpose of the Mizrachi Organization at heart, tried to ease the strained feeling of the meeting. She pointed out the many difficulties that the Committee undoubtedly had to undergo and that we here should be more patient with their movements.

She further suggested that before we definitely refuse to send the $5000 they request - that we telephone the Boston Mizrachi, in order to confirm them of the situation and... [Illegible].

This was done during the meeting and in speaking with Mrs. Rosenthal of Boston. Mrs. Gotsfeld asked that they submit their quota of $5000 to the National Treasury in order to indicate to the Organization that they are in favor of a Technical School only, and unless this would be done, we would be forced to wire our refusal to send this money to the Committee. Mrs. Rosenthal said that their decision in this matter would have to await their next meeting and she suggested further that the money, in the meantime be taken from their National Treasury. This arrangement did not meet with the approval of the meeting, and the following cable was sent subsequently:

Considered all angles. Executive unanimous against building. Will positively not finance agricultural...[10]

The 1930 convention of MWOA, meeting in Baltimore, voted to establish a girls' technical school in Jerusalem with dormitories for out-of-town students. At the same time, members decided to send Gotsfeld once again to Palestine as its "representative," paying expenses only. Representative was a modest title and it fit Gotsfeld's reserved style. Nevertheless no one, in the Yishuv, in America, or in Europe, within Mizrachi or outside, would ever question her authority as the prime mover of the organization.

Awareness that Hapoel Hamizrachi had captured not only the Palestine Committee but also some MWOA women in the United States convinced Gotsfeld to return as soon as possible. Five months after the convention, she was back in Palestine, determined to use her authority to pursue organizational objectives.

Gaining Mizrachi Allies

Gotsfeld's third trip to Palestine followed the World Zionist Organization's recognition of the need for female vocational education. This was important because of residual opposition by Rabbi Fishman's confederates who considered MWOA's money better spent on traditional yeshiva education.

It is a wonder that Gotsfeld's mission met with success, as inefficiency, possibly duplicity as well, had clouded its first efforts in Palestine. In 1925, after the consolidation of the MWOA, Mrs. Buchanan, the woman in whose house the organization began, had volunteered her services. She had already planned a trip to Palestine with her husband and agreed to scout out a site for a school. Upon arrival in March, she sought out Rabbi Yehudah Leib Fishman, the head of Mizrachi's Central Committee. He recommended a property owned by Mizrachi in Motza, on the outskirts of Jerusalem. Mizrachi, he said, would lease or sell it to the women for $500.00.[11] The New York office sent the money, but Gotsfeld, an experienced businesswoman, secretly fretted. She realized that the paltry sum was insufficient seed money for any educational institution and feared that the money would disappear into a general fund. That her fears were well founded Buchanan revealed to her upon her return in August. A lingering memory of this episode would color future transactions with the Mizrachi establishment.

Upon return to Palestine in 1930, Gotsfeld tried to get the money back, arguing that Motza was too far from Jerusalem to attract either students or faculty. Rabbi Fishman, her opponent since 1919, temporized but never returned the money. Undeterred, she sought another ally. Rabbi Meir Berlin was unavailable; he would not settle in Palestine for a few months. Not to be put off, Gotsfeld contacted Rabbi Wolf Gold, then resident in Tel Aviv, and he agreed to argue her case before Rabbi Fishman. Nonetheless Gold's efforts proved fruitless. Fishman's response or rather, non-response stiffened Gotsfeld and Gold's resolution. Sitting on a bench in tree-lined Rothschild Boulevard, they solidified plans for a Religious Girls' Technical High School in Jerusalem.[12]

When Gotsfeld finally reached Rabbi Berlin, he unhesitatingly agreed to join the MWOA Palestine Committee. Perhaps he wanted to compensate for his dictatorial change of MWOA's original name. More likely he was gratifying a lifelong propensity to expand the Mizrachi into every area of Jewish life. A university-educated man, he realized the changing status of women in the modern world. A convinced Zionist, he understood the potential benefit to the Yishuv of trained female minds and hands. This belief was already manifest in long hours devoted to the Mizrachi Female Teacher's Seminary. A vocational high school would fill in the picture.

Another factor was also in operation. In the '20s and '30s Mizrachi was small and underfunded, its leaders not yet conversant with new procedures and social experiments. Religious Zionists, as zealous in safeguarding traditional Judaism as anti-modernist devotees of Agudat Israel, differed from them in an important respect; they appreciated economic and societal innovations and utilized the appropriate ones, even as they retained their religious fidelity. We have already noted the founding of Kibbutz Rotges; in most respects, it replicated the secular

Labor kvutzot. Later Gotsfeld would follow this trend when she patterned agricultural youth villages on Ben Shemen, a children's village founded by Dr. Siegfried Lehmann in 1927.[13] But that was far in the future. In 1930, when she consulted Rabbi Berlin, both knew that Hadassah was considering a vocational school for girls. (In time it would create a vocational high school in Jerusalem and name it after Alice L. Seligsberg, the first Hadassah representative in Israel.) This is probably an additional explanation of Berlin's decision to join Gotsfeld's committee.

The Jerusalem Building

Almost immediately Gotsfeld began the search for a building suitable for conversion into a school and dormitory for non-local girls. Utilizing the contacts of her friend Fradelle Haskell, she located a substantial Arab house on Rashi Street in the deteriorating Makor Barukh section of Jerusalem. Eventually the institution's very presence would help sustain the neighborhood. The building was a stone mansion, solidly built on a corner lot and set in a small but adequate plot. To secure it for MWOA, Gotsfeld signed a contract with the owner, a Dr. Valero, and obtained a municipal permit to remodel the existing structure and eventually add to it.

Bessie Gotsfeld was not a bookish intellectual, but she was blessed with a quick mind capable of absorbing diverse information. This is how her niece described her preparations for each new project:

> She familiarized herself with architects' plans, learned about builders' materials, and became knowledgeable about all the laws governing the erection of a school, from zoning to safety, from health to curriculum. Her daily reading became the stack of catalogues of supplies that kept growing in her home. What was the best bargain in wood, in stone? Who could do the plumbing and wiring at the lowest cost without sacrificing quality of fixtures and workmanship? Was it more economical to bring refrigerators from out of the country, and if so, from where? How about parts and service? What kind of import regulations governed their case?[14]

After extended study Gotsfeld recommended outfitting the building with modern equipment, some never before seen in Palestine. Then she considered the exterior. In line with a standard — never to be abandoned — that every facility be both functional and attractive, she insisted upon meticulous landscaping. She sanctioned plans for a handsome wrought iron fence and gate. Inevitably, complications soon surfaced; as in most real estate transactions, nearly everything cost more than anticipated. Legal procedures, such as registering the organization and securing power of attorney in order to purchase the house, stole time and money and drained energy. MWOA, struggling to pay for the building and its renovation, could barely afford a secretary. The entire venture remained in the hands of the two volunteers. Haskell lived in Haifa and was often unavailable. Gotsfeld's base was Tel Aviv and travel between Jerusalem and her in-laws' house involved a bus ride over difficult terrain. Many a night found her in a Jerusalem guesthouse.

Dropping the Bombshell

Gotsfeld ached to return to the United States. She wanted to convey her enthusiasm about the building while emphasizing the commitment of resources that the purchase and remodeling demanded. To assure that nothing would impede the house's conversion into a school, a letter urged the women to make peace with the Boston group. Then she dropped the bombshell. Realizing that progress was dependent upon the presence of a full-time overseer, she volunteered to settle in Palestine as the Mizrachi Women's permanent on-site representative.

Mendel Gotsfeld

Transfer to Palestine held great appeal for her husband, who had already lived on three continents (four, counting his Egyptian birth). His foundering business was a constant worry. By the 1930 the jewelry store could no longer sustain the partnership and he would have to seek another means of earning a living. Balancing that substantial push was an even weightier pull. Mendel's mother, now widowed, wanted her son nearby and urged him to relocate in Tel Aviv and manage the family properties. As an incentive, she offered the couple a house of their own on Yonah Hanavi Street. She told them that Mendel could earn a comfortable living from the rentals, supplemented by management of some orange groves along the coastal plain owned by American Jews.[15]

A psychological consideration cannot be discounted. Should he agree to his mother's proposal, Mendel, who had dwelled under the Goldstein shadow for two decades, would operate on his own turf. All the same, a contradictory factor was also in play. Having previously functioned as a member of the Goldstein family — in-law, employee, occasional chef and avuncular entertainer — he had nevertheless exercised a traditional function outside of the home. In New York and Seattle, Bessie and Mendel had conformed to a conventional spousal pattern. At home she managed the kitchen; in the business she worked in a back office while Mendel faced the world. Once the couple settled in Palestine, however, Bessie became, in effect, the household head and Mendel the facilitating "wife." Mendel's small real estate business, sufficiently successful to support Bessie's visits to European spas, did not consume most of his time. Bessie, though unpaid, worked in the public arena, while Mendel shopped, did most of the cooking, and looked after his elderly mother and sickly sister in a neighboring apartment. Because of this arrangement, the MWOA got what First Lady Hilary Clinton famously termed "two for one." Bessie made no major decisions without first consulting her husband.

Still, it was his assumption of a traditionally female role that facilitated Bessie's total immersion in the life of the organization and the Yishuv. Mendel, inordinately proud of his accomplished wife, dwelled contentedly and quietly in her shadow. He only stepped out of the shadows to defend her fiercely when anyone criticized her.[16]

By October 1931[17] their life's pattern was set. Henceforth Bessie Goldstein Gotsfeld, with the full support of her dependable husband, would dedicate herself to what she designated "our faith and nationalism."[18] In her soul, Orthodox Judaism and Zionism shone like the harvest moon, eclipsing the sacrifices of vigor and health to which she would willingly submit until her death thirty-one years later.

Maintaining Connections

No record is available as the exact date of her announcement or responses on the part of the organization and her family. We do know that the Gotsfelds returned to New York and then remained there only long enough to settle business and organizational affairs and prepare for a new life in Erez Israel. Withal Bessie managed to tour the eastern cities of Philadelphia, Utica, Rochester and Syracuse and awaken interest in the projected school.[19]

These activities entailed sacrifice of her fragile health. Consequently, while en route to Palestine for purpose of permanent settlement she returned to the spa in Franzensbad, Czechoslovakia. The months of excitement in Jerusalem and New York had taken their toll and a cure was not immediately forthcoming. She did not, however, abandon herself to the pampering but fretted over events in America, Europe, and Palestine.

First the family. From this time forward letters to the family express concern with the welfare of Bessie's brother Izzie: her sister Sarah, the wife of businessman and politician Sol Goldman; and her sister Tillie whose husband Ben Shahan was still a struggling young artist. Though she loved and cherished all her siblings and respected their spouses, she felt a special closeness to her brother Samuel's wife Belle. To this woman, more sister than sister-in-law, she confided intimate details of her medical treatment. It was to Belle that she offered detailed descriptions of her labors on behalf of the organization. In time Belle would publish excerpts in the MWOA Bulletins.

Belle Goldstein was a beautiful and intelligent woman blessed with a stately bearing and a commanding voice. In the early '30s when her children were young, she was not ready for organizational leadership. That would come in due course. Still, from that time forward, the connection to Bessie, her own considerable talents, and willingness to work indicated her own leadership potential.

Gotsfeld's epistolary attention was not confined to her own generation. She sent fond regards to her widowed stepmother. Letters of the childless woman display special concern for nieces and nephews invariably called "the children" or "our children." A 1931 letter mentions a polio epidemic raging in the U.S. and begs her sister-in-law for assurance of the children's well being.[20] They, in return, looked forward to Aunt Bessie's successive visits to America when they would bask in the unbounded affection showered upon them.[21] Nevertheless the larger picture was troubling, especially the Great Depression, and Gotsfeld mused about its effect on the Goldstein family.

Still, concern for the projected school remained paramount. Upon completion of the prescribed regimen in Franzensbad Gotsfeld visited Germany to arouse interest in the new school. Joseph Burg, future BZM teacher, later an Israeli Minister of the Interior, heard her lecture in German before a Mizrachi Youth group. His evaluation: "sharp analysis and frank evaluation of the current situation."[22]

While in Europe, Gotsfeld once again made overtures to Orthodox Jewish women. Some offered resistance, possibly indicating conventional European disdain for overbearing Americans, though this slight and soft-spoken woman was anything but imperious. She cemented her relationship with Anita Müller-Cohen, then living in Luxembourg. The prospect of female religious and technical education excited the imagination of other Orthodox Zionist women. With Gotsfeld's encouragement, they founded the Mizrachi Women's League of Europe, a loose federation of female Mizrachi auxiliaries.[23] Through the 1930s whenever Gotsfeld would take a cure at Franzensbad, she would meet with Müller—Cohen, the organization's president, and other representatives from all over Europe, discuss current MWOA projects, and muster financial support.[24] In preserving contact with Müller—Cohen and the new umbrella organization, Gotsfeld solidified a pattern initiated in the meeting with Rabbi Berlin and followed ever after. For each aspect of the program, she would secure the backing of key people, both volunteers and official functionaries.

At Home in Tel Aviv

In 1931 Mendel and Bessie Gotsfeld settled in a second floor flat in the building that they owned, #29 Yona Hanavi Street. It was located in a relatively old neighborhood in central Tel Aviv. The apartment was very modest:

> One entered the inner courtyard from a small alleyway, climbed a narrow stair to an equally narrow, rather long terrace. The door leading inward brought one to a small entry hall, a kitchen on the right and directly ahead, the dining room, with a living room to the right of that. There was no bedroom, only a bed that folded up under a mantel in the dining room and two others, which were couches by day, in the living room. Outside the dining room was a small balcony... A large table dominated the dining room.[25]

Blessed with a modernist aesthetic sensibility, Gotsfeld preferred simple furniture imported from America. The only touches of luxury were fine china, sterling silver flatware, and choice linens purchased in Czechoslovakia. Flowers and plants infused the small apartment and balcony with scent and color.[267]

Selecting Personnel

Comfortable in her new home, Gotsfeld turned to the job at hand, the creation of a religious girls "technical" (i.e. vocational) secondary school, called Bet Zeirot Mizrachi (BZM). Once again nights away from Tel Aviv were frequent as she took charge of building renovations and set about hiring staff. She was blessed with a singular ability to discover people who shared her eye for the practical and the beautiful. She hired a European architect to remodel the building along modern lines and a contractor to do the work. She found a talented landscaper who carved out suitable spaces for a kitchen garden and poultry raising. Surrounding the property were a wrought iron fence and gate. An artist designed a large sign intended to proclaim the purpose of the building to residents and inspire pride and photographs on the part of visiting Mizrachi men and women.

Plans called for an administrator to supervise the physical plant, the dormitory, social contacts, and extra-curricular cultural and religious enrichment. Indicating the lack of appropriate Orthodox candidates for positions as well as a preference for female staff were Gotsfeld's epistolary complaints about difficulties in finding a "directress": "There is always something lacking. If she has the proper training she is not religious. If she is religious she knows no Hebrew. If she knows Hebrew she has not the training."[27]

Also needed was an educational expert. Before undertaking a search for a school principal Gotsfeld studied educational methodology. She mastered the requirements for accreditation from both secular and religious authorities.[28] Research concluded, she sought candidates capable of administering a female religious vocational school.

The search did not yield immediate results. There was little precedent for female vocational education in Palestine and no model of instruction of adolescent girls in both vocational and religious subjects. Unable to find an overall curriculum supervisor, Gotsfeld selected an expert in Judaica to oversee that part of the curriculum. Jerusalem yielded the perfect candidate, Nehama Leibowitz. Of all the teachers that Gotsfeld engaged, her first choice was the most dazzling. Leibowitz, a recent immigrant from Lithuania, was a Torah scholar and an animated Bible teacher, proficient both in the classical Torah commentaries and in the inquiry method of instruction. She agreed to head the Jewish studies department.[29]

The selection of Dr. Leibowitz as instructor of traditional texts was not only an inspired choice from a pedagogic point of view; it also betokened Gotsfeld's advocacy of modernity. Deborah Weissman's survey of female Jewish education in the Yishuv exposed a noteworthy irony: the more "modern" the (girls') school, the more it taught traditional subjects, whereas for boys, the reverse was the case.[30] In Europe and America girls from middle class Orthodox families were already beneficiaries of secular education. Gotsfeld's Polish education exemplified the trend. Girls' formal Jewish education, however was usually confined to lectures and texts dealing with female ritual obligations, such as the laws of *kashrut* (dietary laws) and *taharat ha-mishpaha* (periodic ritual immersion). To instruct Orthodox girls in biblical and exegetical literature, with Hebrew the medium of instruction, and to engage both female and male instructors, as Leibowitz did, was virtually unprecedented.

After engaging Nehama Leibowitz with the understanding that she would locate a suitable Judaica faculty, Gotsfeld proceeded to the next step, hiring instructors in domestic science and vocational training. Here again she confronted obstacles. Few women were qualified to teach vocational skills and even fewer were available in the Orthodox community. For precedent she had to look at institutions in New York City. Historian Melissa Klapper, among others, argues that the real purpose of New York's vocational schools for Jewish girls (the Clara de Hirsch Home for Working Girls and the Hebrew Technical School for Girls) was to heighten the students' eligibility for marriage and even to provide domestic help for their benefactors. For this reason school administrators steered students towards housekeeping and away from more lucrative and rewarding occupations.[31]

Having lived in New York and having taught household skills to American Jewish adolescents, Gotsfeld shared one objective with the German-Jewish Ladies Bountiful who both sustained and disdained their clients. Happily married herself, she certainly did want to train poor girls "to be the kind of domestic figures their students' economic circumstances would rarely allowed them to be."[32] Indeed the intended school population, indigent daughters of the Old Yishuv, lived under conditions even more straited than those of the Jewish immigrants in New York. Yet because she did not share the German Jewish ladies' patronizing mind-set towards her clients, she set her sights much higher. She was bent on creating a new educational *gestalt*, not mere skills but a total environment, a warm and caring home suffused with the warmth of Jewish tradition. The school would be a total community but also take the individual into account. It would affirm feelings of personal worth and equip students to function in both the public and the private arena. Her students would be trained as full participants in the Zionist rebuilding of Erez Israel.

Final Preparations

Soon the building was ready, but opening it was another matter. In the depths of worldwide Depression, it was difficult to locate the big donors that are always the mainstay of educational and cultural enterprises. To accomplish this, MWOA conducted more fundraisers and increased the publicity. Gotsfeld's controlling hand was discernible in every one of them. In 1932 MWOA published a Yiddish language pamphlet that attested to the school's bona fides as a Mizrachi institution. It outlined the curriculum and indicated future inclusion in the Mizrachi school system. Major Mizrachi figures sang the praises of the projected school. World President Rabbi Meir Berlin and Rabbi Ze'ev Gold, who returned to the United States to become vice-president of American Mizrachi, assured their American and world constituencies of the need for an Orthodox girls' technical school. Gedaliah Bublick, president of the American Mizrachi Organization, had recently seen the building; he proclaimed it a feather in Mizrachi's cap. Changing the metaphor, Anita Müller-Cohen called it a "ray of light and hope" for the Old Yishuv. Articulating German-Jewish concern for *Bildung* she maintained that it would eliminate *Unwissenheit* even as it advanced the reconstruction of Jewish Palestine. Most striking was her rather premature assertion that the fledgling MWOA was already strengthening female Mizrachi worldwide.[33]

American members of MWOA, of course, bore the greatest responsibility for their own project. Just what that entailed was spelled out in every letter that Gotsfeld wrote. Various groups had promised to furnish important spaces. She reminded the "ladies" that to have their chapter's name inscribed on a plaque they had to pay for the room or equipment where they would be placed. Then she would suggest additional fundraisers.

In the absence of adequate resources, the building remained empty for over a year after its completion. This brought on an additional problem. Gotsfeld had engaged a secretary but there was nothing for her to do. Ever frugal, she fretted over the waste of eleven pounds a month, the young woman's (admittedly small) salary. To dismiss her, however, she confided to her sister-in-law, would be to acknowledge, "we are not able to go on."[34]

As if internal problems were not sufficiently burdensome, challenges from other Mizrachi elements did not abate. Officers of the organization in Europe and America continued to demand a share of MWOA's financial resources. Furthermore, controversy with the Boston Hapoel Hamizrachi auxiliary simmered on. When Shlomo Zalman Shragai, leader of the Hapoel Hamizrachi in Palestine and member of the Va'ad Leumi (National Council), entered the picture, the two American women's groups submitted to arbitration. They reached a compromise but Gotsfeld continued to warn the MWOA of the other group's duplicity.

Inflicting the unkindest cut was Rabbi Meir Berlin, Gotsfeld's Mizrachi loadstar. Though a member of MWOA's Palestine Committee, Berlin far preferred the Women's Teacher's Seminary, his personal project, and against all logic, suggested a merger of BZM with that institution. Gotsfeld simply ignored the unreasonable proposal.

Despite disagreement on this issue, Berlin continued to acknowledge BZM's legitimate position in the Mizrachi orbit while Rabbi Fishman, unsurprisingly, continued to question it. By 1932 Gotsfeld had recovered from the humiliation of 1925. A letter belittled Fishman's efforts to deprecate her efforts, assuring Belle Goldman that "his influence in Palestine is naught"[35] and advising the "ladies" to ignore his disapproval.

Leadership from Afar

How did Bessie Gotsfeld hold on to leadership of an American organization after her emigration? A survey of the leadership literature indicates that her personal profile matches some patterns of leadership, but not all, perhaps because most of them use data from the business world. Alice H. Eagly and Blair T. Johnson set forth the two faces of leadership. The first is "task accomplishment," i.e. "organizing activities to perform assigned (such) tasks" as directing rules and procedures and maintaining standards." The second is "maintenance of interpersonal relationships." Men tend to favor the first and give orders from above. Female leaders are more comfortable in the second area. They operate best, the authors conclude, when they meet traditional expectations of feminine behavior and conduct affairs on a democratic basis, whenever possible by reaching consensus.[36]

In a certain sense Bessie Gotsfeld's activities hew to a "masculine" leadership style. Even after she emigrated, she retained control of many aspects of organizational activities, at the same time insisting that she was simply carrying out the organization's will. Despite protests to the contrary, MWOA was her personal fiefdom. By her lights, she had the right to know everything and to control essential policy and specific activities in America as well as the Yishuv. Her first letters from abroad designated every national officer. She expected to be informed about every program, gala, internal altercation, and inter- chapter communication. She searched for information about potential donors and then advised the members how to draw them into her work. She passed judgment on every fundraiser and continued to suggest new ones. When wealthy Jewish tourists expressed interest in the school, she sent their names to New York with instructions to contact them on home ground. Relentlessly she worked out fundraising strategies: plaques on rooms to indicate support, a "Golden Book" of big donors' names, candlesticks purchased by members to be lit at the Yahrzeit of family members. Almost every letter urged the rank and file to raise more money than was possible during the Depression.

In another area, however, Gotsfeld did match the feminine pattern. To reinforce an image of agreement by consensus rather than dictation from above and thus hew to what the sociologists deem "a relatively democratic and participative style consistent with the female gender role"[37] she deliberately downplayed her key role. She refused to take sole credit for policies or programs that she suggested. After settling upon an agenda she persuaded people that decisions were reached by mutual consent.

On the personal level, moreover, Gotsfeld also conformed to cultural patterns. Surveys found that the behavior of female leaders is most effective when congruent with cultural expectations for women. Those who come across as mannish, i.e. autocratic, directive, and unkind, are resented by people needed to carry out their policies.[38] Gotsfeld's natural "gender congeniality" worked in her favor. Bessie Gotsfeld was a woman's woman. She was no stentorian orator but delivered public addresses with quiet dignity. Her Tel Aviv apartment was open to all; she enjoyed serving coffee and cookies to Sabbath guests. MWOA visitors to Eretz Israel considered an invitation to tea in her dining room a great honor and boasted of it upon return home. Flowers adorned her table and her balcony and similar aesthetics governed plans for the buildings and grounds of MWOA schools and farm villages. Her interest in the personal lives of members, moreover, was genuine. To women of every generation she came across as warm and motherly, lending an ear to fearful children, dislocated adolescents, and adults in need.

Perhaps for these reasons, there is no evidence of objections to her domineering control. Two additional factors accounted for this. One was her wholehearted infatuation with the land of Israel, traditional Judaism, and modern education. The other was her unwillingness to distinguish between her own personal needs and those of the organization. She was an unpaid worker, meticulous about expenses she incurred. When carrying on MWOA business, for example, she used public transportation.[39] On occasions of direst need, she raided her own bank account and even borrowed from her mother-in-law. [40]

What most members did not fully realize was that under the round, kindly face and welcoming smile lay an indomitable will. Few were aware of the time, energy, and money involved in maintaining her health. Visits to the Czech spa were efforts to control painful rheumatism. Thwarting complications from diabetes required relentless adherence to the food and injection regimen. Countless were her visits to specialists in three continents in the effort to save her diminishing hearing. Perhaps this accounts for the need to dedicate her life to something greater than herself. Working for a greater good rather than succumbing to personal tribulations, Bessie Gotsfeld probably extended her years on earth.

3

Bet Zeirot Mizrachi, Jerusalem, 1933 – 1935

Nineteen thirty-three brought frustration at first, then accomplishment. In January the building was ready for occupancy, and students and staff were already recruited, but classes couldn't begin until five hundred pounds were available to cover expenses. Gotsfeld's letters are ambivalent, alternately displaying excitement over the school's imminent inauguration and despondency over its financial precariousness. Her own rigorous standards were partly to blame. For example, she demanded tiles in all kitchen and baths, rarely found in Jerusalem buildings of that era, though common in future years [1] Funding ran out before a peripheral fence could be erected, exposing the building to vandalism. Desperate, Gotsfeld begged MWOA for money and suggested schemes for raising it. She courted potential donors and continued to pelt the organization with suggestions for time-tested fund raising gimmicks and new ones as well. To retain the services of the school secretary and to stave off the embarrassment of letting her go, Fradelle Haskell provided the salary. Gotsfeld too advanced money.

Midst all the vexations in her new home, she continued to pine for her family in America and was deeply disappointed that she couldn't attend the bar mitzvah of Eliezer Goldman, her gifted nephew. Nor could she follow the suggestion of Rabbi Gold, who cabled from America requesting her presence at the 18th Zionist Congress, to be held in Prague. She was confident that Anita Müller-Cohen would represent MWOA's interests.

Global issues were especially disturbing, notably the deepening economic depression and Hitler's accession to power. As a result of the Nazi menace, Zionism appealed to German Jews who had not previously embraced its ideology, much less considered relocating in Palestine. Indeed, before 1933, their share of the Yishuv was minuscule, only 35,000 out of 200,000 Jews.[2] After 1930, the American State Department obstructed German Jewish immigration to the United States,[3] making the Land of the Fathers an increasingly popular option. The Yishuv would admit 43,000 German Jews between 1933 and 1938.[4] At the inception of this migration, Gotsfeld and her organization reconsidered the school population. They had planned vocational secondary education for daughters of the Old Yishuv, mostly of Middle Eastern background; now they felt duty-bound to accept European students.

33

Yet the school's classrooms and dormitories lay idle, with only one ray of hope, Fradelle Haskell's forceful advocacy directed at the women of MWOA. Her letter in the organizational bulletin informed, rebuked, and goaded to action:

> That building is now ready - a beautiful, modern, model structure, with all the possibilities and facilities for an ideal vocational school and center for orthodox girls. But, with the completion of that building you have not discharged a wit of your understanding. You have but strengthened and endorsed it. What was formerly a free-will offering you have now converted into a moral obligation. The building is here. You must now clear it of all encumbrances and put it to its intended use. The orthodox girls, both of Palestine and Europe, are impatiently knocking at its doors; they want to know; they want to be taught.[5]

Clearly, Haskell shared Gotsfeld's vision and her forthrightness. In late summer she visited America and submitted an extensive report of progress to date.

> The full plan of activities to which this beautiful building will eventually be put is very wide in its scope and most comprehensive. It is to include all trades suitable for a girl in Palestine and all activities and instructions that will tend to make the religious girl in Palestine a healthy, happy self-supporting woman, and a capable housewife.[6]

Haskell's detailed descriptions, forcefully delivered, helped raise the required funds. Money was also forthcoming from European Mizrachi women, with whom Gotsfeld remained in communication. Groups from Berlin, Breslau, and Hamburg contributed equipment for what was called "the training kitchen." Czech women donated dormitory furniture. Not to be outdone, Mizrachi women from Amsterdam supplied library furniture and Dutch and Swiss women provided linens. Mizrachi women in Palestine also chipped in. The Jerusalem group purchased the dining room furniture and the Tel Aviv chapter equipped the sewing room. Then the Palestine Committee facilitated the final step: erection of fence, gate and sign.[7]

Bet Zeirot Mizrachi

Classes began on October 17, 1933, though there was not money to conduct the planned fanfare. Bet Zeirot Mizrachi (BZM) was its Hebrew name, but the institution bore no uniform English designation. It was called, alternatively, The Mizrachi Women's Trade School and Cultural Center for Girls, The Mizrachi Technical Home and Community Center, The Mizrachi Domestic Science School, and The Mizrachi Household School. The letterhead of the second BZM, constructed later in Tel Aviv, read "Mizrachi Girls Hostel & Vocational School." In an article published in the *Mizrachi Jubilee Publication* (1935), Gotsfeld called it "The Mizrachi Vocational Institution." To German Jews it was "Iwdiheim."

The Curriculum

The curriculum hewed to the Mizrachi philosophy of education, summarized by Ehud Luz as:

> (to) combine the traditional religious education prevalent in the advanced countries of Europe and America; thus the children will absorb Jewish religious values as the basis for their world outlook, will observe the religious commandments on the one hand, and on the other, will acquire the knowledge and qualifications which a citizen in a modern society requires.[8]

Listed under "domestic science" were courses in cooking, baking, housework, laundry, and sewing were The wording catered to haughty Europeans who wanted to "civilize" daughters of the Old Yishuv in modern methods of hygiene, nutrition, and standards of cleanliness. Native girls soon assimilated the western values. From cooking courses they learned preparation of locally grown foods never seen in their parental homes. Lessons in food presentation that reflected Gotsfeld's concern with aesthetics, proved popular.[9] Sewing classes enabled the girls to design as well as fashion their own clothes.

In an effort to gain support, formulators of BZM publicity framed school objectives in conventional terms. They exploited the fact that the so-called "technical" courses were extensions of work performed by homebound women, pointing out that the domestic science curriculum reinforced traditional female roles in the household. Obviously, this line of reasoning was directed at conservative parents from the Old Yishuv and skeptical Mizrachi members. On one level, the propaganda did not bend the truth; some graduates would be content to use skills learned at BZM only in the home. On another level, however, the curriculum subverted the purposes it purported to perpetuate. Graduates, by and large immigrants from Europe, would prove eligible for employment in the public arena.

By the time instruction began the student body had extended beyond the intended population. Twenty-four girls enrolled in the first class, with an equal number on the waiting list. Fifteen were Jerusalem residents who lived at home. Nine others were German-born refugees, housed in the dormitory. Of the latter, about half came from families with the ability to pay full costs. Most others were daughters of migrants from Poland to Germany. Uprooted for a second time; they required full or partial scholarships. Because BZM was a Hebrew-language institution the administration quickly added Hebrew immersion classes for these students.

This population was worldlier than native-born girls, products of the Old Yishuv. Their welcome, if unanticipated, inclusion in the student body advanced the process of westernization and professionalization. Teachers of kitchen work, for example, disdained what the biographer of American cookbook editors Irma and Marion Rombauer criticized as "detailed, quantified scripts."[10] Instead they would instruct the girls in food chemistry, enabling them to modify conventional "scripts" for precise purposes. In the course of time, BZM graduates would fill positions as dietitians and nutritionists, essential to the growing Yishuv.

Later the school would add gardening (flowers and vegetables) and poultry raising, "the hennery"[11]. These departments served a two-fold purpose, equipping some graduates to cultivate urban gardens, and preparing others for life in small villages and collective and cooperative farms. An early graduate would teach gardening in Jerusalem for many years. [12]

The curriculum's second half included subjects that promoted Mizrachi's ideology of Jewish peoplehood, traditional religion, and rebuilding the land. Subjects were Bible, Jewish history, Hebrew literature and a course in rituals, customs, and ceremonies. Department Chair Nehama Leibowitz, a young scholar and talented teacher, became department chairman, in charge of curriculum, hiring, and firing. At BZM, Leibowiz perfected her famous inquiry method of Torah study. Even after she joined more prestigious faculties, she continued to teach there for twenty years.

The beneficiary of a classical European education in a Galician gymnasium, Gotsfeld did not neglect world culture. Academic subjects such as English and civics bolstered assimilation of western mores. Informal lectures by immigrant scholars introduced Japhet's arts and letters into the Shemite school on Rashi Street.[13]

The Larger Purposes

The garden and poultry run, open for neighbors to see, connected students to the larger community. Neighbors and even residents of other Jerusalem sections would purchase flowers on Friday afternoons. The birth of chicks excited not only the school population but also the neighborhood, as this fragment of a letter to Goldstein indicates:

> The incubator was the first time put to use and this time the chickens came out. Good G-d, what excitement! In order to constantly watch the process, the incubator was put into the dormitory occupied by the girls in charge of the hennery. The last few days everybody, even in the neighborhood, walked on tiptoe... We were standing in the room, about ten of us, waiting for the chickens to come out. Mr. Mendelsohn, the teacher, was watching the thermometer to see to the proper temperature when he would open the incubator, take out the chickens, and transfer them to the Hennery. The tension was so great - we all felt

that we were watching the birth of new life. All of a sudden, the little heads began to show so soft, and (we) heard them chirping so softly. It was really a moment to watch.[14]

The dominant messages of the curriculum remained Zionism and Orthodox Judaism. Classes in the geography of Erez Yisrael culminated in an annual ten-day outing, *de rigueur* in Zionist schools, then and now. In line with the movement's cooperative spirit, students placed gifts from abroad and money received from home in a common pool. To establish a connection between ancient religious texts and national reconstruction teacher Eli Feuchtunger invited students to his home, where they read Mishnaic passages on gardening. Thus did he inspire the girls to regard their course of study as a link in the long chain of religious Jewish settlement in Zion.[15] This was a noteworthy departure from the educational philosophy of secular Zionist high schools; for the most part, these schools emphasized change rather than continuity.

Feuchtunger's home lessons pursued an additional objective of BZM, forging community. Young girls removed from familiar surroundings and the case of the refugees, their birthplaces, drew solace from the new environment. It was not easy to create community from a diverse population where German girls from bourgeois homes studied alongside local girls from working-class homes. On the academic side, Nehama Leibowitz attempted to equalize opportunity by offering intensive Hebrew language courses for the Europeans and extra Bible courses for the native girls.[16]

Bessie Gotsfeld's loving care set a standard for everyone associated with BZM. During the application process, she familiarized herself with each candidate's personal circumstance. When the first German girls reached Jaffa, she traveled there and escorted them directly to BZM.[17] For years she would greet each new arrival by name. Whether in Tel Aviv or Jerusalem, her door was open to all. She was a non-judgmental confidante, a loving aunt, and a second mother. Her attitude was contagious. Despite their very disparate backgrounds, the girls got along with one another. They formed clubs that catered to extracurricular interests. They shared gifts from parents. One group raised money for charity. The genuine community formed at BZM became a vehicle of socialization into the larger Jewish society. In sum, Bet Zeirot Mizrachi satisfied multiple requirements: of young women from the Old Yishuv who otherwise would have remained ignorant and unemployable; of uprooted newcomers from Germany; of the New Yishuv, which required skilled workers in the city and on the farm; and finally, of religious Zionists, during the 1930s an unpopular minority. Gotsfeld hoped that competent graduates would put a new face on Orthodoxy and secure its continuity into the next generation.

In years to come, additional courses would be offered, in crafts and secretarial skills. All of these skills were needed in the work place. There were also cooking classes for adult women, initiated even before the building was completed. (These classes were the only instructional activity that brought tuition money into the institution with no strings attached.) Nevertheless the antagonism towards the school on the part of some diehards did not disappear. Remnants of the Old Yishuv, reared under pre-modern conditions, feared losing control of their daughters. Some European-born Mizrachi leaders, moreover, delivered a mixed message. They acknowledged the need for this type of education, but at the same time considered it subordinate to the real business of Judaism. By their lights, a school with female administrators and student body and with a vocational rather than an academic mission would absorb funds better spent on future Torah scholars and redeemers of the land. Rabbi Fishman, unsurprisingly, continued to voice his objections.[18] It would be many years before Religious Zionism would recognize MWOA as an equal partner.

4

Challenges and New Opportunities: Youth Aliyah and a New School, 1933 – 1935

From the beginning, world events helped shape the New Yishuv. The Great War brought about the end of Turkish rule and the creation of the British mandate over Palestine. Just as the Yishuv was getting on its feet, the Nazis assumed power in Germany and began to prepare for a war that would destroy European Jewry. Jewish organizations of the 1930s and 1940s did what they could to recover the bodies and souls of coreligionists who found refuge in mandatory Palestine. The crisis would pit two American Zionists against one another: Bessie Gotsfeld and Henrietta Szold.

Shortly before the Nazis assumed power in January 1933, Recha Freier, author of children's folk tales and wife of a Berlin Orthodox rabbi, proposed a "Committee for Aid to Jewish Youth" (*Jüdische Jugendhilfe*) with the object of settling unemployed German youth on kibbutzim. Freier, a woman of "prophetic vision and fiery temperament,"[1] traveled to Palestine and presented her plan to Henrietta Szold, Director of the Social Welfare Department of the *Va'ad Leumi*. Szold disapproved. The Yishuv is not equipped to absorb the scores of young Germans who have already immigrated, she argued; how can it handle thousands? And what about local children from poor families with their own pressing needs? Soon, however, the brutal circumstances of the Nazi ascendancy and the eagerness of several youth villages and kibbutzim to absorb German adolescents stimulated reconsideration. Furthermore, Arthur Ruppin, chairman of the Jerusalem section of the German Bureau established at the Eighteenth World Zionist Congress (Prague, August, 1933), and a personal friend, approached Szold. He convinced the septuagenarian to head Youth Aliyah, a new department of the Jewish Agency. Its mission was to bring German adolescents aged 15 to 17 to Palestine and to find them a place in the society and economy of the Yishuv.[2]

To transport the youngsters and settle them was no simple matter; obstructions hindered every step. The Jewish Agency was not a free agent; it had to work in tandem with British, German-Jewish, and Nazi authorities. Required from each applicant was approval by the *Arbeitsgemeinschaft für Alijah Kinder und*

Jugend, a joint committee of Jews in Germany who raised money for youth (and later, child) emigration. The *Jüdische Jugendhilfe* would accept only applicants who could demonstrate that their passage and absorption were guaranteed. Once that barrier was surmounted, an even more formidable one loomed. The British mandatory personnel who governed Palestine demanded proof that adequate housing and appropriate educational and vocational opportunities awaited each applicant. To underscore their dissatisfaction with the growth of the Jewish population, they imposed severe numerical restrictions. They doled out only a few hundred certificates in a single time period, usually six months.[3] To its credit, BZM was a pioneer in the resettlement; the school admitted German girls four months before the Jewish Agency took over Youth Aliyah in January, 1934.

In February the first organized Youth Aliyah group arrived in the newly – expanded port of Haifa and settled in Kibbutz Ein Harod. In March a horticultural school in Talpiot, a Jerusalem suburb, admitted a group of German girls. The founder was Rahel Yanait, already a celebrity by virtue of her marriage to Zionist functionary Itzhak Ben-Zvi, the future second president of Israel. In June, a group of Orthodox youth found a new home among the people struggling to sustain the first religious kibbutz, Rotges, near Petah Tikvah. Beset by internal disputes, poor soil, and lack of farm experience, Rotges had never gotten off its feet. Youth Aliyah was a shot in the arm. (In 1940 it would relocate near Gedera and prosper under the name Yavneh.)[4] There followed a small group of Orthodox agricultural apprentices in Tel Joseph, a communal village in the Valley of Jezreel.[5]

Bessie Gotsfeld's reaction was mixed. She delighted in the rescue of Jewish children. All the same, the fact that BZM received no certificates disappointed her. To secure them she enlisted the aid of Orthodox spokesmen in Palestine and European Mizrachi women. In a series of letters to Henrietta Szold and her assistant Hans Beyth, her allies requested certificates for Jewish girls eligible for enrollment in BZM. Then Gotsfeld and a Mrs. Shereshewsky, representing BZM, met with Henrietta Szold. Szold, always punctilious about regulations, replied that BZM, a new institution, had not yet gained the approval of the mandatory government and was therefore not yet eligible to receive Youth Aliyah students.[6]

This altercation must be seen the context of tensions between Orthodox and secular Jews during the 1930s. When Youth Aliyah began operation, British governmental authorities, asked to issue 500 certificates for a six months period, grudgingly granted 350. Orthodox spokesman immediately demanded that a healthy percentage of the total be assigned to their institutions. They knew that the Jewish Agency preferred collective farms to their urban institutions and private families eager to shelter child refugees. With abhorrence, they witnessed the immersion of children not assigned to their agencies and houses in a culture that was at most indifferent to religion, often downright hostile.

Prompting action, furthermore, was longstanding bitterness on the part of Mizrachi adherents. While wholeheartedly dedicated to rebuilding Palestine along

Zionist lines, they were nonetheless alienated from the prevailing culture. An unpopular minority, they considered their achievements undervalued while the socialist factions received full credit for developing Jewish Palestine. They resented the charisma of socialist Zionism that radiated from the Yishuv to every part of the diaspora. The historian Mark A. Raider maintains that during the interwar period, Labor Zionism captured American Jews for Zionism. Despite the relatively small size of Poalei Zion and Pioneer Women vis-a-vis the Z.O.A., Hadassah, and even Mizrachi, he argues, the glamour of kibbutz life pervaded Jewish schools and other institutions.[7] To tout its own credentials before the American Jewish public, Mizrachi tried, with small success, to tarnish Labor with the brush of antinomianism. Thus, when the (Conservative) Rabbinical Assembly of America issued a statement in favor of Labor Zionist efforts, Gotsfeld's friend Rabbi Wolf Gold roundly scolded the rabbis for condoning Godless, communistic kibbutzim.[8]

More troublesome to the Mizrachi leadership than American attitudes was widespread public disapproval in the Yishuv of tactics employed to achieve their objectives. In the mid 1930s, Mizrachi pursued two goals, public recognition of the Sabbath and the maintenance of Jewish dietary regulations in public kitchens. To assure success, they refused to participate in the Nineteenth Zionist Congress, held in Lucerne in August 1935, unless the meeting agreed to adopt those standards. Though they won the day, their tactics further alienated the secular majority (even as they delighted Bessie Gotsfeld.)[9] Because of such procedures and their general disconnect with the prevailing culture, the majority of Jews barely tolerated the Orthodox minority. Orthodox educators, in turn, complained of anti-religious prejudice so intense that when they visited the Jewish Agency building in Jerusalem, they were constrained to remove their head coverings.[10]

To prevent conflict with the Orthodox sector, Youth Aliyah reserved one quarter of the precious certificates for religiously observant youth. In the eyes of Mizrachi leaders, eighty-eight certificates were insufficient. Forthwith, they issued two new demands. First, transfer certificates already granted to the Ahavah Orphan Home, a Haifa institution transferred from Germany and run along traditional but non-Orthodox lines, to the non-Orthodox list, thereby freeing up places in institutions that met more stringent religious standards. Second, include youngsters already settled in Ben Shemen in the total count. Szold acceded to the first request, but not the second. Ben Shemen, should not be included, she argued, as its certificates did not come through Youth Aliyah.[11] At the end of negotiations, Youth Aliyah raised the number of certificates for young people from Orthodox families to ninety-six.

Because Szold and Beyth preferred agricultural collectives and urban institutions with a Zionist outlook to private homes exempt from supervision [12], they granted Gotsfeld's request and assigned the entire lot to Kibbutz Rotges and Bet Zeirot Mizrachi. The kibbutz received fifty-six certificates, and BZM forty, in two installments.[13]

Forty new students: a blessing and a burden at the same time! MWOA was hard put to feed, house, and house the nine German girls already enrolled. Only loans from the Gotsfeld family and a few private donations kept BZM from bankruptcy. To multiply their number more than fourfold seemed insurmountable. Desperate, Gotsfeld turned to Orthodox leaders living abroad. From London Anita Müller-Cohen, an MWOA supporter since 1930, and from Amsterdam a Mrs. Spangenthal-Pinhof advanced her case. They joined rabbis and laymen from all over the world. Sympathizers bombarded German and Palestinian staff with letters. They claimed that the latter favored the Talpiot School of Horticulture and Haifa's Ahavah over BZM and other Orthodox institutions. They pointed out that many Orthodox Jews in Germany were recent immigrants from Eastern Europe, less established economically than Jews with deeper roots in the country. For this reason, they requested extra support to make up the difference between the small sums provided by the girls' families and the bank deposit demanded by the *Arbeitsgemeinschaft* and the British authorities in Palestine.[14]

The response of Szold and Beyth in Palestine and members of the *Jüdische Jugendhilfe* (the corresponding Youth Aliyah organization in Germany) certainly did not please them. The *Jüdische Jugendhilfe* pointed out that BZM was not yet registered with the *Arbeitsgemeinschaft* and Youth Aliyah; it would have to complete the process even to merit consideration. After that, a representative of the British government would have to inspect the building and grounds. Only then would the 40 certificates be made available.

Szold was equally conscientious about following regulations worked out with the British authorities. She lay down a stream of complaints. Three students on the list were not between fifteen and seventeen years of age, and therefore *prima facie* disqualified. Even the eligible had not submitted all requested data. The list of candidates was incomplete. Furthermore Gotsfeld had already requested money from Youth Aliyah in the form of a loan for a third floor addition to the Rashi Street building. Szold's scolding letter to Gotsfeld warned that the loan depended upon fulfillment of all the regulations and impeccable arrangements for financing. To top it off, she threatened to withhold twenty-eight of the forty certificates.[15]

As quickly as possible, BZM complied with the directives, but another problem soon surfaced. The institution had to guarantee financial coverage for each student before her departure from Germany. Few parents could pay all the tuition, or even half; they required full or partial scholarships.

Letters from American and British rabbis and Mizrachi personnel in Europe demanding special consideration for Orthodox girls and BZM flooded Szold's office. So much mail on that issue reached her desk that in letters to her own intimates, she grumbled about "the constant complaints and worriments (sic) of Mrs. Gotsfeld." She found them excessively time-consuming and "obtrusive."[16]

The American Scene, 1934

All this exacted a toll on Bessie Gotsfeld's health. Reluctantly, she left Tel Aviv in pursuit of a cure in Europe, first in consultation with a Viennese physician, then in the familiar Franzensbad spa. Rested, she boarded ship for America, with plans for a speaking tour to raise money for BZM. That appeared necessary in light of the fact that Mizrachi men continued to regard MWOA as an auxiliary rather than independent organization and their leaders continued to urge the women to support *their* projects. Gotsfeld feared that while she was engrossed in running BZM and expanding its enrollment, MWOA members were succumbing to their entreaties. A letter to Belle Goldstein, written while the building was under construction, had expressed outrage that the organization did not prioritize it. Why, she had queried in a fit of pique, was it placed tenth on the list of topics discussed at an annual meeting?[17]

Since December 1932, when the letter was written, and the summer of 1934, when she reached the United States, the situation had improved. Flush with delight at the actualization of their first project, a large delegation of MWOA women appeared at the national convention of the Mizrachi Organization of America held in Detroit. Determined to formalize their independent status. they chose Dvorah Rabinowitz, a rising star, as their spokesperson. She mounted the podium and proposed a motion declaring autonomy for MWOA within the religious Zionist framework. Quickly, male opponents consulted Robert's Rules of Order. "Point of Order!" they shouted, and "Point of Information!" Sage Adela Goldstein, longstanding MWOA president, stood beside the young woman and chided the men in Yiddish: "You must let Dvorah speak. She must not be aggravated; she is pregnant!" Cowed, the obstructionists sat in silence while the motion was seconded and passed with a show of hands.[18] By exercising a prerogative unavailable to men, Gotsfeld's stepmother and her followers secured the formal independence of the organization. It was a signal victory, yet only the end of the beginning.

Acknowledgment of the importance of BZM to Mizrachi education came in the form of a small monthly stipend from World Mizrachi's central bureau, *Mercaz Olami*[19]. Nevertheless, many Mizrachi leaders would not come to terms with female sovereignty. This was true of friends as well as opponents. If Rabbi Fishman didn't even pretend to grant the MWOA its due, Rabbi Berlin, probably the most important catalyst of Gotsfeld's commitment to Zionism, used tactics that she considered underhanded to woo Mizrachi women's funding away from BZM in favor of the Mizrachi Teachers Seminary for Women. Even Rabbi Wolf Gold, who had helped the organization get on its feet, seemed poised to join the obstructionists. In Gotsfeld's eyes these were besetting sins. She never wavered from her 1929 affirmation: "Nothing effective can be done unless we have the *entire national organization* in unison. We need the people and the money and our forces are scarce."[20]

The fund raising tour went well, topped by a farewell luncheon in which members outdid themselves in honoring MWOA's "Palestine representative," the title that Gotsfeld held until late in life. Assured that the women would no longer divert attention from their own projects, Gotsfeld concluded her six-month stay in the United States and sailed for home.

Return to Palestine

With eager anticipation, Bessie contemplated reunion with Mendel, yet parting from beloved sisters and brothers, nieces and nephews, and a very special sister-in-law had been excruciating. A stopover on the island of Madeira, "a bower of flowers in the midst of the ocean,"[21] eased the transition and bolstered the spirits of a nature devotee and lover of beauty. Nevertheless MWOA was never far from Gotsfeld's mind. A letter written on the Aquitania examined the fund-raising progress, suggested new American contacts, and proposed new publicity. Gotsfeld's involvement extended to a request for recipes for the BZM cooking course. [22]

The end of the journey was especially tiring. After greeting Mendel in Haifa and resting a few hours, she met with Fradelle Haskell, who informed her of current developments. Her subsequent return to Tel Aviv offered no opportunity for relaxation and recuperation. There were well-wishers to entertain and tourists to woo.

The Jerusalem facility was on its feet now, though Gotsfeld constantly complained about overdue payments from America and insufficient funding from Youth Aliyah. Money matters notwithstanding, the original wrinkles had been smoothed. The school had a full staff, including educational and administrative directors, and competent teachers. Its reputation was solid. The waiting list was long. Students from Germany studied alongside local girls. Graduates located jobs easily. But the school's very success introduced new problems. In 1935 sixty students enrolled, a remarkable increase from the original twenty-four in two short years. The overwhelming majority were Youth Aliyah wards requiring dormitory accommodations. Their enrollment, though welcome, increased costs far beyond original projections. A balanced budget remained a distant dream.

Then there was a husband to placate. Mendel fretted over the tax on his wife's energy and was jealous of time spent away from him. Bessie too complained of no time for a private life, but did nothing to change the situation. She was indispensable and she knew it. For these reasons, she did not take advantage of her selection as a delegate to the Nineteenth World Zionist Congress, but remained at home in Tel Aviv.

The Second Bet Zeirot Mizrachi

From the beginning there had been vague talk of a network of vocational schools. By 1935, the Jerusalem school was stable enough for Gotsfeld to lay the groundwork for a second BZM in Tel Aviv. Before launching the new endeavor, she helped formulate new fund-raising procedures. A donor could purchase a pair of candlesticks for Friday night use of a single student. Other devises included a Golden Book inscribed with names of "patronesses," a *Sefer Hakavod* (Book of Honor) with pictures, and individual "sheets" inserted into a second beautiful volume. Local chapters with deep pockets could "donate" rooms, to be acknowledged with wall plaques. A major gift would entitle the donor to see his or her name attached to a wing of the building.

In pre - World War II usage, "propaganda" was a neutral term denoting publicity. The most basic "propaganda" was a prominent display of the MWOA name on the building. Tourists, Gotsfeld reasoned, would remember it and open their pocketbooks. MWOA members would return to America and recount with pride what they had seen, with similar results. Gotsfeld relied heavily on visitors from America, regaling them at her home. Letters to New York urged members to badger non-members who had seen the building and expressed interest in it.

Nor did she neglect the written word. When asked to describe the new school in the trilingual Jubilee Publication celebrating twenty-five years of Mizrachi in America, Gotsfeld composed a six-page article. In obedience to the maxim "conventionality is the best shelter for new aspirations," she phrased her extensive article in terms intended to satisfy the most tradition-minded Jews:

> The girls are equipped with sufficient knowledge and training to enable them to fill responsible positions as cooks, seamstresses, etc. What is of equal importance — during this time they learn to be economic and efficient housewives, bringing to the task in the home a scientific approach and creative spirit that are the secret of the successful homebuilder.[23]

The article ends with a note about the unanticipated but welcome new population and a tug on the emotions of the reader:

> We must therefore rededicate ourselves to renewed and intensive efforts to create new opportunities for these unfortunate victims of Hitlerism and make possible the expansion of our institution, give them a home and enable them to become Builders of Zion. May this coming New Year find you a tower of strength ascending the highest productivity in this part of the upbuilding of Eretz-Israel.[24]

Letters to New York suggested various "propaganda" devises, among them audio-visuals such as pictures and film and pamphlets reviewing the story of the organization and its projects. Excerpts from the letters appeared in MWOA Bulletins (that unaccountably underwent frequent name changes). Gotsfeld took delight in a 1934 Hadassah Newsletter article that cited BZM as an institution that accommodated German refugees; she suggested wide distribution of the piece.

Funds raised this way, however, were small change in light of the enormous sums required to launch a wholly new institution. After the MWOA National Conference of 1935 voted to found a new BZM in Tel Aviv, Gotsfeld approached Mayor Meir Dizengoff, Vice-mayor Yisrael Rokah (soon to be mayor), and the Municipal Council. With quiet assurance she presented the case for a second school. She described the Jerusalem school's program and convinced the officials that the all - Jewish city would benefit from a similar institution. Proudly, she displayed a European architect's modernistic design and touted the benefit of a handsome building to the urban landscape. The Council agreed to donate a large lot, centrally located near Dizengoff Square, and worth $50,000, provided that MWOA lay down a sizable down payment and persuade a bank to grant a mortgage for the rest.

Finding patrons capable of large donations was the obvious next step. Luckily, a generous South African couple with the picturesque name of Gesundheit settled in a Tel Aviv mansion and remained major supporters for many years. A wealthy Philadelphian named Ellis promised a big gift and then, disappointingly, changed his offer to a loan for a mortgage. In the end the Ellis Fund did donate generously, but the happy conclusion arrived at considerable cost to Gotsfeld's energy and nerves. Fortuitously, the manager of the Mizrachi Bank in Tel Aviv was a member of the Municipal Council; his bank assumed the mortgage. Much work needed to done before the completion of the second BZM, but Gotsfeld and her supporters had surmounted the principal obstacles.

5

Facing Competition, 1935–1936

Like many chronically ailing people, Bessie Gotsfeld was already past her physical prime by the time she reached her late forties. Hard work, rheumatism, and diabetes in particular had exacted a toll. Her red-gold hair, the glory of her youth, had lost its color and sheen and her blue eyes had surrendered their clarity. A youth who met her at this time described her as "short, poorly dressed...her face was heavily freckled, her eyes blood-shot, her lips full and protruding." Only a rigorous personal discipline kept her going. Before every meal, she carefully measured out her food. Three times a day, she retreated to a place where she could inject herself in private. Just as significant for her well-being was a refusal to wallow in self-pity, her concentration on other matters outside of her own person. The same young man who described her so ungraciously went on to say that she exuded such sympathy for him and all young people that long after he lost contact with her, he continued to feel a kinship. Years later, he brought his new bride to meet her.[1]

In the mid 1930s, Gotsfeld tried to normalize relations with other organs of Mizrachi. It was not possible to disregard the incessant demands for support of the Mizrachi Teachers Seminary for Women on the part of Rabbi Berlin and his daughter Judith. All the rabbis regarded MWOA, by now the most successful fundraiser in Mizrachi, as a cash cow. Gotsfeld was willing to participate in Mizrachi programs under what was called *Keren Erez Yisrael* but only if she controlled their dispersal. She told Judith Lieberman, Rabbi Berlin's daughter, that the money earmarked for MWOA endeavors should "at least go to the institutions that (the)money is collected for."[2]

When Leon Gellman assumed presidency of the Mizrachi Organization of America, Gotsfeld hoped that the men would no longer try to prevent MWOA from pursuing its own course and collecting the money due it from general funds. Instead she found herself once again bickering over status and money. In the United States, Mizrachi was a beneficiary of the U.P.A. (United Palestine Appeal) and its various arms were entitled to small sums from that pool. When MWOA needed funds earmarked for the Tel Aviv BZM, however, the Mizrachi Organization in America held back the money. Some cash came from the *Mercaz Olami*, the World

Mizrachi Central Committee, but not enough; this group was equally strapped for funds and consequently tightfisted.

To reduce long-standing friction with *Hapoel Hamizrachi*, Gotsfeld convinced MWOA to take on a joint project with that organization: *Meshek Poalot*, a new farm for female workers. The concession to the long-standing antagonist was also intended to reinforce discipline in MWOA, for between the lines of the agreement there was an unwritten caveat. In order to acquire the funding, the Boston group would have to refrain from soliciting money from MWOA members.

AGREEMENT BETWEEN THE HAPOEL HAMIZRACHI AND THE MIZRACHI WOMEN'S ORGANIZATION
March 17, 1936

AGREEMENT is hereby made between the HAPOEL HAMIZRACHI OF ERETZ YISROEL, represented by Mr. S.Z. Shragai; the HAPOEL HAMIZRACHI OF AMERICA, represented by its national President, Mr. Isidore Epstein; and the MIZRACHI WOMEN'S ORGANIZATION OF AMERICA, represented Mesdames. A. Shapiro and B.J. Goldstein; and with the participation of Rabbi Meyer Berlin and the national President of the Mizrachi Organization of America, Mr. Leon Gellman.

POINT NO. 1: That the Mizrachi Women's Organization of America shall participate in the establishment of a Meshek Poaloth of the Hapoel Hamizrachi and thereupon takes upon itself to raise $5,000. (£1,000) within two years from date. For this purpose, $500 shall be supplied by the Mizrachi Women's Organization of America by Passover.

POINT NO. 2: These funds namely $5,000. shall be used only for building and equipment purpose and not for any other phase of the Meshek Poaloth work and undertakings.

POINT NO. 3: The Mizrachi Women's Organization of America shall be given due credit for its assistance in the erection of the Meshek Poaloth inasmuch as the Meshek shall bear the following label: "Meshek Poaloth of the Hapoel Hamizrachi - Erected through the Assistance and Participation of the Mizrachi Women's Organization of America".

POINT NO. 4: Mrs. B. Gotsfeld or any other member of the Mizrachi Women's representative in Palestine that shall be designated by the Mizrachi Women's Organization of America, and with the consent of the Hapoel Hamizrachi shall represent this organization in those Hapoel Hamizrachi committees that shall engage themselves in the establishment of the Meshek, in all details.

POINT NO. 5: All monies from individual contributions as well as from Mizrachi Women's Chapters in America, also from those groups who are not connected with the Mizrachi Organization donating for the Meshek Poaloth, shall from to date go into the treasury of the Mizrachi Women's Organization of America and shall be credited towards the $5,000.

POINT NO. 6: The Hapoel Hamizrachi in Eretz Yisroel and America shall not arrange any financial campaign among the groups of the Mizrachi Women's Organization of America without their consent, and shall not organize any women's groups for moral or financial support of the Hapoel Hamizrachi.

POINT NO. 7: The Hapoel Hamizrachi of America shall extend to the Mizrachi Women's Organization moral support in this work, among the women of America.

Signed - HAPOEL HAMIZRACHI OF PALESTINE
s/S.Z. Shragai
HAPOEL HAMIZRACHI OF AMERICA
s\Mrs. Abraham Shapiro,
Pres., MIZRACHI WOMEN'S ORG. OF AMERICA[3]

Once again Gotsfeld's leadership role is downplayed; she is only the replaceable "representative." Even so, she does not lose her identity but is designated by her own first initial, not her husband's. This was, notably, not the case for the national president of MWOA.

Gotsfeld's leadership role is apparent in another area. MWOA set aside money for the Jewish National Fund, seasonal campaigns, and emergency drives for various religious and national causes. Gotsfeld did not oppose these donations, but insisted upon control from the top. Funds, she insisted, must come from the MWOA treasury, sanctioned by her approval. With great care, she supervised MWOA's annual contributions to the *Meshek Poalot* and the Mizrachi Female Teachers' Seminary.

At the same time, there were problems of internal management. For reasons of immaturity and poor mental or physical health, some German girls were not the proper material for BZM. One recommendation called for returning a young woman to Germany on the basis of her emotional immaturity. A teenager lost her way en route, to the consternation of her parents and the institution. That story turned out happily when the girl showed up at the school. Other young women were not so fortunate; budgetary pressures necessitated turning away potential students.[4]

Gotsfeld attempted to fill another need as well. Young women from Orthodox homes and no longer in school were often at loose ends. Some were local residents on their own for the first time; the majority were recent immigrants from Central Europe. To house them in a caring and religious environment until they could support themselves she set up a working girls' hostel, *Bet Haluzot*, adjacent to the school. This, of course, increased the strain on the budget.[5]

Gotsfeld's fragile constitution could not long sustain the unending enforcement of discipline, the quest for sovereignty, the fiscal worries, and the fluctuating promises on the part of the Ellis Foundation to fund a second BZM. Nor could her delicate health tolerate extremes in temperature. Tel Aviv's idiosyncratic weather — rain in the winter turning sand into mud and rendering some streets impassible, suffocating humidity in summer — forced her to abandon husband and home at peak times. She enjoyed Tiberias in winter; the mild climate and daily bathing in its hot springs did her good. However, when she spent a late summer month in Jerusalem, where a desert climate cools the night air, she could not follow her physician's orders to refrain from activity. Even when she resisted the temptation to visit the BZM, she complained to her sister-in-law, it made no difference.

> Mendel let me come here with a faithful promise that I don't go to Bet Zeirot but what is the difference? Bet Zeirot comes to me. This is the most difficult time of the year in our institution, the adjustment of the staff, and how difficult it is to do that with an unbalanced budget you can well imagine. I have meetings everyday and what makes it even harder for me is that I have not the support of Mendel because he claims that my health comes first. It is a vicious circle, my dear. I can't neglect my health and I must stand by the institution.[6]

Two Losses and a Gain

The year 1936 was one of turmoil, organizational, personal, and national. At that time, the Tel Aviv municipality finally fixed its imprimatur on a second BZM. Diminishing Gotsfeld's joy, however, was the loss of two women who were very important in her life. One was Fraidelle Haskell, who died suddenly in January. Haskell had been her closest friend in the Yishuv, the champion of her work even before her immigration. Haskell, moreover, had been bookkeeper of the Jerusalem school since its opening and Gotsfeld would be hard-pressed to find a replacement. Of her friend's death, she wrote,

> Like thunder out of a clear sky this terrible tragedy came to us. We knew Mrs. Haskell was sick with typhoid and were very anxious about her, but nobody for one moment thought it would be fatal. Helpless we stand before fate, not even being able to give ourselves completely to our sorrow because of the demands life makes on us.[7]

A personal tragedy was the death of her stepmother Adela, of which she was informed in April. She deeply mourned the woman who had come into her life in early adolescence and sustained her for thirty-five years.

Nineteen thirty-six nevertheless introduced a measure of compensation; it was the year when Gotsfeld's nephew Eliezer Goldman arrived in Palestine, After his graduation from Yeshiva College with honors in mathematics, the family had expected him to continue his studies in the Rabbi Itzchak Elhanan Rabbinical School of Yeshiva University. But what attracted the brilliant youth was not American Jewry but Erez Israel, not the rabbinate but the Zionist experiment. He dallied for a year, and then emigrated. The Gotsfelds welcomed him into their Tel Aviv home. At that point, he had not yet decided whether to remain in Palestine, and used it as a home base while Mendel and Bessie joyfully assumed the *in loco parentis* role.

Youth Aliyah

Outside events took their toll. The Berlin Olympic Games of 1936 brought temporary respite to the mounting social, economic, and legal removal of Jews from German life, a lull before the storm. The same year, however, ushered in three years of agony in the Yishuv. Arabs, alarmed at the mounting Jewish population, rioted against the British and attacked Jews. They concentrated on the fragile physical links between Jewish communities, in particular the twisted mountainous road that conveyed vehicles between Tel Aviv and Jerusalem. Gotsfeld's first letters to her sister-in-law had bemoaned the depredations of 1929 from the safety of a Czech spa; those of 1936 conveyed first-hand experience. Her home was in Tel Aviv, where she was preparing a second BZM, but the only functioning Mizrachi Household School (one of its English-language titles) was in Jerusalem. Braving the perils of land travel, she went there as often as she could and lingered as long as she was needed, much to her husband's distress.

The dangers heaped new financial burdens upon old ones. Because of the explosive political and military situation the British governor imposed a 7 p.m. curfew. Now it was necessary to provide services not anticipated in the budget. Gotsfeld had to find teachers and counselors to supervise forty-five resident émigrée girls during the summer, when the regular staff was on vacation. Faculty and students wanted to be kept abreast of the news, but forays away from the building, even in daylight, were dangerous. A radio was the obvious conduit of information, but the school operated so close to the bone that it had to rent one. Gotsfeld redoubled her efforts to locate a donor, and found one.[8]

When not occupied with fund raising, municipal machinations, organizational discipline, school management, and precarious local conditions, Gotsfeld's attention centered on Youth Aliyah. Within religious Zionism, she always demanded her due, but in exchanges with non-Orthodox Jews, she closed ranks with Mizrachi and Hapoel Hamizrachi. Before the Youth Aliyah bureaucracy, she defended two nascent Orthodox farm villages, Kibbutz Rotges, near Petah Tikvah, and *Kfar Noar Dati* (The Religious Youth Village) in the Haifa area. She felt a special kinship with the former, the first Orthodox institution to reap benefit from Youth Aliyah, partly because BZM was the second.

The *Jüdische Jugendhilfe* selected candidates for *aliyah* (immigration) in Germany, then turned them over to Youth Aliyah. Youth Aliyah, in turn, arranged for British certification of the children, settled them in institutions in Erez Israel, and subsidized their absorption. The problem was that the only Orthodox institutions prepared to receive young people were Bet Zeirot Mizrachi, Kibbutz Rotges, and Rambam and Nehemiah, two boys' trade schools in Haifa. Non-Orthodox Zionism, by contrast, boasted thirty kibbutzim; scores of agricultural villages; and two founding constituents of the *Arbeitsgemeinschaft* , the Ahavah orphanage and the Ben Shemen Youth Village.[9]

Orthodox groups in Palestine and the Diaspora alerted sympathizers to the imbalance. Religious parents in Germany, they complained, had registered their children with the *Jüdische Jugendhilfe*, but there was nowhere to send them. Rumors, some true, others exaggerated, proliferated about the placement of children from Orthodox homes in schools and collective settlements which encouraged them to abandon religion. Partisans warned that in the absence of Orthodox institutions, a thousand deserving children would abandon Jewish tradition. Rabbi Joseph Hertz, Britain's Chief Rabbi, demanded that no German child be placed in any "a-religious or anti-religious place." Other Orthodox spokesmen hit upon a discrepancy between Russian-born residents of the New Yishuv and potential immigrants from Germany. The former, they maintained, had been nurtured in atheism and socialism, while the latter hailed from bourgeois homes. Even those who did not attend synagogue on a regular basis, they opined, were not skeptics and nonbelievers.[10]

For their part, non-Orthodox citizens were nonplussed at the implication that they were responsible for the imbalance. Was it a crime, they asked, to maintain institutions that reflected their own ideology? Why hadn't Orthodox Jews built more of their own? Some even balked at the 25/75 agreement, hinting that well under a quarter of the applications came from Orthodox candidates.

In response to the observation that they had not prepared places for Orthodox *olim* (new immigrants),[11] Mizrachi partisans again made distinctions between German and Russian Jews. They argued that because the Orthodox youth were essentially children of recent émigrés from Eastern Europe, they needed more aid than Jews long resident in Germany. They added that Orthodox Jews in Europe and America were, as a rule, less affluent than their liberal co-religionists, hence less able to support the causes that they espoused.

To put an end to the squabbling Youth Aliyah created Kfar Noar Dati. It arranged for the Jewish National Fund to consign an "oak-clad hillside," an undeveloped area next to Kfar Hasidim, an Orthodox settlement in the Haifa environs. Children would be housed in the new village but receive religious education and agricultural training at Kfar Hasidim.[12] Promptly, two problems materialized. First, it took a full year for the transfer to take place, during which time many Orthodox groups, including MWOA, duly briefed by its "representative," raised a hue and a cry. Henrietta Szold, ever punctilious in hewing to regulations, would not proceed with plans until the transfer was complete.[13] Even before that was accomplished, another problem surfaced. Kfar Noar Dati, according to Szold's estimate, would cost £P13, 500, but Youth Aliyah was hard pressed to squeeze out £P10, 000.[14] Again Orthodox spokesmen protested the scarcity of places for children from religious homes. Some went back to their original argument and insisted that religious children could never be fully served by a mere 25% of the certificates.[15] To all this, hard-pressed Szold responded,

> The real explanation of our difficulty is this: the Youth Aliyah became possible in its present form only because the Kewutzot (sic) gave us the possibility of maintaining, educating, and adjusting young people to agricultural pursuits at a minimum expenditure of funds, and the religious elements in Jewry had not provided Kewutzot."[16]

Eager to settle differences between Jewish factions, Szold convinced Hadassah to come to the rescue. Hadassah's contribution of $15,000 (£P3000) covered the building costs. Dormitories housed eighty boys and girls at first, then 150, later 200. Subsequently, Youth Aliyah provided funds for general management, farm equipment and livestock.[17]

Gotsfeld was a vociferous advocate of the first Orthodox youth village, but occupying most of her attention was another matter, BZM's financial dependence upon Youth Aliyah for the support of the German girls sent there. The rescue organization had agreed to subsidize each client at £3.5000 a month. With a bit of belt-tightening, rural cooperatives, collectives, and farm schools could manage with "a minimum expenditure of funds;" but urban facilities with dormitories could not. At one point, BZM had to turn down the *Jugendhilfe's* offer of ten new students, stating that with only a per capita £3.5000 subsidy, it could support only five.[18] After a three year struggle on her part as well as that of her allies — in this case sweetened by Szold's advocacy — [19] Gotsfeld achieved her goal: each BZM student would receive a stipend of £4.2000 per month. Later on, even that sum would prove inadequate.[20]

All the while, the American scene was never far from Gotsfeld's mind. Letters of 1935 and 1936 indicate bitter feelings towards Henrietta Szold. Long after she settled in Palestine, Szold remained the idol of Hadassah, by this time 100,000 strong. Responding to her charisma, the National Board acceded to her suggestion that the organization become Youth Aliyah's fund raising organ in America, paralleling the *Arbeitsgemeinschaft* in Germany. That fact dominated Gotsfeld's attitude towards Henrietta Szold and Hadassah. Gotsfeld's view of Szold is conveyed by the Hebrew expression *kabdehu v'hashdehu* (respect and suspect); her stance towards Hadassah was one of unconcealed enmity.

Actually, on the organizational level there was no parity between Szold and Gotsfeld; only Gotsfeld was the official representative of a Zionist organization. Szold was Hadassah's honorary president, but the title had no bearing on her work.

It was in her dual capacities of head of the *Va'ad Leumi*'s Social Service Department and Director of Youth Aliyah that she convinced Hadassah to assume the costs. The Jewish world nevertheless continued to associate Szold with Hadassah.

Strained feelings between the two organizations, initiated in 1933 and augmented in 1934, proliferated after December, 1935, when Rabbi Wolf Gold informed Gotsfeld that Hadassah had become the sole fiscal body securing the means for Youth Aliyah. For the two of them this was proof of Hadassah's desire to monopolize the appeal for German children. The benefit to German Jewish youth notwithstanding, Gotsfeld soberly evaluated the effect on the organization that she represented. German children, she observed, are an obvious a "selling point" a recruitment tool. "Our organization, she warned Belle Goldstein, "must be very much on its guard that it should not lose out by all these negotiations." [21] As the head of an organization that regarded Hadassah as a major competitor for Orthodox Jewish women's hearts and pocketbooks, Gotsfeld was convinced that Hadassah's new undertaking would slow down MWOA recruitment and weaken its authority. She and the other MWOA leaders had long chafed at the membership of Orthodox women in both organizations, curtailing the size of their contributions to each. It was one small step from resentment to certainty that Hadassah intended "to swallow every other group."[22]

Some Mizrachi women fought back with whispered insinuation. The source of the canard that Hadassah's support of secular kibbutzim contributed to unbelief and loose sexual morals in the Yishuv is obscure[23] but it reached Szold and did not endear MWOA to her. Rumors are, by definition, vague and ambiguous; in this instance they conflated Hadassah, Youth Aliyah, and Szold.

That issue aside, Gotsfeld feared that the fund raising mechanism of MWOA would collapse under the collusion of these powerful forces, especially in light of the fact that American donors were not allowed to earmark their contributions for Orthodox refugees. Hadassah alone could collect American dollars, the *Jugendhilfe* alone could move certified refugees, and only Youth Aliyah could place the children. This led to unpleasant interchanges between Szold, Harry Fischel, an Orthodox Zionist and philanthropist, and Anita Müller-Cohen, resettled in Tel Aviv. To Müller-Cohen's complaints Szold responded: "Monies intended for our work come to us direct in the Agency, and we have no connection with any of the Mizrachi offices, banks, etc."[24]

At this time MWOA's immediate requirements were a third floor on the Jerusalem BZM and an entirely new structure in Tel Aviv. Since no building, however indispensable, could match the emotional appeal of an endangered child, Gotsfeld and her cohort anticipated shriveling funds when they were most needed. Another factor was also in operation. Despite Gotsfeld's advocacy of Orthodox agricultural farms and cooperatives, during the mid 1930s her heart was in the cities, sites of the present and future BZM. Henrietta Szold, on the other hand, agreed to sent Youth Aliyah girls to urban schools but preferred settlement in the countryside, as she indicated with these words: "We do not want to multiply city education to the detriment of agricultural training."[25] Szold took little notice of the fact that the "Household School" offered training in gardening and poultry raising. (Indeed, several graduates would settle on kibbutzim and moshavot).[26]

Mizrachi stalwarts had hoped that new immigrants from Poland and Rumania would alter the balance between religious and freethinking Jews. That did not happen. To bolster religious education of young newcomers, Rabbi Berlin became a partisan of MWOA. On its behalf he pressed a spirited demand: "The Women's Mizrachi Organization is the only organization qualified to care for the religious training of children in Palestine."[27] Emboldened, MWOA, under Berlin's direction, proposed a three-point plan intended to establish parity with Hadassah in Youth Aliyah:

1) That Hadassah endorse a statement for the press showing that Mizrachi Women's Organization of America was participating in Youth Aliyah.

2) That Hadassah recognized representatives of Mizrachi on the National Youth Aliyah Committee - in their official and not in their individual capacity.

3) That copies of all correspondence, reports, etc. re Youth Aliyah be sent to the Mizrachi Woman's Organization.[28]

The Hadassah leadership considered Berlin's demands a nuisance rather than a serious proposition. They pointed out that MWOA was already a participant in Youth Aliyah, but as a recipient, not a donor. They had already noted Orthodox Zionism's representation on the Religious Committee by Rabbi Yehudah Leib Fishman (kept out of the debate by his very membership). Rose Gell Jacobs, National Hadassah President, reminded Jrena Shapiro, MWOA'S National President, "Hadassah is interested in all the Jewish youth." To prove the point, the Hadassah Board stepped up the drive to obtain the $15,000 for Kfar Noar Dati. To Hadassah leaders it was obvious that Youth Aliyah should chose their organization on the basis of its proven ability to raise money for projects in Palestine. For the same reasons the Jewish Agency did not take MOWA's proposal seriously.[29]

Institutional suspicions were not confined to one side. A letter from Jacobs to Szold curiously mirrors Gotsfeld's complaints about Hadassah. Were Youth Aliyah to accept Rabbi Berlin's demands, she maintained, "The Mizrachi Organization would built itself up on the back of the joint Youth Aliyah Appeal and Hadassah would hold the bag of fund raising responsibility."[30] Henrietta Szold was more charitable. Despite her irritation at Gotsfeld's "constant complaints and worriments,"[31] she compared the MWOA representative favorably to the rabbi. "Rabbi Berlin's interest therein should be kept quite separate from the Mizrachi Women's," she wrote. "The latter issue is purely organizational; his is political and pseudo-religious."[32] What Szold meant by "pseudo-religious" will be discussed below. More pertinent to this discussion were her diagnoses of Berlin's position and the MWOA predicament. Berlin pursued his objectives by participating in the political backbiting that has marked Zionist politics for a century. The two women, on the other hand, prided themselves in their distance from politics. What Gotsfeld really needed, Szold surmised correctly, was additional money for MWOA programs. Of course that is what virtually every letter to MWOA 's national office in New York demanded.[33]

An additional point that Gotsfeld reiterated time and again was that not all BZM students received Youth Aliyah funding. Even in the face of Nazi outrages, she held fast to the school's earliest objective: to educate and socialize young girls long resident in Palestine. Since few students could afford tuition, this imposed an added financial burden. A few of the German refugees, moreover, had not immigrated through the Youth Aliyah mechanism and were therefore not eligible for funding.

Most pressing was the enduring budgetary crunch. Still harboring jealousy of Hadassah, which, to her mind, had money to spare, she bemoaned Szold's expectation that the BZM budget include shoe repair, damages, and accident insurance. Szold's reasoning — that the Meier Shfeyah Children and Youth Village did this without complaint— she considered unfair.[34] Comparatively wealthy Junior Hadassah sponsored Meier Shfeyah, Gotsfeld noted, and therefore the youth village did not suffer BZM's financial difficulties.[35]

As far as Rabbi Berlin was concerned, Szold was correct. The rabbi was indeed less interested in bolstering a woman's organization than in strengthening Mizrachi. Education along Orthodox lines, he argued, was the birthright of every young immigrant.[36] The son of the great scholar who directed Europe's most prestigious yeshiva, Berlin assumed continuity from the pre-Emancipation past when rabbis controlled every aspect of Jewish life, especially education. In the graceful prose of Jehuda Reinharz, "East European Orthodoxy... regarded the whole Jewish community, its sinners as well as its pious, as an integral whole - one, to be sure, in which traditionalists were accustomed to exercise dominant authority."[37] To maintain that authority, Berlin plunged into political life. The struggle over Youth Aliyah took place in the mid-thirties, the period when Mizrachi, under his leadership, imposed public Sabbath and *kashrut* observance upon a reluctant majority. Because the rabbi, triumphant on that score, still distrusted MWOA's insistence upon independence, his advocacy of its right to supervise Youth Aliyah education must be seen as a tactical ploy, not a change of heart.

Gotsfeld faced more immediate worries. In June 1936 the promised new funding for Youth Aliyah students had not yet materialized. Desperate for money, she threatened a separate appeal for religious youth. Hadassah, she complained, "monopolize (d) the appeal for Youth Aliyah and (did) not pay in full for their charges. The money we get from the M.W.of A. we use for girls who are not of the Y.A. and have nobody else to appeal for help. We shall certainly not use that money to pay their debts."[38]

The money did come through, however, and the unpleasantness abated. The issue would resurface during the war years, amidst mounting pressures. By that time Bessie Gotsfeld and Henrietta Szold, chastened by experience, were ready to collaborate for the larger causes of child rescue and rebuilding the Jewish homeland. [39]

6

Never a Rubber Stamp

There was a discrepancy in pre-state Zionism between original assumptions and sober reality. Zionism's formulators envisioned a nation peacefully settled in its historic homeland, enjoying cultural integrity and physical security. All too soon, reality overwhelmed theory. The Yishuv became an arena for Jewish cultural wars of European origin; and simply to date eruptions of Arab fury — 1920-21, 1929, 1936-39, 1947-8 – is to attest that peace and security remained a distant dream. During the late 1930s and the early 1940s, political events shaped Bessie Gotsfeld's life and labors. The Arab riots, the Peel Commission, the MacDonald White Paper, the mounting desperation of European Jewry, then global war - all occupied her mind and troubled her soul. The state of America affairs as well elicited her interest and even governed her vocabulary, as for example, when she equated MWOA's quest for sovereignty with the United States' embrace of the Monroe Doctrine.[1] Furthermore, her brother Samuel's involvement in New York politics made Roosevelt's re-election a matter of personal interest.

Though alert to regional and international events, she nevertheless shied away from political engagement, verifying Szold's observation that her concerns were organizational rather than political per se. Defying her closest lieutenants, she never allowed MWOA to stand for election as a separate party.[2] The only purely political opinion that she voiced at this time was criticism of the British Royal Commission, formed in the wake of the 1936 Arab riots. The Peel Commission Report of July 1937 recommended dividing Palestine into Arab and Jewish states while retaining British control of the Jerusalem-Galilee promontory and key ports. Unlike the major Zionist leaders who consented to its proposals, though unhappily, Gotsfeld could not accept partition of mandated Palestine. Her position hardened after she attended the Twentieth World Zionist Congress, held in Zurich in August 1937, as one of three delegates from MWOA in the eighty-person Mizrachi contingent. Joining hands with the parent body and most American delegates, including Szold, she voted to oppose the Peel Report.[3]

After the Congress, Gotsfeld returned once again to Franzensbad for a cure and remained for the High Holydays. Vexed by declining hearing, she proceeded to Vienna to consult an otologist. Her body was in Europe, but "Palestina," as she sometimes spelled the name, was ever on her mind. Soon she was home, confronting problems, old and new. Aside from the viability of the Yishuv, the mounting Nazi menace, and the welfare of her relatives across the seas, the issues that caused concern were internal and organizational, with personal implications.

Maintaining Principles and Prerogatives

Dissatisfaction with other religious Zionists did not decline even in the face of mortal danger to world Jewry. Gotsfeld was often at odds with Shlomo Zalman Shragai, spokesman for Hapoel Hamizrachi. She was not opposed to his party per se; early quarrels with the Boston group had been turf battles. Her advocacy of Kibbutz Rotges and Kfar Noar Dati, moreover, indicated willingness to join hands with ventures undertaken by the religious kibbutz movement (*Hakibbutz Hadati*). Pursuant to the March 1936 agreement, signed by Shragai as well as herself, she helped the *Meshek Poalot* get on its feet. Yet she opposed Shragai on several grounds. She chafed at the slow pace of his work. She suspected that he used money designated by MWOA for the religious girls' farm for his own purposes. What most upset her was his irresponsible handling of money. Unlike MWOA, which kept track of all income and budgeted expenses, Hapoel Hamizrachi, she was convinced, undertook assignments without considering their long-range costs.

An ideological factor sheds additional light on Gotsfeld's antagonism to Shragai. At this time (though not later) she got along well with Moshe Hayim Shapiro, another Hapoel Mizrachi leader, a man of great political savvy, more inclined to action than philosophical musings.[4] Shragai, on the other hand, was more thinker than doer. Like many revolutionaries, he justified the new in terms of the old. A died-in-the-wool Marxist, he interpreted religious socialism in Torah terms:

> The believing Jew sees and judges every idea in light of faith and God's Torah. To the believing Jew "God's Torah is perfect" and serves as the basic foundation for all ethical teachings in all of its various revelations. The faith of the believer does not tolerate any partnership with any other authority. This [would] lead us to the conclusion that there is no room for a believing Jew to see himself as a "religious worker or a "religious socialist," etc. [However] a believing Jew *can* come with his faith to Zionism, to working-class-ism, to kibbutzim, to socialism, to ethicism (sic), etc. - if the Torah requires or justifies them. And he who is not able to merit this must examine his ways and strengthen his belief and "repent and be healed." Faith and life, according to the Torah, are not a type of "second front;" they are the foundation.[5]

Gotsfeld's social views, as far as can be determined – for she never stated them explicitly – were closer to those of her old mentor, Meir Berlin. Her father, brothers, and husband were businessmen. Governing her life and work were bourgeois values of careful planning, rational organization, and budgetary constraints. Mizrachi laymen were predominantly smallholders and merchants who shared her middle-class background and bias. Rabbi Berlin, their champion, was not happy with the plank in the Poalei Hamizrachi platform that decried the exploitation of workers, He maintained that socialism attracted Jewish workers only because greedy entrepreneurs strayed from Torah principles. It followed that the solution to economic problems was a Jewish community living in the spirit as well as the letter of God's law.[6]

During the '30s and '40s, Hapoel Hamizrachi captured the imagination of the younger and progressive rabbis and laymen in Mizrachi . Among them was Rabbi Wolf Gold. Formerly a champion of MWOA, he appeared to be losing interest. The same was true of editor Gedaliah Bublick.

That Gotsfeld was not at home with Hapoel Hamizrachi is indicated by her acceptance of Mizrachi's opposition to a controversial Hapoel Hamizrachi decision. During Hapoel Hamizrachi's formative years, it had split over the question of whether to join the Histadrut (General Federation of Jewish Workers in the Land of Israel). After much debate, the majority contingent decided to affiliate, a sign of accord with the social values of the majority labor parties. Many years would pass before the two factions would reunite.[7] Histadrut members received a major benefit, enrollment in *Kupat Holim* (Sick Fund), its health insurance plan. The Histadrut permitted Hapoel Hamizrachi to set up its own *Kupat Holim*, making members equally eligible for low-cost treatment in hospitals and clinics and for prescription drugs at nominal cost. Mizrachi leaders, on the other hand, shunned the Histadrut as militantly anti-religious. Rabbi Judah Fishman-Maimon, for example, refused all contact with the organization.[8] For many years, the issue remained a source of dissension within religious Zionism.

In the Yishuv, only paid workers could receive benefits under *Kupat Holim*. Since MWOA was an independent entity with no corporate ties to either Mizrachi or Hapoel Hamizrachi, Gotsfeld could have established personal eligibility for *Kupat Holim* medical benefits, but she chose not to. Consequently, she had to render full payment to the physicians who treated her numerous ailments, and for the medicines that they prescribed (though she received some from America). Her decision seems to have been a matter of principle, either disapproval of the Histadrut or the conviction that compensation for MWOA work should be personal satisfaction rather than monetary remuneration.[9]

Gotsfeld's fidelity to Mizrachi social philosophy notwithstanding, she continued to oppose Mizrachi male hegemony. She was convinced that the *Mercaz Olami* (World Central Mizrachi Committee) respected neither her projects nor her methods. The Batei Zeirot Mizrachi were of little concern to rabbis who continued to equate education with yeshiva learning. Her American-style accounting methods and distribution of resources was as foreign to them as was Justice Brandeis's comparable position to his East European opponents.[10] An east European herself, she nevertheless shared Henrietta Szold's endorsement of the Brandesian requirement of fiscal responsibility.

Most distressing was the realization that neither *Mercaz Olami* nor its American affiliate acknowledged MWOA's sovereignty. In response to (male) Mizrachi meddling, she declared, "I never in my life was a rubber stamp and don't expect to be." The personal merged with the organizational: "I hope you see their point very clear (sic). The object is to have your representative in Palestine out of the picture." [11]

New evidence of Mizrachi's disregard for Gotsfeld's sensibilities and MWOA's independence surfaced in 1937. By that time she had lived in Palestine for six years. She was a proven leader. She represented an organization that had been self-sufficient for twelve years and legally independent for three. She had built one school and capably guided it for four years. A larger school was under construction in central Tel Aviv. She stood up to politicians in the Yishuv as well as the Youth Aliyah leadership. Her organization was the most efficient fundraiser in World Mizrachi. Twice she was selected to represent Mizrachi at the World Jewish Congress. These factors notwithstanding, *Mercaz Olami* continued to demand a voice in MWOA affairs. She always refused. In her estimation, men enjoyed the grand gesture, while women performed the real work. Her disdain for the *Mercaz Olami* was clear: "They have nothing to do, and since they are not doing anything constructive, they want to meddle with our work." [12]

Injury followed insult when *Mercaz Olami* sent Gotsfeld a check for the *Bet Haluzot* in Tel Aviv. This was an institution for young women not much older than her adolescent students. Female workers who lived in the cities were especially vulnerable to exploitation by employers and other men. To give them a safe place where they could nurture their finer instincts, she supported *Batei Haluzot*, religious and cultural centers for working girls, one located in the Jerusalem BZM, the other in Tel Aviv. Her budget, however, separated funds for those institutions from those dedicated to the BZMs. This accounts for her fury at receipt of that check, especially because she was anticipating a larger one earmarked BZM. Did that mean, she wondered, that that in the eyes of Mizrachi officialdom, female institutions were interchangeable? Aware that the umbrella organization treated Hapoel Hamizrachi as a separate unit, she demanded equal consideration. Anything less, she knew, would imply MWOA's return to a position of subservience, "an enormous setback." Time and again she reiterated the position that policy must be "formulated and determined by the MWOA, and, of course "carried out by its representative in Palestine." [13] No rubber-stamp she!

Personal prerogative and institutional independence aside, BZM took up most of her time and absorbed nearly all her energy. In the middle thirties, conditions in Jewish Palestine were far from luxurious. Gotsfeld was willing to live in a cramped apartment with few conveniences. Her sole personal indulgence was clothing from America, either sent by family members or brought in by visitors. Amenities common in America elicited were hard-won prizes in the Yishuv. The laundry in the first BZM had opened with no hot water heater. BZM didn't even have a radio until she located a donor.

Bet Zeirot Mizrachi, Tel Aviv

With the waning of Arab violence in the late '30s and the influx of Jews fleeing persecution in Germany, Poland, and Rumania, financial stability returned to the Yishuv. The Depression in America was easing, loosening the purse strings of American religious Zionists. For these reasons the second BZM, completed in 1938, was physically superior to the first. No remodeled house this one, but a new structure designed by a European-trained architect. It was an L shaped building of two (later three) stories, strategically positioned on a handsome plot. In front was a small garden, laid out by a landscape artist. The entrance was of polished stone with a marble-like gleam. When the structure and grounds were finished, they attracted visitors from the entire Yishuv. For its day it was a wonder, the more so because it was planned and executed by an American woman for an Orthodox organization.

Furnishing the building was a challenge and a joy. Gotsfeld instructed Betty Gafni, a local committee member, to find library equipment in old Jaffa. When the chairs and tables did not please her, she sent Gafni back to exchange for those she considered more suitable. With the modest Gotsfeld apartment on Yona Hanavi Street in mind, Gafni observed, "She (Gotsfeld) was more concerned about those things than about her own comforts and furnishings."[14]

The lower level of the new building contained the common rooms: large kitchen and dining room, offices and classrooms, and a space that was a gym on weekdays and a synagogue on the Sabbath. The second floor, and later the third as well, functioned as a dormitory. A school objective was to teach young women to get along with one another while at the same time enjoying personal privacy. The configuration supported the purpose; an outside terrace connected the rooms, but each girl could retire to her own space.

BZM Tel Aviv specialized in sewing, cooking, household management, and crafts. Food prepared in class was served as the next meal. During the war years the administration would add a commercial course to prepare secretaries for growing businesses in the Yishuv. Girls who selected it learned Hebrew typewriting and stenography and familiarized themselves with English business terms.

The BZM synagogue satisfied both religious and social objectives. After Friday evening services and a special Sabbath dinner, the girls enjoyed folk dancing. Teenaged boys and girls from the B'nai Akiba youth movement attended Saturday morning services and socialized afterwards. There were bar mitzvah celebrations, usually of teachers' sons, and galas for local Mizrachi members. Festivities took place at night in the same space. Students who served the meal, then later cleared tables and swept floors earned pin money.

On weekday and Saturday evenings young men would call for the girls and take them out. A curfew (typical for the period even in American women's colleges), was strictly enforced by a monitor at the school's reception desk. Students had to sign out when they left and sign in when they returned. All this conveyed the message that they were dignified young ladies expected to behave accordingly. Still, no Big Brother or Sister kept them under surveillance. Nor did anyone censure a bareheaded boyfriend or his date.[15]

After the Tel Aviv building's completion and dedication, Gotsfeld traveled to the United States for a cross-country fund raising tour. World War II erupted during this visit, but she left before this country joined the war effort. Nevertheless, it was in America that Gotsfeld would face the first challenges of that terrible conflagration.

7

Wartime Propaganda, Peaceful Activities, 1939 - 1942

A few months before war broke out Bessie Gotsfeld sailed to the United States on the Queen Mary, arriving in June 1939 to find Meshulam Kerstein of Mizrachi waiting for her. To her surprise, her teenaged nephew Jacob Goldman also managed to find his way to the place of quarantine.[1] Soon there was a joyful reunion with sisters, brothers, and sister-in-law Belle. The fly in the ointment was the distressing predicament of her sister Tillie, married to the artist Ben Shahan. In the early years of their marriage she had supported him, but fame brought estrangement and, eventually, divorce.[2]

There was little time to fret over family matters; immediately Gotsfeld turned her attention to organizational matters. She discovered that eight years of work in the Yishuv had enhanced her reputation, yet for the first time her leadership style was a subject of dissatisfaction. Tempering the cadre's appreciation of her selfless devotion was irritation with her controlling ways. Rank and file members, however, continued to regard her with unqualified awe, especially the young among them. At one conference, a group of Junior Mizrachi women sat in a circle on the floor at Bessie's feet, delighting in her obvious interest in each one of them. She encouraged the young women to expand their special project in Palestine, children's houses in religious settlements.[3]

A personal charisma carried her far. She arrived in time for the first MWOA annual convention not held in tandem with the men's Mizrachi convention and was one of two featured speakers at the second evening's celebration, "Palestine Night." Her presence and the novelty of the independent convention against a background of impending war succeeded in filling organizational coffers. After the convention, Gotsfeld attended the ill-fated 1939-40 New York World's Fair, enjoying "Mizrachi Women's Day."

Some problems encountered in Palestine followed Gotsfeld to the New World: male Mizrachi's *de haut en bas* attitude; conflicts between Mizrachi and Hapoel Hamizrachi; competition with other Zionist women's groups within Mizrachi and outside. As to her own organization, she was pleased with its effective fund-raising mechanism, but exasperated with the dearth of organizational know-how.

On a personal level, she had to assuage her sister Sarah's fears for her son, then pondering permanent settlement in Palestine. Eliezer Goldman was an idealist drawn to religious socialism. He left the university, married, and settled in Kibbutz S'de Eliyahu. After the birth of Israel, Pinchas Churgin, his Yeshiva University professor, would recruit him for the new Bar Ilan University. Goldman completed the PhD in philosophy and taught there for many years. Throughout his long life he retained his kibbutz membership, and handed over his entire salary.[4]

While he still lingered in the Gotsfeld home, Sarah was vexed with uncertainty. She worried that Eliezer would be subject to the American military draft and was afraid that he would abandon Orthodox Judaism. Neither fear materialized. Eliezer did not qualify for the military and he never abandoned his religion. Underlying the suspicion that he would was the family's mistrust of Zionist religious socialism, both its sophisticated and complex rationale and its challenge to the Mizrachi establishment. Gotsfeld concentrated on the facts as she saw them. More than her sister, she was aware of the allure of secularism in the Yishuv and told her to be content that Eliezer opted for a religious kibbutz.

The problem of citizenship during wartime was a further source of worry. Bessie was an American citizen, but Mendel was not. She fretted over Mendel's legal status in Palestine should war come. Her politically connected brother Samuel had been working on it for some time, but in 1939 nothing was resolved.

The onset of war in early September brought terror to her heart. She fretted over the distance from her husband and the children under her care; she trembled for the harassed Jews of Europe and the uncertain future of the Yishuv. More immediately, the fate of her sister-in-law Belle Goldstein was unknown for a few days. Goldstein was a Mizrachi delegate to the Twenty-First World Zionist Congress that convened in Geneva, Switzerland and closed abruptly just one week before the Nazi invasion of Poland.

To the family's relief, Belle reached New York on September 7, but she conveyed harrowing news. Because of the MacDonald White Paper permanently limiting Jewish immigration to 75,000 and the mounting oppression of Jews in central Europe, Goldstein reported, spirits were low even before the Congress opened on August 16. As it progressed edginess gave way to despondency. The third day brought a public announcement advising Polish citizens to return home immediately. On August 24, the Congress, awash in rumors of border closings and military mobilization, shut down altogether. Chaim Weizmann closed the final session with these prescient words:

> If, as I hope, we are spared in life and our work continues,
> who knows — perhaps a new light will shine upon us from the thick,
> black doom...There are some things which cannot fail to come to pass,
> things without which the world cannot be imagined.[5]

That most European delegates had an appointment in Samarra was beyond the imagination of even the wildest prophets of doom. The Americans, of course, would return to a safe place, but their immediate predicament was terrifying. They traveled to Paris on a blacked-out train, registered at the American Embassy and then undertook the difficult chore of securing reservations for ship passage home. Goldstein later recalled sitting in our hotel room in the evening when an excited porter in the hotel rushed in to draw the heavy black-out drapes.

> Europe was acquainted with bombs, as we fortunate Americans were not. At night, the streets of Paris were dark and deserted, but during the day one could easily mark the fear of approaching war on each face. We sailed in complete darkness, once night fell. Radios were taken away from the passengers, cables to the U.S. were not permitted — no one was allowed a lighted cigarette on deck at night. It was a very rough voyage with practically everyone confined to their rooms. We had taken a northern route to avoid a possible submarine attack. It was a harrowing experience, but I kept remembering that we were going home to our families, to the safety of our homes —while millions of our fellow Jews, what of them? The joy of reunion with my family a week later could not erase the picture of those sad good-byes in Geneva.

With the beginning of the war, transoceanic communication sharply declined. Weeks would pass with no word from Mendel. Worried to the point of distraction, Bessie often resorted to airmail (via the Pan Am Clipper) and, when a matter was most pressing, transatlantic cable. The best mode of communication was private. Americans, living in a country that remained neutral for more than two years, traveled to Palestine with surprising frequency. Whenever possible, Gotsfeld entrusted packets of letters, personal and organizational, to people she deemed reliable.

Her wartime letters to Mendel conformed to the same pattern as those addressed to Belle in peacetime, i.e. confessions of love and longing coupled with detailed directives on the conduct of MWOA business. The major difference was the nervous tone. Eager to retain control of MWOA projects, Bessie repeatedly inquired about BZM personnel, Youth Aliyah certificates, wartime shortages, and money promised by *Mercaz Olami*. She reminded her husband to be kind to major donors.

For Mendel this was an enormous responsibility. Formerly his wife had been in charge, though she undertook no major task without first consulting him. Now he had to depend upon unpredictable mail services to convey her wishes. On many occasions, decisions rested upon him alone. Longtime family friend and MWOA associate Jrena Shapiro acknowledged the difficulties in a holiday greeting.

> We realize how incomplete the holidays must be to you without Bessie at your side. And yet we know that you must derive some gratification from the knowledge that although she is here, she is veritably

in Palestine at the same time; for Bessie and our Homeland are inseparable... This invaluable piece of work which she is doing here must be a source of spiritual joy to you, and an inspiration to you to carry on the work which you have so willingly undertaken to do for us in her absence... We know that under your supervision, the many girls to whose care we are dedicated are thriving, and that the administration of our affairs is being carried through successfully and smoothly.[6]

Despite these concerns and in the face of persistent ill health, Gotsfeld determined to fulfill her promise to MWOA. In November and December she undertook a strenuous cross-country tour by rail with the object of insuring the solvency of existing projects and stimulating interest in new ones. She started in Chicago at MWOA 's Northwest Regional Conference. A special reason for attending the conference while suffering from a throat ailment was competition with Hapoel Hamizrachi supporters who maintained a strong presence in that city. A private session with younger women so impressed them that they organized three Junior Mizrachi chapters.

While in Chicago, Gotsfeld introduced an entirely new project. In 1939, plans were underfoot for moving members of the Rotges group from land near Petah Tikvah to two new locations. Some had already joined Kibbutz Tirat Zvi; others were planning K'vuzat Yavneh, south of Tel Aviv. Gotsfeld reminded MWOA women of the historic connection between BZM and Rotges, the first Orthodox beneficiaries of Youth Aliyah. Noting the expanding activities of all Zionist groups in light of the wartime crisis and the need for her organization to follow suit, she urged MWOA to purchase the property. The leadership acquiesced and sent Rotges a cable that indicated interest and proposed terms.

Nevertheless, Gotsfeld was happy to leave the Windy City, where the thermometer dipped to fourteen below zero. As she proceeded to the Twin Cities, Milwaukee, Des Moines, and Kansas City, her modest demeanor and moving speeches boosted membership and raised money. From the Midwest she also arranged to send food and medical supplies to the Yishuv. Proceeding westward, she addressed a small crowd in Denver and a larger one in Los Angeles. Then followed a sentimental journey to Seattle, where memories of her early marriage years and her first Zionist activities warmed her heart. With the Anches, Buttnick, and Genauer families she renewed old friendships. Within the Orthodox community Gotsfeld was a celebrity, and women arranged a gala featuring her as guest of honor. There, as in Chicago, she organized a Junior Mizrachi chapter.[7]

The fall and winter of 1939 - 40 was the time of the "phony war" in Western Europe and North Africa was not yet a war theatre. The Nazi devastation of Poland, heart of European Jewry and birthplace of many members, was well publicized, but the fate of Polish Jewry still hung in the balance. For these reasons, Gotsfeld did not focus on European conditions but followed a scheme planned before her arrival in America. She appeared not only as the MWOA representative but also as a messenger from Zion. In the second capacity she railed against the MacDonald

White Paper, issued just six months before. The White Paper of May 17, 1939 granted a quota of 10,000 Jewish immigrants for the next five years plus an additional 25,000. Without Arab agreement to admit more Jews, the total was not to exceed 75,000. Gotsfeld let the women know that the Yishuv's response was "no surrender and no despair."

As she traveled, she gathered new statistics to indicate valiant Jewish resistance to a sinister British policy.

> In 1939 - 16,370 immigrants entered Palestine on certificates. 10,823 came in so-called "illegally." During the period since the war, that is since September 1st until the end of the year, 4300 immigrants came in with visas and 3700 came with Aliyah B[8]. Of the numbers mentioned above, 3840 were adolescents and children. It is a great tribute to the Yishuv to have been able to absorb these numbers.

And then a heartening summary: "Fifty new settlements, some in more dangerous strategic zones... Palestine absorbed 60,000 homeless refugees and 5000 young people uprooted by persecution from their countries of origin." Following a reassurance that "every Jewish household in the country is prepared to meet any crisis as a people," Gotsfeld tried to impress her listeners with their own critical role in the effort.

> The Galut must be harnessed and do its share in this struggle so that those actually engaged in the process of creation may not stop for one moment and that the builders and defenders can take heart in this day by day struggle. The real answer of the Jew to the attempt to stifle his national rebirth lay in our continuing the settling of the land and the rebuilding of its ruins in the face of all obstacles, as only untiring creation will secure the final victory.

Every speech included a pitch for the organization, its major enterprises, role in resisting the British, and emblem of persisting hope.

> It is a particular tribute to the Mizrachi Women of America for creating institutions whose task is the training of the Jewish woman for participation in this great struggle. It is in these institutions, the Batei Zeirot Mizrachi, refugees from Central Europe and Palestine girls are imbued with the spirit of the Torah which gave the Jew an eternal deed to Eretz Israel. It is the goal of the pupils trained in these institutions to supply a reserve force for the army of religious youth which is carrying on the fight of the Yishuv at the front at Tirat Zvi, K'vuzat Arieh, and other points. The opening of the Tel Aviv building constructed during the disturbances is therefore of great significance and symbolic of the dauntless determination to carry on in spite of everything.[9]

Some addresses appealed to feminine pride, dwelling upon female participation in "industry, commerce, culture, civil service, social service, women in kibbutzin, women on guard, and women in politics." She also reminded members of their duties as religious women. It was their special duty, she asserted, to maintain religion among the young. "We are confronted with a twofold duty, save their lives and save them for traditional Jewry." She detailed her personal role in rescuing and rehabilitating children from religious homes and bragged about the eighteen to twenty-five percent of Youth Aliyah children placed in religious institutions.

Each address closed with a ringing peroration. For example:

> Three and a half millions [i.e. in Eastern Europe] are not able to conduct a Jewish life. We must preserve Judaism in Palestine. It is incumbent upon every Jewish woman to register under the banner of Mizrachi Women to perform this holy duty. In Palestine 150,000 men and women, young and old, answered the call of National Service. Let us rise to the height of the great task that lies before us. Let this emergency not find us wanting. Let everyone give till its hurts. I will conclude with the words of our leaders. "The eternal tie which unites G-d, His people, and their sacred soil will not be cut."[10]

The speeches and galas and endless meetings near completion, Gotsfeld traveled to San Francisco for another meeting and a needed vacation. Then she recrossed the continent and rejoined her New York family for a short time. After tearful good-byes, she returned to Erez Israel. Though the Yishuv was a potential war zone — during her absence a few bombs had fallen on Tel Aviv and Haifa — she was happy to be home with husband, staff, and the young women on whose behalf she toiled.

Mizrachi Ventures, 1941-1942

In 1930 Rotges had been the only religious kibbutz. Between the mid-thirties and the mid-forties the number increased tenfold.[11] Although Gotsfeld was no special partisan of Hakibbuz Hadati, affiliated as it was with Hapoel Hamizrachi, she encouraged all efforts to shore up religious Zionism in Palestine. Consequently she applauded the decision of Junior Mizrachi (founded in 1940) to furnish children's houses in religious collectives as well as cooperative settlements. In February 1941, when war lapped the Eastern Mediterranean shore, her article in the MWOA bulletin honed in on a serene scene, the cornerstone laying of a Children's Home in K'vuzat Tirat Zvi. To bolster spirits, she injected an amusing but problematic anecdote into her report.

> Recently they had a dentist there who looked over the children's teeth. They were all assembled in the room assigned to the dentist and were curiously and fearfully watching his doings. One small boy had disgraced his manhood by ignominiously turning tail and running. The doctor, wishing to prevent the kids from being assailed by mob feelings and following his example, called out: "There goes a coward!" The rest of them, though quaking in their shoes, pluckily remain(ed) and suffered themselves to be examined, poked at and

sprayed by the sprayer. On leaving the room they were stopped by their erring comrade, who inquired what was done to them. "Oh, he just watered our teeth that they should grow better," was the rejoinder of a three-year old."[12]

Here Gotsfeld abandoned her normal sensitivity and made light of the child's humiliation, preferring to draw a lesson from the second tot's statement:

> I related to you the above incident as it is illustrative of the spirit in which these children are brought up of tending, of cultivating, of having things to grow. Even at this tender age they already think in the agricultural terms of their environment.[13]

Behind the stated explanation probably lay another motive. Gotsfeld wanted to direct attention to the Rotges property, for she was in the process of negotiating its purchase. For years she had envisioned a religious children's agricultural village on that site.

At the time, though, the urban institutions remained her principal concern. This was the period of innovative programs at the two Batei Mizrachi. MWOA had long subvented the Mizrachi Teacher's Seminary for Women, though never delivering as much money as Rabbi Berlin requested. Now Gotsfeld wanted to launch a seminar for teachers of vocational subjects. When the rabbi flatly refused her appeal, she created a teacher-training program in BZM for graduates who excelled in their studies.

Nehama Leibowitz and Informal Adult Education

Gotsfeld also instituted innovative programs for Orthodox women with no previous connection to BZM. To enrich the cultural life of religious kibbutzim, she brought a select group, two young women from each kibbutz, to Jerusalem for a five-month very intensive seminar in Torah studies. Nehama Leibowitz directed the program, aided by three or four other BZM teachers.

An unanticipated but far-reaching consequence emerged out of this modest program. After completing the program and returning to the kibbutzim, students requested a follow-up. Leibowitz complied, each week sending out thought questions on the Torah portion (*parashat hashavuah*) read in synagogue. Soon BZM received additional requests for inclusion in the mailing list. To facilitate the growing enterprise, Gotsfeld enlisted the aid of Joseph Burg. As a young leader of the Mizrachi students' association in Berlin, he had heard her lecture to the group in 1929. After his immigration to Palestine, he lived in the same neighborhood as the Gotsfelds, befriended them, and studied Talmud with Mendel. At this time he taught Talmud at Herzliah High School and at BZM. He responded to Bessie's request with enthusiasm, and soon arranged a correspondence course. Each week he sent out mimeographed copies of Leibowitz's observations and questions on the week's Torah portion. Leibowitz read each response, then corrected answers and offered further comments.[14]

BZM students and kibbutz women were only the first to benefit from Leibowitz's lessons. When other people requested the mimeographed sheets, Burg distributed hundreds of *gilyonot* (circulars) to teachers and Sabbath study groups throughout the land. To pay for it, Gotsfeld depleted the discretionary fund that she retained to cover unexpected costs. Years later Nehama Leibowitz commented on this support with these words: "Money should be spent but not wasted on trivial, meaningless objects. She (Gotsfeld) herself in her personal life put this code into action."[15]

Eventually the program and the budget grew too large for Burg and BZM to handle, and the Torah Education Department of the World Zionist Organization took it over. Still later, it published yearly collections and translated them into English for distribution abroad.[16] Whether delivered in person or in writing, Leibowitz's teaching would impart a love of Torah to three generations of young Jews. BZM benefited from her pedagogy and scholarship for a full twenty years, ending only in 1953, when she left to instruct older students, among them hundreds of Jews from the diaspora, including college students one one-year study programs.[17]

Gotsfeld's cultural mission extended beyond formal education. Joseph Burg put it this way:

> She understood that in a country of immigrants not only is the vocational training of young girls a basic necessity, an act of first priority, but there is also a need to create a social atmosphere around the nucleus of education — for youth, for adolescents, and for adults."[18]

To satisfy social and cultural cravings of urbane Orthodox adults, Gotsfeld asked him to set up an ambitious series of programs in the Tel Aviv BZM. Several evenings a week the dining room became a lecture and concert hall. Among the speakers were Burg himself (later Israeli Minister of the Interior) and Jacob Katz, later a highly-respected historian but then a teacher at BZM as well as the principal of the Talpiot Teachers Seminary.[19] Among the featured speakers at the "Torah and Haskala" program were Nehama Leibowitz, who traveled from Jerusalem with her blind husband, as did her controversial brother, Yeshayahu Leibowitz, Hebrew University polymath and gadfly. An "Institute for Jewish and General Learning" featured European refugee scholars of the highest caliber, who lectured on many subjects. Refugee musicians performed. Housemothers encouraged BZM students to attend the cultural events, but did not compel them to do so.

These peaceful diversions also served the purpose of calming a public deprived of reliable information about their relatives caught in the Nazi net. Little did they know that in 1943, the reality of war would reach their shores in the form of little Polish refugees known to history as *"Yaldei Teheran,"* the Children of Teheran.

8

The Children of Teheran

It will be remembered that the original mission of BZM was vocational education for girls from the Old Yishuv. As it turned out, the school opened in the fateful year of 1933. Because of the pressing need to find homes for girls fleeing Nazi persecution, that objective, though never abandoned, assumed a secondary position. During the thirties and early forties, European girls constituted most of the school population. When wartime exigencies and British policy placed overwhelming obstacles in the path of immigration from Europe, Gotsfeld, ever flexible, took that fact into account. At her request, a 1942 memo announced: "Due to the fact that at the present moment there is a scarcity of immigration, it has been deemed advisable to turn over the facilities of the Bet Zeirot Mizrachi to the vocational guidance and training of the religious Palestinian girl."[1] Soon enough however, political circumstances forced further readjustment. Educational institutions throughout the Yishuv became involved in the celebrated episode known as the "Children of Teheran."

In February 1943, at the height of the Holocaust, eight hundred young Jews reached Palestine. Every one of them had suffered harrowing adversity. Hapless youngsters, infants, school-aged children, and adolescents, 80% without parents, they comprised one sector of 14,000 Polish citizens: Jewish and Christian, military, and civilian, who fled from the Nazis under the leadership of General Wladislaw Anders. The refugees had moved eastward to Siberia, then turned south into the central Asian Soviet republics. As they plodded along, adults and adolescents worked in forests and labor camps until compelled to resume the journey. Thousands died of exposure, disease, and malnutrition before survivors reached Pahlevi, the Persian port on the Caspian Sea.[2]

During the perilous journey, the refugees suffered conditions that Jews pray to avoid during the Rosh Hashanah synagogue service: poverty, hunger, thirst, pestilence (lice), and infectious disease (typhus). Involuntary nomads for three years, many children had to abandon parents too sick or exhausted to proceed. Others buried mothers, fathers, and siblings along the roadside. Like animals, some roamed in packs. As they trudged through village, wilderness, and forest under scant adult guidance, not a few confronted wild beasts.

73

After reaching Pahlevi in the summer of 1942, the refugees proceeded to Teheran, the Persian capital. Once there, Jewish adults among them gathered Jewish children in a separate camp outside the city. During the seven-month Persian sojourn, these counselors endeavored to provide good food, clothe half-naked bodies, and bring order into chaotic lives. Help came from the Polish Red Cross, which donated food, clothing and medical treatment to all Polish nationals.[3]

Finding refuge on neutral ground did not assuage the pain of the "Children of Teheran," as the group was soon designated. Compounding the misery of malnutrition and illness was emotional distress, later indicated by one of the children:

> We cried for our lost childhood and for our fathers and mothers. And when we thought we'd cried ourselves out, another awful truth hit us all at once - we children had deserted our fathers and mothers to save our own lives. And then we discovered that we still had more tears left to shed.[4]

What would become of them? Wounded by Jew-baiting on the part of Polish children in the cohort, some Jewish children refused to acknowledge their origins. Most, however, hoped to reach Palestine but despaired of ever achieving that goal. Adults could not hide the British limit on immigration certificates. But a double scandal — early rumors of genocide and the disgraceful Struma incident (when a refugee ship, unwelcome in any port, sunk, with a loss of 428 men, women, and children) – moderated their position. Whitehall allotted immigration certificates to the Children of Teheran, including them, to be sure, in the 75,000 total stipulated in the White Paper.

While the children lingered in Persia, David Laumberg (Laor) from Pinsk, a Hashomer Hazair member in his late twenties, organized The Teheran Children's Home outside of the city. He selected a staff from members of HeHalutz, a loose organization of young Zionists already planning settlement in kibbuzim. Younger volunteers, among them seventeen year old Rachel Drexler, his future bride, learned on the job.

Soon after the refugee children reached Persia, sixty-nine Jewish women, detained in Europe by war and exchanged for Germans resident in Palestine, returned home. The women authenticated the rumors of unspeakable atrocities. It was at that crucial juncture that Laumberg contacted Henrietta Szold. While acknowledging that the children did not conform to Youth Aliyah criteria in age, health, parental consent, and Zionist training, she immediately included them anyway.[5] Ben Gurion negotiated for help in bringing the children to Palestine,[6] at first unsuccessfully. He sent Zipporah Meirov Shertok, wife of Moshe Shertok (later Sharett) head of the Jewish Agency's Political Department, to Teheran. With boundless energy, Shertok undertook diverse tasks, negotiating group transfer to Palestine with British, Polish and Persian authorities and problem solving within the camp itself.[7]

When agreement was finally reached, it took seven months to plan the transfer and seven additional weeks to complete the journey. British ships transported the Teheran Children and their guardians via a circuitous route, the only one available to them, through the Gulf of Oman into the Arabian Sea, thence to Karachi and Bombay, where they lingered for two weeks. Then they sailed through the Suez Canal to Egypt. Hans Beyth, Szold's deputy, met them in Egypt, along with Palestinian Jewish soldiers serving in the British army. Two trains delivered the children to Palestine. They reached the border on February 18, 1943.[8]

News of the children's miraculous escape from the Polish Gehenna had, from the start, kindled passionate emotion. Szold's report uncharacteristically gave way to sentiment even as it soberly indicated differences between the ragged Teheran Children and previous Youth Aliyah clients, adolescents from stable homes.

> The young refugees range in age from a year and a half to eighteen. By far the larger proportion, over 600, is of school age, from seven to fourteen. The overwhelming majority, perhaps all but the forty babies below kindergarten age, have been wandering from place to place for three years, since the invasion of Poland by the Germans and the slicing off of a considerable Polish terrain by Soviet Russia. They have been sleeping in the woods, half-naked, exposed to disease, eaten up by vermin, starved, guiltless, innocent, badly used victims of the war and the war lords.[9]

The Children Arrive

Despite their heart-melting condition, the mere fact of their survival provided a much-needed boost after the revelations of Nazi atrocities. Language in a Mizrachi report indicates the excitement that pervaded every sector of the Yishuv.

> For a long time the population awaited the child refugees from Poland and Russia with nervous anticipation. The day of their arrival was a time of great excitement. Like firebrands plucked from the fire they emerged as heralds of redemption for brothers and sisters who remained alive, tiny embers smoldering in snow-covered forests.[10]

Newspaper headlines broadcast their arrival. Articles lavished attention upon the bedraggled children and printed harrowing details of the torments they had endured. At the same time, the publications offered comfort to the frightened Yishuv. People regarded these children as the first of thousands who would find temporary asylum in neutral countries and permanent settlement in Palestine.[11] Sadly, this was not to be. Only about 150 additional children joined them the following summer. Nevertheless, expectations that many more would follow turned the Children of Teheran into a cause célèbre.

Intimations of Trouble

Sad to relate, the exhilaration that accompanied the children's appearance did not unite the Yishuv for long. On the contrary, it renewed the *Kulturkampf* between Orthodox and secular Jews, with repercussions down to our own times.[12] News of the Teheran Children ignited long-smoldering resentment on the part of the religious leadership for its puny sliver of the national educational system. While the refugee children were en route to Palestine, the Zionist Mizrachi and separatist ultras of Agudat Israel joined forces. Arguing that 90% of Polish Jewry had been religiously observant, they demanded traditional instruction for all children and enlisted aid from prominent Orthodox figures in the English-speaking world.[13] The Agudah threatened that in the absence of an agreement requiring universal Orthodox education, they would press their claim before the Polish government-in-exile, which was helping to maintain the Teheran Children's Home.[14] When this proved unfeasible, they insisted that schooling for Teheran Children replicate Polish yeshiva education. The Zionist Orthodox establishment concurred on the demand for religious education, but parted ways on important details. Chief Rabbi Isaac Herzog and Mizrachi president Rabbi Meir Berlin demanded education of all Teheran Children in a school system controlled by the Chief Rabbi.[15]

Stuggles over Placement

When the children finally reached Palestine, the squabbles gave way, briefly, to joy. As the train moved slowly northward, representatives of all groups in the Yishuv lined the route to salute them. Even Arabs joined them. At every stop the populace showered them with sweets and oranges, the latter remembered as a rare treat in wintry Poland.[16] At the Rehovot station, Bessie Gotsfeld stood beside Sarah Herzog, wife of the Chief Rabbi, the two women representing Mizrachi.

The train proceeded to Athlit, a British detention camp near Haifa, previously set aside as a site for "quarantine, disinfection, and similar matters."[17] Social workers hospitalized sick children and escorted tots under five to the WIZO Baby House in Jerusalem. Representatives of each party in the Yishuv, from leftist Hashomer Hazair to ultra-Orthodox Agudat Israel, sat uneasily at tables beside each other. Eighty-two year old Henrietta Szold, representing Youth Aliyah, was seated in the center.[18] After a few days of light questioning, officials sent the youngsters to eleven transit camps. Those over fourteen years of age could choose their own placement.

At this point, verbal debates gave way to battles for the bodies, minds, and souls of the children. Tussles over permanent placement highlighted divergent assumptions entertained by various segments of Yishuv society. Youth Aliyah prioritized rehabilitation and Zionism and preferred kibbutzim. Orthodox groups focused on Torah education and demanded placement in religious residential and educational institutions.

The two positions reflected dissimilar, incompatible contexts. The founders of Youth Aliyah were Jews with a western upbringing who cherished the Enlightenment values of rational inquiry and individual choice, foundation stones of Jewish Emancipation. In a period when Sigmund Freud's theories achieved popularity, they were sensitive to damage inflicted upon fragile psyches. That Szold was of this mindset is evident in the following statement "It has been our habit in the Youth Aliyah to deal, not with children, but with the child."[19] Consequently she expected Youth Aliyah workers to determine the physical and psychological requirements of each boy and girl and to take into consideration his or her institutional preferences. This is not to say that Youth Aliyah objectivity was absolute. As an organ of the Zionist Jewish Agency, the organization directed children and youth to institutions that fostered Hebrew language, productive labor, and land reclamation.

Ashkenazi rabbis in the Yishuv, on the other hand, upheld a premise that reflected their East European experience. For them education was a function of the Jewish community as a whole, properly entrusted to learned religious leadership. In their eyes, the refugee children were a compact bloc, a pathetic remnant of Poland's holy community. Noting that most were either orphans or sons and daughters of parents whose fate was unknown, they declared themselves the legitimate guardians of the entire cohort. Chief Rabbi Issac Herzog pronounced "We are convinced that we represent the general will of the nation, the source of its historic continuity."[20] Following this logic, Agudat Israel brooked no compromise; it insisted upon its right to educate all children and supervise them until age twenty.[21]

The more practical Mizrachi leaders agreed to a compromise. Retreating from their original demand that all Teheran children be sent to religious institutions, they now requested only children reared in traditional homes.[22] They did manage to extend the age of consent from fourteen to fifteen, thereby accepting free choice for older adolescents.[23] Furthermore, although the Mizrachi rank-and-file did not air their feelings in public, they, like Szold, were unhappy with old-fashioned yeshivas on the European model that preached anti-Zionism. Fueling that fire were rumors of children snatched from Mizrachi and transferred to Agudah institutions.

Mizrachi leaders nevertheless remained adamant on the issue of the education of religious children. They won the permission to settle and educate Orthodox refugees in institutions attached to the Religious Sector of Youth Aliyah, represented by Rabbi Y.L. Fishman. [24]

Transit Camps

Of eleven temporary reception centers, only three followed strictly Orthodox lines: Kfar Noar Dati; Mikveh Israel; and BZM, Jerusalem, which took care of seventy children. In the other eight centers Youth Aliyah provided kosher food, set aside rooms for daily and Sabbath worship, and accepted 150 prayer books sent by Mizrachi.[25] Yet Sabbath observance, though mandated, was often honored in the breach. Mizrachi and Agudah joined hands in demanding religiously observant *madrikhim* (counselors)[26], but fewer than half came from their ranks.[27] Most were secular Jews from kibbutzim, observed smoking and sewing on the Sabbath.[28]

While the transit camps were in operation, Youth Aliyah personnel assumed the thankless chore of assigning children to permanent settlements. After evaluating each child's physical stamina, intelligence, and mental stability, they tackled the controversial area of religion. They had already agreed to determine placement on the basis of parental practice and to settle children from traditional homes in institutions under Orthodox auspices.[29] At a psychologist's suggestion they did not venture into theology or philosophy. Instead, they determined a child's religious background by posing simple questions: "Did you father have a beard? Did he wash his hands before meals? Did he wear a *tallit kattan*? Did your mother kindle Sabbath candles? Did you recite the *Shema Yisrael* at bedtime?[30]

Most children who responded in the positive were assigned to Mizrachi institutions; some were already there.[31] Because of Agudat Israel's anti-Zionist orientation, Youth Aliyah assigned it only students who specifically requested this placement.[32] Problems arose when children from traditionalist homes refused to accept assignment to Orthodox settlements, either out of newfound conviction or from the dread of separation from older siblings who opted for non-religious institutions.[33] After decisions became public, temperatures reached the boiling point. Orthodox spokesmen attacked Youth Aliyah, the Jewish Agency, and the Yishuv's educational system. Some blamed children's preference for non-religious *kibbutzim* on the free thinkers who had organized the Children's Home in Teheran and the anti-religious bias of transit camp counselors. *Madrikhim* accompanying children on tours, they maintained, deliberately selected the most attractive secular kibbutzim and the most primitive religious ones.[34]

Mizrachi leaders dusted off an argument set forth in 1934 and modified it to meet the conditions of 1943. Disingenuously, they maintained that they had previously not challenged secular education for German Youth Aliyah children because so many were products of assimilated households. Children of Teheran, by contrast, were not scions of secular western Jews but of Polish Jewry, which was overwhelmingly observant.[35] Nevertheless as we have seen, Mizrachi did not challenge the choices of young people beyond their mid-teens. Agudah polemicists expressed themselves much more stridently. Some went so far as to blame the European catastrophe on Jews who abandoned the Torah. They proceeded to repudiate Youth Aliyah regulations that older teenagers be given choice of placement and that non-primary relatives have a say in their education.

The short-lived liaison between the Agudah and Mizrachi came to an end while the temporary camps were in operation. Agudah representatives who slipped into the reception centers told gullible youngsters that Mizrachi was not genuinely religious, but rather a stepping-stone to atheism. Their words only harmed the religious cause. Many children could not distinguish between the Zionist Mizrachi and the anti-Zionist Agudah, leaving an opening for leftist ideologues to tar both groups with the brush of parasitism and lack of national resolve.[36] For their part, the Agudah considered Mizrachi's compliance with the final allocation little short of treason.[37]

In my opinion, the final distribution was a triumph for Mizrachi. Youth Aliyah placed 716 children from the first cohort of Teheran Children. Small groups went to relatives (26), the Baby House for children under 5 (30), and hospitals (16). Agudat Israel received 32 students and Mosad Ahava, 36. Mizrachi installations admitted 278 children, a number equal to those who settled in non-religious institutions (298).[38]

Bet Zeirot Mizrachi and the Children of Teheran

Gotsfeld did not participate in public skirmishes over the Teheran Children, though she undoubtedly supported the Mizrachi position. For years she had blamed Szold, Hadassah, and Youth Aliyah for insufficient funding of Orthodox institutions. When one received a subsidy in 1936, she credited her organization:

> Do they (Hadassah women) for one moment realize that this was done because they could not stand the pressure of the criticism of the world that the religious youth receives so little consideration and because there is a M.W.O.A. to stress that point? [39]

Her November 1943 internal report to the MWOA averred: "No one can doubt now that the vast majority of these children were religious and that the demand that they be given a religious education was justified."[40] She regarded their arrival as an opportunity to strengthen her original objective of wielding education as a tool to advance religious Zionism.

> If in the past, the bulk of Zionist upbringing was the work of non-religious groups that had espoused Zionism out of their own national consciousness or because of the pressure of circumstances, we shall in the future increasingly employ educational means in order to bind people to our national endeavor... These new groups with whom we shall be dealing... consist in the main of religious Jews reared in the traditions of Torah. If we desire that in assimilating them to the political, social, and cultural values of our national revival we do not lose them for the Torah, we must be able, ourselves, to provide the *instruments* whereby they shall be absorbed into the new life. Others may supply special expenses. *Only we can forge the fixed capital of this great educational enterprise.*[41]

An unforeseen consequence of the Teheran Children episode was the extension of Gotsfeld's endeavors into new directions. Prior to 1943, female adolescents were her only concern; after that, the exigencies of war placed boys and girls of all ages under her care. Bet Zeirot Mizrachi in Jerusalem served first as a preparatory camp, then a long-term haven for some Teheran children. Little ones under five years old previously housed in the Wizo Baby House soon became too old for the facility. Wizo representatives approached Gotsfeld and Dr. Jenny Thaustein, director of BJM Jerusalem from 1940 to 1948, requesting to house them in that facility. At first the two women demurred on grounds that BZM was dedicated to adolescent girls, but the sight of the pitiful children changed their minds. They took in all thirty-five along with their counselors and installed them in the top floor of the building. The children remained there for a full year. In Thaustein's words, "We sent them to schools nearby, but this was their home, and how we spoiled them! [42]

Accommodating older newcomers called for sacrifice. Resident Youth Aliyah students interrupted their studies for two months and vacated their rooms. The girls went to two Orthodox kibbutzim, Tirat Zevi and S'de Eliyahu, to join the "labor mobilization" intended to alleviate the wartime farm worker shortage. For a time non-resident Jerusalemites continued their studies in the *Bet Poalot,* but they soon left to make room for the children. [43]

Bessie's heart went out to the boys and girls for whom BZM supplied temporary housing, medical care, and Torah instruction. Like Szold, she observed the psychological damage resulting from their wartime experience.

> The educational and psychological problem which they present is enormous. Here were children who at the age of twelve had undergone experiences which, spread over an entire lifespan of a mature person, would suffice to make his life one of harrowing adventure. The struggle for existence has pressed itself indelibly upon them. They have no faith in anyone. Whosoever they come in touch with is a potential enemy, putting up a pleasant front in order to deceive them. [44]

Even though she did not mince words about the children's failings, she offered the MWOA members solace in the Jewish tradition, in the same breath touting her organization's effectiveness.

> That they (the children) have succeeded in retaining the characteristics of human decency is a tribute to the Jewish family and its power to mold the souls of the children in their earliest years. Only by unrelenting devotion and kindness can they be won over... OUR UNDERSTANDING OF THE PROBLEM AND OUR ABILITY TO HELP IN THE ADJUSTMENT OF YOUTH WAS A GREAT ASSET IN DEALING WITH THIS DIFFICULT SITUATION. [45]

After a two month stopover in the Tel Aviv BZM, many children found permanent placement. Some older girls remained there, calling for a modified curriculum to compensate for lost years. To minister to small children, MWOA rented the house next door; it accommodated forty children aged six to fourteen and included some from the original Teheran group. Classes for these children took place elsewhere, but the BZM students and staff cared for their other needs.[46]

There were additional efforts on behalf Teheran Children. Gotsfeld convinced MWOA to supply basic equipment for children transferred to agricultural settlements S'de Ya'akov, Kfar Haroeh, Yeshivat B'nai Akiba, and Yavneh. She also set aside funds for two new institutions formed for younger Teheran children. One was the Bet Hayeled in Pardes Hanna; the other was the Meshek Yeladim in Talpiot, which absorbed children formerly housed in the *Bet Poalot*.

MWOA was not the sole group that provided for Orthodox children; it joined hands with *Moezet Hapoalot* of the Poel Hamizrachi and the Mizrachi Women of Palestine. All this generosity, however, left a hole in the budget of its primary institutions, the *Batei Zeirot Mizrachi* in Jerusalem and Tel Aviv. According to prior arrangements, *Mercaz Olami* (World Mizrachi Central) was supposed to supplement their budgets, as well as the teachers' program initiated in the 1940s. The money, however, was not always forthcoming.[47]

For all the drama, the Children of Teheran episode is but one example of personal accomplishment and institutional transformation during the 1940s. How Bessie Gotsfeld and her organization weathered the storms unleashed upon the Jewish people in general and the Yishuv in particular during the remaining war years is the subject of the next chapter.

9

Wartime Expansion, 1943 – 1945

The darker the night, the brighter the stars. After the Teheran Children's arrival, the Yishuv redoubled efforts to assist other Jews fleeing near-certain death in Europe and murderous persecution in Arab lands. Instruments of rescue and rehabilitation were brilliant stars piercing the gloom of that long and terrible night.

Bessie Gotsfeld's success in broadening MWOA's operations rested upon three essential facts. Most compelling was the European Jewish tragedy. Second was the wartime prosperity of all Americans, including Orthodox business and professional people, and the consequent availability of money for philanthropic purposes. A third factor, connected to first two, was the purposeful activity that marked all Jewish organizations at this time. Ever ideological, in addressing MWOA members reluctant to increase their responsibilities she argued that augmented effort on their part would open the way for religious Zionism to gain acceptance in the Yishuv and by the American Jewish public. That the MWOA membership was willing to assume new and costly obligations also arose from a fortuitous circumstance; the national president during the critical period of 1942 to 1946 was Belle Goldstein, Gotsfeld's talented sister-in-law, correspondent, and soul mate.

First MWOA had to hold on to what it had. Wartime Great Britain, fighting for survival, did not hesitate to ride roughshod over populations under its control. The new Tel Aviv BZM, located in the heart of the city and displaying superior amenities, drew the attention of British military authorities. Peremptorily, they requisitioned it for an ordinance school and depot. To prevent BZM from closing, Bella Gesundheit offered her large Tel Aviv villa on a temporary basis. Gotsfeld supervised the transfer of personnel and equipment to the Gezundheit house. It was hardly an ideal situation, and she boiled with anger at the contempt for Jewish children that the choice of that facility betokened. At her insistence, Mizrachi Women in America lobbied their congressmen for a redress of this wrong. Their complaints and subsequent pressure did not move Austin Colonel Godwin, commander of troops stationed in Sarafand, Palestine. Indeed, after British and American forces defeated Rommel and the ordinance depot was no longer needed, he explored alternatives to justify retention of building. Nevertheless, General Ekserdjian, the British Hirings Officer, agreed to meet Bessie Gotsfeld and Sarah Herzog. That man, fortunately, did not share Godwin's antisemitism nor did he know that the women operated under the clandestine guidance of Joseph Nelson, an American Jewish officer. As a probable result of Nelson's plotting and the women's pleading, BZM Tel Aviv reverted to the legal owners in 1943.[1]

Expansion and Growth

MWOA's first wartime innovations entailed enlargement rather than innovation. Both Batei Zeirot Mizrachi added rooms to house the new resident girls. After the British military's withdrawal from the Tel Aviv school, Gotsfeld reorganized the complex into four divisions. Each of the first three was labeled a *Bet Poalot*, with vocational and recreational programming. "Vocational" indicated the program for teenaged girls, the original mission of the school. "Recreational" included social and cultural activities for the larger community conducted in the evenings. The Tel Aviv *Bet Poalot* was modeled after the successful Jerusalem hostel.

The fourth division was a new project under the auspices of the Educational Department of the *Va'ad Leumi*. In 1943 that agency determined a need for "pre-vocational instruction" in the seventh and eighth grades and chose BZM as its first site. Every week about seven hundred young girls from Mizrachi elementary schools entered the school to receive instruction in sewing and basic handicrafts.[2] To her membership Gotsfeld crowed: "Thus we receive a definite status within the general educational system and became officially recognized as one of the factors participating in the school set-up in Palestine."[3]

A group of Mizrachi women in England opened a small BZM in Haifa.

New Fields of Activity

For Bessie Gotsfeld in the 1940s, as for Henrietta Szold during the 1930s, a felt need dictated assuming the responsibilities of social service. At her suggestion, MWOA earmarked money for the construction of children's homes in Hapoel Hamizrachi kibbutzim in the *Bet Shaan* valley and day nurseries and afternoon schools in *Schunat Shapira, Ben Zvi, Petah Tikvah* and *Pardes Hanna*. They enabled mothers to leave their children in capable hands and work in orchards and farms, thereby abetting the survival of religious collectives and cooperatives. Industrial workers brought needed cash to religious settlements, and their factory work served Zionist and wartime purposes as well. Before the war, the British mandatory authorities had administered Palestine as a colony, expected to produce raw materials for British industry. They had not permitted Jews to open large factories or learn innovative industrial techniques. Wartime exigencies removed those restrictions. Now Jews produced war matériel, repaired ships, machinery and weapons, and manufactured specialized scientific apparatus, optical instruments, and pharmaceuticals as well as textiles. Female factory workers helped expand the Yishuv's economy even as they freed men for military service.[4] Later in the decade, the economic strength and military expertise gained during the war would facilitate the realization of independence.

Social service held special appeal for Junior Mizrachi, and the young women looked to Gotsfeld for guidance. Recalling her own youthful struggles, she encouraged them to adopt a program that was exclusively their own. They followed her advice and took upon themselves the construction of Children's Houses in Orthodox villages and collectives. By 1945 five were fully functioning in *Kfar Pines, S'de Eliyahu, Tirat Zvi, S'de Ya'akov* and *Yavneh* and a sixth was under construction in *Kfar Aza*.

In twelve years, the MWOA program had grown from one small school to numerous programs in education, child rescue and absorption, social service for children, and general social service.[5]

"Housing, Physical Care, Social Rehabilitation, Religious Guidance"[6]

With these words, Gotsfeld summarized MWOA's wartime programming. One theme persisted in the face of vigorous growth; Gotsfeld insisted that all MWOA-sponsored agencies adhere to the original standards set for the BZMs. For her, environment was everything. The BZMs were much more than schools. Their Hebrew name and all English language appellations designated them homes. Students inhaled an air suffused with Zionism and religion, of course, but also comity and loving care. Gotsfeld's accessibility and concern for every individual set an example that the students themselves emulated. At times they would arrange charitable projects. Some girls fashioned handcrafted articles and sold them to the public for the benefit of the school.

To accommodate young boys from the first "Teheran" contingent, MWOA moved women out of apartments in the *Bet Poalot* in Jerusalem. The boys remained there until MWOA rented apartments in *Talpiot*, a more centrally located neighborhood. Girls joined them. After a year, Gotsfeld expressed mixed judgment on the children's progress: "One can scarcely recognize the smiling children who arrived a year ago. [Still] the impressions left by their tragic experiences cannot be easily effaced and their rehabilitation and education requires much tact and patience."[7]

Meshek Yeladim Motza

Between 1943 and 1946, MWOA founded three children's villages, *Meshek Yeladim Motza, Mosad Aliyah*, and *Tel Raanan*. All pursued Gotsfeld's grand objectives: the rehabilitation of child refugees, physically and psychologically, and the inculcation of religious and Zionist values. To keep happy expressions on their faces, MWOA joined *Omen* (*Irgun Neshai Mizrachi*, The Mizrachi Women of Palestine, a local Orthodox organization, itself an amalgam of 3 groups). They funded the transfer of the *Meshek Yeladim* (Children's Farm) to a more rural environment, the terraced slopes of Motza , outside of Jerusalem. MWOA paid for 60% of their upkeep, *Omen* the remaining 40%.[8]

Rehabilitation was not trouble-free. The children wrestled with terrifying demons. Many had watched the murder of close family members; others did not even know whether their parents were alive. Having grown accustomed to hiding in the forest and running from place to place, they trusted no one. Some ran away from photographers, imagining that evil people would locate them through the pictures and strike them in their sleep. Like Johanna Spry's Heidi but with more deep-seated angst, some children hoarded rolls under the mattress.[9]

There was much to be done, first to recover the children's trust in humanity, then to prepare them for participation in the Zionist enterprise and the Mizrachi program. To begin the process, staff members lived on campus. An obstacle to normalcy was the abrupt cessation of most children's formal instruction three or four years before. Some required individual tutoring. Still, most proved malleable and after about three years were indistinguishable from local children (though years later demons would emerge to haunt some survivors).[10]

Mosad Aliyah

Difficulties encountered in *Meshek Yeladim Motza* only sharpened Gotsfeld's determination to create new institutions. One site had been on her mind even before the war. Early in 1939 she learned that members of Rotges, BZM's companion beneficiary under Youth Aliyah's Religious Department, were leaving the kibbutz to found Yavneh and other religious kibbutzim. During her American fundraising tour later that year, she requested and received endorsement of a plan to transform Kibbutz Rotges into a children's village under MWOA auspices. After the return home, she completed the arrangement, but there was no movement until the Teheran Children's arrival stimulated attention in child rehabilitation. In 1943 Rabbi Meir Berlin addressed MWOA's Eighteenth Annual ("*Chai*") Convention and specifically appealed for a Children's Village and Farm School for refugee children and orphans of soldiers.[11] In response, the women pledged $75,000.00.

Adjacent to Rotges was a parcel of land owned by Germans that the British had confiscated as enemy property. In 1944 The Jewish Agency, prodded by its Youth Aliyah division, leased the old kibbutz and the additional land and prepared them for occupation. It hired workmen to renovate a large house for an office and convert barns into dormitories. MWOA provided clothing and food, furniture, beds, linens, utensils, and agricultural equipment. Initially there were accommodations for about a hundred children. That 150 refugee children would live there in 1948 and that the number would double by 1961 was inconceivable when Rotges was first recast as *Mosad Aliyah*; in 1944; everyone regarded it as an emergency measure slated for termination after the war.[12] Need and opportunity, however, transformed a stopgap measure into a permanent installation. *Mosad Aliyah* would prove capable of caring for young refugees who were either admitted legally or who slipped into the country illegally. Following the War of Independence, the J.N.F. became its official owners and then promptly leased it to MWOA.[13]

Long before the procedure was completed and the acreage increased, Mosad Aliyah Rotges[14] was fully operative. In 1948 it encompassed 120 dunams, half dedicated to agriculture, the other half to living and learning facilities. The children, aged 9 to 16, cared for chickens, ducks, geese, and six cows. In workshops boys learned tinsmithing, and instruction for girls included handicrafts and sewing.[15] Officially MWOA shared management with Hapoel Hamizrachi, Kibbutz Rotges's original backer, but Gotsfeld's hand guided every move. Her right-hand man was Yoel Shiftan, whose work with refugee children awaiting placement in Athlit had previously caught her attention. The young man's informal pedagogy in the transit camp and his choice of Zionist subject matter — Hebrew, the biblical book of Joshua, and poems about the land — had impressed her, as did his scrupulous supervision of daily prayers and the fact that he alone of the Athlit staff lived on the premises and made himself available at all times. For his part, Shiftan admired Gotsfeld's determination to find a suitable home for every child and to take extraordinary measures to accomplish her goal.

Flowing from their mutual respect was Gotsfeld's offer of the position of administrator. Shiftan accepted on condition that he, unlike other workers, receive a written contract. Gotsfeld did not want to change her policy, and the job lay unfilled for a while. When she realized that his services were indispensable, she agreed to hire him on his terms.

That original give-and-take betokened their relationship, sincere esteem alongside a studied distance. Gotsfeld admired Shiftan's social instincts and practical know-how so much that when the director of education left, he assumed that position while retaining his own. Most administrators grouped children according to country of origin; he permitted them to retain friendship groups formed on their own. Gotsfeld also appreciated Shiftan's intimate knowledge of the physical plant. When a donor offered to pay for cabins, for example, he knew exactly how many were needed, and what kind to order. Because of his obvious intelligence and concern for children, she trusted his decisions. Any item that he considered essential did not require her signature. But she would not let anyone in Israel or the home office in NY learn about the arrangement.[16] So much for her role as " "representative" simply implementing organizational directives!

Despite their closeness, Shiftan detected ambivalence in Gotsfeld's relationship with the staff. Teachers and administrators were free to make suggestions, but she controlled major operations. For anyone to circumvent a budget that was worked out to the penny was out of the question. Nevertheless Gotsfeld managed to locate resources for individuals and programs that she considered exceptional. Years later Shiftan marveled at her dogged persistence in scouting out places for Orthodox children detained at Athlit even when all rosters were filled.[17]

Tel Ra'anan

In 1945 MWOA established a third children's farm school, Tel Raanan Children's Home (*Mosad Tel Ra'annan*), in B'nai Brak. *Tel Ra'annan* children, like those at *Motza*, were younger than the pre-teens and adolescents at *Mosad Aliyah*. Of the three groups, they were the least isolated. *Tel Ra'annan* boys and girls attended the local Orthodox school with local students and soon were caught up in a fight between their new classmates and children from a rival religious school. Happily, they retreated to their irenic quarters, set in a beautiful orchard. There they took additional instruction in practical skills considered appropriate for their age and sex. Gotsfeld especially enjoyed the atmosphere of *Tel Ra'annan* and visited often.[18]

Other Wartime programs

Urban programs also increased. MWOA rented a house across the street from the Jerusalem BZM, where a new staff cared for 28 boys. Their story is as nearly as dramatic as that of the Teheran Children. Jewish orphans in Yemen became wards of the state and were forcibly converted to Islam. To hold on to them, agents from the Yishuv surreptitiously stole them from the authorities and transported them first to Aden, thence to Palestine.[19] A 1945 joint bar mitzvah ceremony for thirteen of them galvanized the Yishuv. Chief Rabbi Isaac Herzog spoke at the event, which drew officials from all religious Zionist organizations. Moshe Shertok (later Sharett) represented the labor parties, accompanied by his own children.[20]

In the final months of the war, 1142 children, of whom roughly a third were refugees, enrolled in MWOA institutions. The organization supported schools and youth villages that cared for 365 refugee children: 80 in BZM-Jerusalem BZM, 49 in the Yemenite house; 36 in BZM- Tel Aviv, 49 in *Motza* (and planning for another 10) and 100 in *Mosad Aliyah*, along with fifteen pre-schoolers at the Bet Hayeled in *Pardes Hanna*.[21] By May 1945 MWOA donations to other Mizrachi-run institutions raised the number to 2000.[22]

Other wartime projects under MWOA sponsorship and Gotsfeld supervision were clothing collections, a (Passover) *Maos Hittim* fund, and a large JNF fund. Nearly every letter and memo contained an appeal for used clothing and linens. It was an open secret that new clothes were to be included as well. To avoid the stiff tariff levied on new items, the women removed labels and mixed them with older items before shipping. That some members had little understanding of conditions in the Yishuv is indicated by Gotsfeld's request that they not include high-heeled shoes. So important were these collections that she put her husband in charge of the warehouses where they were sorted.

This period saw the dissipation, though not the disappearance, of a long-term MWOA grievance. Responding to the criticism of other groups, Hadassah relinquished its monopoly as fundraiser for Youth Aliyah, though it retained the title of official agent for Youth Aliyah in America. Four organizations joined a coordinating committee for Youth Aliyah collections in America. Mizrachi Women of America was one; the others were Hadassah, United Palestine Appeal, and Pioneer Women, an affiliate of the Poale Zion (Labor) movement.[23] For MWOA, the chief benefit was the right to use the term "Youth Aliyah" in fund raising.[24] At this juncture, Hadassah hegemony became less of a hurdle than squabbles with other organs of the Mizrachi movement.

Internal Dissensions

Soon the emphasis shifted from disputes with secular organizations to the uneasy alliance with women's groups that shared Gotsfeld's religious and Zionist orientation. As MWOA did not have sufficient resources for full maintenance of its ambitious agenda, Gotsfeld sought the aid of outside agencies. At her behest, the Jewish National Fund and the Jewish Agency prepared the ground for new projects that were shared with other organs of World Mizrachi. MWOA joined hands with Omen, the Palestinian Mizrachi woman's group, to fund *Meshek Yeladim Motza* on an unequal basis (60% from MWOA; 40% from *Omen*);[25] Mosad Aliyah retained ties with Hapoel Hamizrachi; and the Pardes Hanna *Bet Hayeled* (Children's Home) was a product of partnership with the *Moetzet Hapoalot* of the Hapoel Hamizrachi.

Joint ventures, however, did not stifle Gotsfeld's mistrust of the other religious women's organizations. *Omen*'s champion was Sarah Herzog, attractive and self-assured wife of Isaac Herzog, the Ashkenazi Chief Rabbi of Palestine. When Rebbetzin Herzog, as she was universally called, had visited America shortly after Gotsfeld's departure in 1940, MWOA hosted a luncheon in her honor at the Warldorf Astoria Hotel. The hall was packed with representatives of twenty-two women's organizations, eager to see the wife of the Chief Rabbi and another luminary, the wife of Baron James-Armond de Rothschild. Sarah Herzog, the principal speaker, praised the MWOA schools and asked the women to build others like them. After the luncheon she met privately with MWOA's national board and asked the group to amalgamate with *Omen* and the *Moezet Hapoalot* into a single overall organization. MWOA would not even consider the prospect without first consulting Gotsfeld.[26] Many transatlantic cables thrashed out the issue. All along, Gotsfeld on one side of the Atlantic and Goldstein on the other received emissaries from the other women's groups. Gotsfeld's response was always a resounding no. She considered Sarah Herzog's proposal little more than a scheme to milk MWOA, the wealthiest organ of Mizrachi, to nourish the other groups' projects. No respectful entreaties, no reproachful pleas for unity within a beleaguered minority, could move her. No would she allow her followers to participate in Yishuv politics, insisting that educational institutions were the best means of strengthening religious Judaism.

Not all MWOA members agreed with her a-political stance. Their ambivalence is manifest in a short MWOA Bulletin article about the 1944 election to the *Asefat Hanivharim* (Jewish National Assembly). Headlined "Mizrachi Women in Palestine Enter Politics," it reported the success of a rival woman's group with unconcealed jealousy:

> The Mizrachi Women's Organization of America, *which does not participate in Palestine politics,* is nevertheless pleased to note that the Mizrachi Women's Organization of Eretz Yisroel [i.e. *Omen*] has become a factor in the political life of the Yishuv... Though the total number of votes received by the Mizrachi Woman's ticket was a modest one... it compares most favorably with the number of votes received by the combined ticket of the Woman's International Zionist Organization [WIZO] and the Women's Organization for Equal Rights... more than 22% of the total vote which, we are impelled to editorialize, is not so bad.[27]

Equally ambivalent was the relationship between Gotsfeld and Rabbi Meir Berlin, long-time head of World Mizrachi. Complicating matters was the rabbi's outlook on America. Unlike Rabbi Fishman, who had left the United States immediately after World War I, Berlin had remained for seven more years, establishing educational programs, forming a rescue organization, and advancing Orthodox causes. He returned during World War II. Though his respect for this country increased in light of pan-European indifference to Jewish suffering, he nevertheless continued to dismiss American Jewry as little more than a cash cow for the religious community in the Yishuv. Once, when asked to comment on American yeshivas, he was reputed to have replied that there were none worthy of the name.[28] More the wonder, then, that when Berlin participated in a cultural series held at BZM Tel Aviv, the topic was "American Jewry, Life and Values!"[29]

The rabbi did respect the woman who invited him to deliver the talk, despite her American background, but this did not alter his position. He never stopped badgering Gotsfeld for money, and he refused to get involved in any of her new educational ventures. For many years, MWOA had contributed the Mizrachi Teachers Seminary, but in 1945, when she asked him to endorse a Teachers Seminar to train instructors in crafts (*Handskunstsarbeit*), household management, and nursery school teachers, he turned her down. Her response was to create one of her own, and then introduce other new programs. Dismayed at the paucity of religious *madrikhim* (counselors) and kindergarten teachers in religious schools, she also provided instruction in those skills.[30]

Gotsfeld was not a little peeved at Rabbi Berlin's dismissal of her priorities, yet she also recognized their fundamental accord on key issues. All of her educational programs operated in the National Religious Zionist system at a time when liberals, led by Henrietta Szold, questioned the division of the national educational system along religious and political lines. Gotsfeld, like Berlin, remained adamantly opposed to union. In 1944, exasperated by the enrollment of Orthodox elementary school graduates in the Alice Seligsberg Trade School (a recent entry into vocational education under Hadassah sponsorhip) she invoked the rabbi's aid in steering those girls to BZM, lest "the effort of eight years exerted by teachers of a Mizrachi educational system is wasted and ends in a successful achievement for the promotion of a unified educational system."[31] There is no record of Rabbi Berlin's response. It is, however, indisputable that without his participation in Yishuv politics and faith in Gotsfeld's abilities, her most memorable achievement would not have advanced so smoothly.

10

Postwar Pressures and Accomplishments, 1945 - 1947

War and its aftermath did not reduce tensions within religious Zionism. Efforts to combine Mizrachi and Hapoel Hamizrachi proved premature. In America Mizrachi was more popular than Hapoel Hamizrachi, and MWOA leaders, still smarting from altercations with the Karlsberg group from Boston, identified with the former rather than the latter. Hapoel Hamizrachi in the Yishuv, however, continued to attract progressive Orthodox Jews.[1]

In June, 1946 Moshe Shapiro, leader of Hapoel Hamizrachi, addressed a MWOA Administrative Board meeting in New York. He burned with indignation at Gotsfeld's intransigence based, he declared remarkably, on an assumption of superior female intelligence:

> I want to tell you that in the years I have been working with Bessie Gotsfeld, when she asks anything I always give in. But it has never happened that she should understand that anyone else understands anything and that sometimes she must also give in ... Mrs. Gotsfeld acts as though Rabbi Berlin and the other members of the movement know nothing... The Mizrachi Women must recognize that the men may not be too smart, but they are also not too stupid and they do have an understanding of what is going on.

After condemning MWOA for presenting a united front, he faulted Gotsfeld and her followers on two grounds. The first was their refusal to meld with Omen and Hapoel Hamizrachi Women in a single organization. Here he pitted the genial wife of the Chief Rabbi against intractable Gotsfeld. "Mrs. Herzog is a wonderful woman. She has wisdom and understanding. One can work with her. I do not understand why she must constantly complain that no matter what she asks is refused." It all boiled down to what really troubled him, MWOA's refusal to increase its financial obligations. Aggressively, he barraged the women with impossible demands, asking them, for example, to send representatives to Europe in order to present the Orthodox position and to increase the population of clients in MWOA institutions tenfold. Peevishly, he declared that he was wise to Gotsfeld's tactics.

When we ask Mrs. Gotsfeld, she says she is only a representative and only follows out the decisions made at 1135 Broadway (the MWOA national office in New York). We ask her to bring this to the attention of the Mizrachi Women of America. We cannot understand that they don't realize the importance of this matter. Then we say, if you won't do it, then we will go to America and raise money for this. Mrs. Gotsfeld says, America? No. The money raised in America must go only to the Mizrachi Women's Organization of America. If you do this, you will hurt the work we are doing for the children.

In the attempt to invalidate her arguments and arouse sympathy for his cause, Shapiro resorted to hyperbole, implying that the distress for which she was responsible was worse than tribulations suffered in the beleaguered Yishuv.

I want to tell you, though, that we are working in very hard times and under very trying circumstances. Our nerves are strained in Eretz Yisroel, especially those of the people in responsible positions. You cannot understand what a day like yesterday means in Eretz Yisroel. It is not a question of the nine Jews who died. This is the beginning of great things. The religious youth finds itself in grave position. We have to fight the Goyim and the Jews. But it is even worse that you don't get along with the Mizrachi Women of Palestine. We should work together with them to attain the maximum achievement.[2]

Clearly, Shapiro's economic and social radicalism did not extend to the area of gender. It seems to me that Shapiro was expressing traditional male discomfort with female authority. What he actually resented was Gotsfeld's determination to prioritize female interests. In his eyes, Gotsfeld's actions neither met traditional expectations about female behavior, nor corresponded to Jewish traditions about "kingship" i.e. leadership, which must be male. Gotsfeld, unlike Herzog, was no *rebbetzin*; her identity and interests were not determined by connection to a man. Shapiro did not state outright that Sarah Herzog's behavior conformed to the conventionally feminine——i.e. controllable——and he did not lecture that decisions in the all-important area of the pocketbook belonged to men alone. Instead he paid Gotsfeld a backhanded and snide compliment, turning her intelligence into a liability.

Gotsfeld was not present at that meeting. But its fierce attack was obviously painful to her. This is how Dvorah Rabinowitz expressed her predicament:

When you come to Palestine representing an organization, especially a new country like Palestine where everybody is anxious to do and build things (and there isn't one phase of Palestine life that can't use more money), you are approached from all sides for assistance and all causes seem important. For someone to have had the courage and stamina to withstand all the beggings and pleadings for important work and carry out what we set ourselves to do required super-human strengths. I do not know of anyone who could have withstood it and carried it through, as did Bessie.[3]

Despite Shapiro's complaints MWOA continued to work alongside Hapoel Hamizrachi and its women's branch in certain areas In October 1945 Gotsfeld announced the construction of children's homes in five Hapoel Hamizrachi kibbutzim, and, in tandem with Moezet HaPoalot of Hapoel Hamizrchi, additional day care centers. Together the two women's organizations maintained youth clubs in Tel Aviv and Jerusalem.[4]

Even satisfaction of her own cohort required tact and gracious diplomacy. Gotsfeld had to withstand "beggings and pleadings" from MWOA members and supporting foreign groups demanding inappropriate tokens of their donations. Responding to a proposal that names of Uruguayan donors be inscribed on children's beds,[5] she wrote:

> Your suggestion to equip beds [in the as yet unnamed Children's Village at Ra'annanah] is a very important one. However, may I point out to you that we endeavor to train these refugee children in such a way so that they shall forget the horrors of Europe and feel that they are once again part of a family with loved ones near them? Because of that, we have made it a policy not to put a donation plaque on each chair or table or bed. We do not want the children to feel as if they are in an Orphan Asylum. We want them to feel that when they have come to Eretz Yisrael, they have come – home.[6]

To satisfy the craving for recognition, she suggested "Loyalty Certificates" or inscription of the chapter name in a Golden Book to be kept in the main office of the projected Children's Village.[7]

Residue Of One War, Prelude To Another

With the end of World War II, Gotsfeld eagerly anticipated happy reunion with her family and colleagues. When, however, MWOA made plans to send a delegation to Palestine in the summer of 1945, the ever-practical leader suggested a delay until after the resumption of classes.

The group that arrived in May, 1946 included her sister-in-law Belle Goldstein as well as Rabbi Simha Rabinowitz, the new director of Tel Ra'annan and his wife Dvorah, long active in MWOA. (It was Dvorah whose forceful arguments and fortuitous pregnancy at a Mizrachi Convention twelve years before had facilitated the Mizrachi Organization's reluctant acceptance of MWOA independence.) During the year that the Rabinowitz family—parents and three small children—was in Palestine, she worked tirelessly with Gotsfeld to implement MWOA's growing programs.

Upon arrival, the Americans found themselves in a war zone. The end of World War II had not terminated Jewish distress. Thousands lingered in European displaced persons camps, some subject to harassment by antisemitic detainees from their lands of origin. Many longed for Palestine, but the British refused to open the gates more than a crack. Their policy during and after the war forced clarification of Zionist objectives. The Biltmore Platform of 1942 had called for a Jewish state. The British position, inflexible even after the destruction of European Jewry became known, resulted in Jewish repudiation of the mandate and the call for armed struggle. Haganah blew up bridges; Etzel targeted British military installations. Mandatory authorities, in turn, inspected every corner of the land for weapons and military leaders. The search began on what the Jews called "Black Sabbath," June 29, 1946, and continued for two weeks. Many were arrested, among them Jewish Agency officials, but few weapons were uncovered.

Gotsfeld would not allow political events to stand in the way. The dedication of an annex to the Jerusalem school proceeded as planned. On way to the event, the taxicab ferrying the American delegates from their hotel had to stop for the funeral procession of two young men killed in a scuffle with the British military. The delay over, the women proceeded to the ceremony, which celebrated a new space to accommodate seventy-five additional students.[8]

The notorious bombing of the King David Hotel took place on July 22; the British responded with a curfew on Tel Aviv and Jerusalem. For four days shops were closed and Jews were forbidden to leave their homes. This did not stop strong-willed Bessie Gotsfeld. On the second day, she found a police officer willing to escort her to BZM, where thirty refugee children from the Motza Children's Home had repaired for vacation. She convinced him that the sight of soldiers patrolling the streets and the noise of loudspeakers barking orders would evoke still-fresh memories of Nazi horrors and reinforce psychological damage already inflicted. Upon her arrival, the children gathered round their "*doda*" [aunt], consoled by her reassuring smile and calming words. Officers soon demanded her departure and she complied, but only after receiving assurance that there was sufficient food to sustain the children through the crisis.[9]

An Aborted Journey

Belle Goldstein, observing her conduct, was loath to leave, but her duties as national president of MWOA compelled her departure. To ease the pain of parting, the sisters-in-law promised to meet in December, at the 22nd World Zionist Congress. The choice of Basel, Switzerland, where Theodore Herzl had convened the first congresses, they agreed, was surely a sign that, despite the decimation of the Jewish people, Zionism would advance unflinchingly towards the goal of Jewish state.

Gotsfeld looked forward to what would be her third Congress, and began the journey, but illness prevented its completion. The Mediterranean was so rough that even seasoned travelers could not eat. What is uncomfortable for a healthy person can be lethal for a diabetic, for consumption of food is necessary for the administration of insulin. After disembarking, she was so dehydrated that Dvorah Rabinowitz, who accompanied her, rushed her to the nearest hospital, situated in Besançon, near Lyons. Her condition improved under the physician's care, and she was soon ready for nourishment. Rabinowitz determined to secure for her friend the best Jewish medicine, chicken soup, but didn't know how to obtain it. Her limited French had been sufficient to inform a physician of Bessie's condition but was unequal to the task of securing a kosher-killed chicken and finding someone to prepare a broth. She finally discovered a local Jewish storekeeper and comically indicated the requirement with chicken-wing arm gestures and high-pitched "kukurikus." When the woman, a Mrs. Reingowertz, got the gist, she called her son in Lyons and he brought a *shohet* (ritual slaughter.) The "Jewish medicine" revived Gotsfeld, but she was not strong enough to attend the Congress. Disappointed but thankful to be alive, she recovered in a Swiss Jewish home that her sister-in-law Belle located.

Inspiring the Membership

Upon return, Gotsfeld kept members informed of the parlous situation in Palestine. To cement attachment to the Yishuv and MWOA she appealed to the brain with edifying information and to the heart with poignant anecdote. One was the report of a heartening meeting. While waiting in Rome for a plane bound for Palestine, Gotsfeld and Rabinowitz met a widow awaiting the certification required for entry into the British-controlled land. The woman informed them that her three daughters were already there. When she showed them the children's picture, Dvorah realized that she herself was the photographer; the girls were residents of *Tel Raanan*, where her husband was the director. [10]

Meanwhile troubles in the Yishuv multiplied: more curfews, martial law, incarcerations, and new reprisals, as furious argument rocked the UNO at Lake Success. It all came to a head on November 29, 1947, when the world organization voted to partition Palestine into a Jewish and an Arab state.

All the while, it was business as usual at the various MWOA institutions. The small children of *Tel Ra'anan* were allowed to remain awake all night during the eve of the *Shavuot* festival to study Torah; seven Yemenite boys celebrated a joint bar mitzvah at the BZM Jerusalem annex. [11] To assure the members that all was well, Gotsfeld sent an upbeat message to the New York office:

> From the outside, the Land appears to be in a state of upheaval
> and disruption. Nothing could be farther from the truth. There have, of
> course, been days such as those following Black Saturday on June 29
> of last year or the period of martial law in Tel Aviv when it appeared as
> though the normal life processes of the Yishuv were being paralyzed.

These, however, have been exceptional times. On the whole, the economic, social, and cultural life of the community goes on as usual. The frequent curfews and other restrictions have been more of an embittering nuisance than a real check. Moreover, the expansion of the Yishuv has continued. During the past year it has even been accelerated. As these words are being penned, news has just arrived of the twenty-fifth settlement on the land this year, a new link in the chain of settlements in the Negev. Without much publicity, work has already commenced on development of the water resources in the southern part of the country. Industry too has not been at a standstill. No matter how one evaluates the fortunes of Zion during these past years, they have *not* been years of stagnancy for the Yishuv.[12]

The purpose of the extravagantly optimistic letter was less to console the members than to connect them to the issue at hand. Opposed to the violent and separatist actions of the radical *Etzel* and *Lehi* fighters, she cleverly utilized their violence acts to justify new projects and spur further action.

The great source of strength of the Yishuv lay always in the fact that it maintained a national discipline even though it did not have a formally recognized state- that our organized representative and executive institutions not only performed various State functions, but wielded the moral equivalent of state authority on the basis of voluntary consent. It is this greatest of achievements of the Yishuv which is being challenged by the separatist military organizations which have become a menace to the integrity of the Yishuv.

From what source do these organizations derive their rank and file? If we disregard the top rank of leaders motivated by a definite political philosophy, we find that their membership comes largely from those parts of the Yishuv which have always been more or less maladjusted to the new life in Eretz Israel and have been living more or less on the periphery of the new Yishuv. Often enough, the youth has torn away from the cultural environment of its parents but has not succeeded in adjusting itself to the new environment and has been left floundering about without spiritual anchorage. It is this youth which is drawn to the separatist movements, not merely by their political naiveté but largely by association of their own frustration with those of their people.[13]

This report rested upon four remarkable assumptions, all of them debatable. One was that Jewish suffering in British-controlled Palestine troubled American Jews more than those who actually experienced it. The second was that national unity was the *summum bonum*. The third was that recipients of the report condemned the terrorist tactics employed by *Etzel* and *Lehi*. Connected to the third was the fourth and most original; ingeniously it employed current events for her own purposes. Gotsfeld blamed the aggressive insurgency on societal conditions rather than the political situation. Young peoples' violent, society-splintering actions, she declared, result from the loss of religious moorings. The answer to terrorism and disunion, then, was education in a religious and caring environment.

This, then, was the rationale for the most ambitious project undertaken by MWOA, initiated, remarkably, during the period when the Jewish state was struggling to be reborn. It was a large children's village to be built near Ra'ananah, seventeen miles north of Tel Aviv.

From Dream to Realization: Children's Villages and Farm Schools

A large comprehensive youth village was already a gleam in Gotsfeld's eye during her 1939-40 tour of the United States. In Chicago she had sought and gained approval to organize one for young refugees. Did this gesture indicate changing priorities? It will be remembered that her first efforts were urban rather than rural; the two BZMs established during the 1930s located in cities, emphasized skills of the home and light industry rather than the farm. I do not think that MWOA's sponsorship of children's villages on the outskirts of small towns during the early 1940s signified a turnabout; it indicated rather that Gotsfeld's assessment of how best to utilize resources was not static but dynamic. The tilt towards the countryside was not a reversal but rather a shift in direction.

BZM was a Zionist institution and all Zionists cherished the land and valorized its reclamation for the Jewish people. Hewing to this proposition, Gotsfeld had justified the inclusion of gardening in the first BZM curriculum as "a practical preparation for farm life; and (to) inspire them with a love for this life on land, so foreign to most immigrant youth, yet most essential if they are to help in the rehabilitation of this country." Poultry raising, she wrote, was "one of the essentials of colony life in Palestine."[14] Her depiction of student and neighborhood excitement over the birth of chicks is, in my opinion, the most charming report in her correspondence.[15] BZM, moreover, encouraged graduates who chose to live on a collective farm or cooperative farm village. Indeed, it was to promote "life on the land," that Gotsfeld championed Kibbutz Rodges and *Kfar Noar Dati.*

Youth Farm Villages in Palestine

Long before Gotsfeld launched a farm village in Ra'annanah, two large agricultural youth villages had already made their mark on the Yishuv. One was *Shefeyah* (later *Meier Shefeyah*) organized in the 1920s by Alice Seligsberg and Sophia Berger, friends and colleagues of Henrietta Szold. At Szold's suggestion, Junior Hadassah adopted the village as its special project. The second was Ben-Shemen. Its founder and director for thirty years was Siegfried Lehmann, whose original ideas attracted the attention of world-famous Martin Buber and Albert Einstein. Responding to Lehmann's prestige, the Jewish National Fund (JNF) leased a large parcel of land near Ramleh and prominent German Jews donated sufficient funds to bring about his dream. In 1927 the first group of children, aged 11 to 14, arrived in the village. When Recha Freier proposed sending German young people to Palestine, Lehmann, visiting Berlin at the time, agreed to accept them. In 1933 *Ben Shemen* became one of two founding organizations of Youth Aliyah.

Siegfried Lehmann, influenced by European social thinkers of his day, carried out a program that featured "education for community in small groups; division of the school day into lessons of general education and work in the field; "self-government of the children's groups, guided by a *madrikh*, and, finally, education for life in a village." That is how legal scholar and author Norman Bentwich summarized the program. He went on to define the *madrikh* as "literally, guide or pathfinder... on the one hand an outdoor educator for fieldwork and recreation, and on the other hand, youth leader... an educator... (but) it should be borne in mind that the *madrikh* may not be a regular teacher or instructor in the school."[16]

Eventually *Ben-Shemen* affiliated with Mapai. (Shimon Peres was educated there.) At both *Ben-Shemen* and *Meier Shefeya*, recreation and spiritual regeneration marked the Sabbath, but not in strict accord with religious tradition. For this reason, neither was an appropriate model for an Orthodox institution. *Ben-Shemen* nevertheless must have influenced Mosad Aliyah, for the latter followed similar guidelines: the emphasis on farming, the divided day, *madrikhim* as well as teachers. But the religious village that most closely resembled *Ben-Shemen* was the one that Gotsfeld launched in 1947.

The New Village

Kfar Yeladim Ra'anannah's birth pangs were long and sustained. A proposal accepted by MWOA in 1939 saw the light only in 1945, when Gotsffeld renewed her efforts to secure a large parcel of land adjacent to property already acquired near Raananah a centrally-located village, At first the JNF offered twenty dunams; Gotsfeld categorically refused them as insufficient for a village planned for hundreds of children. As in her efforts to retrieve BZM Tel Aviv from the British military authority, she pursued her goal relentlessly. She petitioned many people, including Aryeh Gellman, an American Mizrachi leader, persuading him to meet with JNF board members.[17] As luck would have it, Rabbi Berlin was the JNF president at the time. Gellman's support and Berlin's position turned the tide. The rabbi found a large and arable plot of land adjacent to the MWOA property and JNF leased it to MWOA.

The following is an eye-witness account of Gotsfeld's first visit to the site, as told by Israel Friedman, a Mizrachi professional. Some details are unclear, probably because of its source. Friedman was fourteen years old, overwhelmed with admiration of the woman who feted him with smiles and cookies before the journey. Furthermore, his speech was committed to paper long after the event, and the typescript does not flow from the author's typewriter but that of the secretary who took down his testimony. Nevertheless, its animated tone captures fifty-seven year old Gotsfeld's bright-eyed enthusiasm and illustrates her determination to implement an ambitious plan.

> I remember like today and will never forget it. On this nice summer's day in the afternoon, Rabbi Berlin asked for a car, took me and [a JNF] official. We went from Jerusalem to Tel Aviv. We came to Yona Hanavi 27. He sent me up to her house on those narrow steps, you know, on the 2nd floor. I went to call her. She was sitting and shaking – "Why are you so late?" She was expecting to see the land. She ran down from the steps like a young girl of 12.
>
> We were waiting in the car and drove out to Raananah. On the way, not far from Petah Tikvah, we had some sort of traffic jam. Although the traffic then was not as heavy as the traffic now in Israel, we had a jam. So she got angry and she said to me: Tell the driver to make it faster, faster. She was running to it like G-d knows what. And finally we reached Raananah, and this man from JNF himself wasn't exactly aware of where it was. He took out the map, and together with the driver [searched] until we finally spotted the place, and he pointed it out to her. You should see that woman at that moment. First of all, we young men were standing in the middle. She asked the JNF [official] to point out the borders exactly. You should have seen her face. East, west, north, south. She began to walk over the whole length of the place, all around it looking, and it was rocky land and grass: nothing. But a nice view, not far from there we saw all the roofs of Raananah and the highway leading to Haifa. I was standing with Rabbi Berlin in the middle. He was older, upporting himself on a cane, and he said to me, "Look at her, I envy her. I wish I had men like her."
>
> Her joy of creativity... She was standing just in the middle of the lot and she began to call out plans and projects like the greatest architect, visionary. She said – "Here on this place I will have not just plain houses for children, but palaces. This will be the center, the *meister* – she used the German word – the *meister Anstalt* of Eretz Israel [first class educational institution], for my children. The children will come in and I will need more- increase- more space." And he said – "Don't you worry. You will get as much as you need. First build what you have in mind." And she said – "it is going to be the greatest place in the world."[18]

Having secured some 275 dunams of land (about 70 acres) from the JNF, and another 32 from private individuals, with more promised, Gotsfeld decided upon an ambitious plan. Though members informed her that they could not support more than 200 children, she was determined to create a physical plant that could eventually accommodate more than twice the number. To accomplish this required modification of the original plan. She suggested using money sent by MWOA for infrastructure that would one day have room for 500 students and a large staff: roads, water and electricity, central buildings, preparing the land for planting. The rest would have to wait. As usual, this task-oriented woman saw the whole picture.

As per her custom, Gotsfeld conducted an extensive search for the right person to devise an overall plan. She looked for a town planner and architect capable of designing a campus that was functionally appropriate and aesthetically pleasing. She chose M. Ben Ury of Haifa, drawn to his suggestion of single story buildings that hugged the ground and blended into the landscape. The plan may have reminded her of Frank Lloyd Wright's Usonia communities, popular in post-war America. Buildings would be grouped in zones, distinct zones for distinct tasks: housing for students, teachers, and staff; dining hall, school buildings, cultural buildings, administration, workshops, and eventually, a synagogue.[19]

The Children's Village opened in 1947, with about eighty children previously detained on Cyprus. The children were placed in four dormitories. This was an unusual set-up for the day. Gotsfeld, who cherished the aesthetic almost as much as the practical, disapproved of the common practice of constructing two boxy institutional-type structures, one for boys, the other for girls, set in an area with no landscaping. Seventy children, among them Children of Teheran, soon joined the original group. Alongside the *madrikhim*, the entire cohort planted gardens and primed the land for agriculture.[20] With an ear to the radio and an eye to the future, these young pioneers prepared the way for the village that would soon bear Gotsfeld's name.

11

A Climactic Year, 1947 - 1948

Pursuing Normalcy in Abnormal Times

In October 1947 Bessie Gotsfeld entered her sixtieth year. The previous months and the year that followed nearly exhausted the limits of human experience, encompassing creative activity, personal honor and private tragedy, jubilation at national independence, and alarm over the safety of the innocents under her care and the independence of her organization.

Nineteen forty-seven was the year when the United States Special Committee on Palestine (UNSCOP) considered the Palestine question and recommended partitioning the country into a Jewish and an Arab state. While international debate raged and Arab attacks multiplied, the Goldman-Goldstein family presence in the land swelled. Eliezer Goldman had settled permanently in *Kibbutz S'de Eliyahu*. Belle's daughter Leona Goldstein and two other young women came to Palestine as trainees in the children's homes. Leona's sister Raisel arrived with her new husband Leon Rauchwerger, who planned to study at the Hebrew University. To Bessie's delight Raisel soon gave birth to a daughter. Just as her sister and brothers' children were "the children" so did Ora Rauchwerger's birth in May, 1947 initiate Gotsfeld into surrogate grandparenthood.

She had little time to share her happiness with Dvorah, for in June the Rabinowitz family, unable to renew their visas, returned to the United States. Dvorah, who assumed MWOA's vice-presidency (later the presidency), reported on her year in Erez Israel. First, the tenor of the times:

> I lived through curfews, martial law, seizing our leaders and taking them to Latrun. But I witnessed the splendid spirit and tempo of the Yishuv. The keynote was "carry on" - keep the stream of life flowing: send children to school, plant, reap, sow, build, open new factories, establish new kvutzoth.[1]

To indicate MWOA's participation in constructive action, she vaunted the 640 refugee children, "whose numbers are daily increasing" under MWOA care in numerous institutions, including the vocational high schools and *Batei Haluzot* in

Jerusalem and Tel Aviv. At the same time MWOA also helped support several teacher-training programs. One was the Mizrachi Teachers' Seminary, Rabbi Berlin's pet project. Then there were the programs that Berlin had deemed superfluous, training BZM graduates as kindergarten teachers, vocational teachers, and *madrikhot*.

The Children's Village and Farm School

The *piéce de resistance*, the Children's Village and Farm School in Raananah, Rabinowitz noted, was already in operation. Additional JNF land increased the campus to 312 dunams. It was a time of furious building. At the time of the dedication, October 21, 1947, (just one month before the November 29th UNO vote on partition), eight of the twenty-five planned buildings were ready, with others under construction. Four dormitory buildings already housed 150 students.[2]

During the first months of operation, Gotsfeld went to Raananah often to inspect the construction and to establish a personal presence. In the process, she exposed herself to personal danger. Once she traveled there with Herman Hollander. Hollander was a refugee from Nazi Germany who had transferred the family fur business to the United States and later emigrated. In Israel he worked for Mizrachi and the new state as a "dollar a year man." En route to Raananah, a surprise Egyptian air attack forced Hollander and Gotsfeld to run for cover. [3]

Hayim Zvi Enoch

For headmaster of the new school Gotsfeld chose Hayim Zvi Enoch, already celebrated as a brilliant and innovative educator. Born and educated in Berlin, he studied in Zurich, Switzerland between 1932 and 1934, where he assimilated educational theories advanced by Pestalozzi and Rousseau and their contemporary successors who championed Gestalt psychology and holistic education. After "ascending" to Palestine, he taught at the Mizrachi Teacher's Seminary for some years and in 1948, at age 43, was impatient to shape education in a pristine environment.

It had long been Gotsfeld's policy to select competent educational directors and then leave them to their own devices. To do so in this case was particularly appropriate because, in important respects, Enoch's educational vision resembled her own. At the time most farm villages featured institutional-type dormitories for the entire student population. Against the grain, Gotsfeld suggested individual cottages, each with its own kitchenette, dining room, utility room, and clubroom. Each building would house about thirty-two children and their *madrikhim*. Like Enoch, she knew that children seldom flourish in large institutions where no adult seems to care about them. In the urban schools she had counted on administrators to foster a home-like atmosphere for the children. Gotsfeld and Enoch shared the conviction that refugee children, so cruelly torn from their families, required the companionship that small spaces foster.[4]

Together, Enoch and Gotsfeld fine-tuned the cottage system. They did not group children according to age or seniority, as in a kibbutz, but deliberately mixed ages, as in a family. One room might accommodate a boy or girl of seven, another of twelve, a third of sixteen. Younger children would rely on older "brothers" and "sisters" so that the adolescents who cared for them would develop a sense of responsibility. Each house was divided down the middle, half boys, half girls. *Madrikhim* slept in private rooms at opposite ends of the building, with easy access to the children. Staff and children ate the two lighter meals in the dining area, older students helping the younger. Only the weekday main meal and Sabbath repasts would be shared with the entire population -students, teachers, and staff - in the large communal dining room. Enoch's vision, like Gotsfeld's, glowed with lofty expectations. At the dedication ceremony he proclaimed: "This will be neither a children's institution nor an orphanage but a children's educational center where the children will return to family life and be brought up in the spirit of Torah, Mitzvah, work, and realization."[5]

To help children realize their potential, he undertook a program that took into account occupational, emotional, intellectual, and spiritual requirements. Since neither Gotsfeld nor Enoch experienced the "divided soul" that bedeviled many modern Jews, they did not differentiate among them. Gotsfeld's Orthodox father had educated his daughters in Jewish law and custom at home even as he enrolled them in a Polish gymnasium; her husband, who studied Talmud all his life, declaimed selections from Isaiah, and courted her with Shakespeare. Enoch, who happily submitted to the religious precepts of Shem, was equally at home in the tents of Japheth. With Gotsfeld's encouragement, he tailored holistic educational theories to suit the young refugees. Schooling at the Children's Village was religious, humanistic, democratic, and practical.

A Religious Environment

As in all MWOA institutions, environment was all-important and Jewish tradition a paramount factor. Because the campus was an autonomous unit, it was easier to control than urban schools. City planner Ben Ury deliberately set buildings far from the highway and the town so as to isolate the children from neighbors who did not observe the Sabbath in accordance with Jewish tradition.[6] The staff did everything to create a pleasurable and spiritual Sabbath. After Friday afternoon cleanup girls donned navy skirts and white blouses. Boys wore white shirts and navy trousers, long or short, depending on the season. Friday evening meals featured white tablecloths, sparkling candles, fresh flowers, and special delicacies. After the meal everyone sang Sabbath songs and *birkhat ha-mazon* (grace after meals) together. Students and staff attended Saturday morning services in the dining room, refitted for that purpose.

Embracing World Culture.

Enoch, a Renaissance man who matched wits with Yeshayahu Leibowitz and Baruch Kurtzweil, reveled in the arts, especially music. He did all he could to transmit his passion to the culturally deprived youngsters. Mornings everyone awakened to the exuberant strains of Hayden's Trumpet Concerto. During their half-day in the fields, children heard classical music. Instrumental instruction was available. Every child had access to a recorder and those with talent and interest could join the "flute band." The school choir was a popular choice. Student vocal and instrumental ensembles performed for the entire school.[7]

Creating Responsible Citizens

The student population was divided into *hevrot* [groups], each with about forty members. Each *hevra* had a committee that supervised order and cleanliness, sports, and religious observance, and arranged the roster of duties. Children were responsible for their own rooms, their cottage, and the outside garden. Daily services in the cabins were the boys' responsibility and they selected their own Torah readers and cantors.

More distinctively, the Ra'ananah institution, like Ben-Shemen, was a self-governing village. Boys and girls over twelve voted for a Children's Council headed by a "Prime Minister." The council passed judgment, for example, on new students' Hebrew knowledge and determined when they were prepared for academic work and vocational training. *Madrikhim* operated solely as advisors and they testified that the children's decisions invariably proved correct.[8]

Integral to the holistic education that Enoch provided was sexual equality. The Raananah institution was fully co-educational. Girls wore skirts to class but trousers for work in garden and field and while playing sports. For proficiency in several sports, they won prizes. On *tiyulim* (excursions by foot) boys and girls hiked together and male and female endurance were prized in equal measure. Like the boys, girls worked four hours a day in the fields and devoted the other four to their studies. All students performed calisthenics before breakfast.

Sexual Parity: Gender Differentiation

Leisure time activities also exhibited sexual parity. Girls sang and danced with the boys and swam with them as well. Together they watched films in many languages as they squinted to decipher handwritten Hebrew translations running along one side.

When a new opportunity arose, Enoch made sure to grant it equally to girls and boys. Kfar Batya was dedicated to agricultural and vocational education, yet when several academically inclined teenagers approached Bessie Gotsfeld and requested immersion in college-preparatory courses, she was willing to consider their proposal. After consultation with Enoch[9] she arranged for the students to remain in the village, and help teach younger children to pay for room, board, and tutors in science and English. These bright and ambitious adolescents also instructed each other. To save money the group purchased only one textbook in each subject. Each individual became an expert in a single unit and then taught it to the others. David Eliach taught them advanced Talmud, accepting no pay. So motivated were they that the entire group passed the stiff entrance exams to the Hebrew University. One was a girl, Yaffa Sonenson (later Eliach), who would become a professor at Brooklyn College and a Holocaust writer.

(Another scholar is Jacob Klein. Awarded a doctorate at the University of Pennsylvania he returned to Israel as professor of Assyriology at the new Bar Ilan University. He credits Enoch with teaching him to think clearly).[10]

Sex roles were nevertheless clearly differentiated in other arenas. In the student houses, where children were responsible for cleanup after meals, boys removed dishes and cleared the dining room while girls washed and dried the utensils. Although boys and girls studied academic subjects together, workshops trained the sexes in different skills. Boys learned shoemaking, carpentry and electrical and metalworking, while the girls' vocational curriculum resembled that of the BZMs. All students worked in fields and the flower gardens planted near the houses, but boys did the heavy lifting and took care of the early stages of cultivation: sowing, spading, and weeding. Poultry raising was a female task and milking cows (by hand) a male one. Traditional Judaism, of course, sharply distinguishes between active male roles and passive female roles. Boys only were obliged to participate in daily prayers conducted in the houses. Still, girls as well as boys studied religious texts and attended Sabbath services.

This atypical institution, obviously, required an unusual staff. If teachers were officers in command subject to General Enoch, *madrikhim* were non-coms with hourly contact with the children. Out of displeasure with the conventional training of *madrikhim*, Enoch formulated his own. He molded his own students into *madrikhim* and *madrikhot* sympathetic to his principles and methods. They learned through observation, practice, and Enoch's formal instruction. Eventually some of them became prominent pedagogues. Like masters in Yale dormitories, some instructors would perform the double duty of teacher-*madrikh* and teacher-*madrikha*.

An Innovative Curriculum

David Eliach, the seasoned and well-liked Talmud teacher found Enoch's type of pedagogy inappropriate for text-based Jewish studies.[11] Instructors in other academic subjects, on the other hand, would imitate Enoch's methods. To introduce geography to young children, for example, Enoch would not impose terms such as ellipse, continent, ocean, longitude and latitude at first, nor would he begin a lesson with questions. Instead he would excite natural curiosity, setting a globe on a table and silently inviting inspection. "What do you see?" his eyes and hand gestures would inquire as children circled the table. He would remain mute until one bold youngster would observe that it was round. Another would correct him: "Well not exactly round, it's somewhat flat on top." Another would remark on the presence of huge land masses surrounded by even larger bodies of water. Another would draw attention to vertical and horizontal lines. Their interest piqued, the children would pump the teacher for terms to express their observations. Despite the exceptional methods of instruction, or perhaps because of them, standardized tests posed no problems for these fortunate students.

Not that Enoch was a warm puppy. To the contrary, he was a stern disciplinarian, respected rather than loved. His flaws were those commonly attributed to people that Israelis call *yekkes* [German Jews]. A stickler for order and cleanliness, he would twist the ear of a boy who appeared slovenly or allowed a stray sheet of paper to remain in the lawn. At times he spoke sarcastically to the youngsters and sometimes he was excessively caustic. Yet there was method to his severity. He was determined to turn dispossessed orphans into independent men and women who would not expect compensation for their early suffering. There was a communal goal as well, to produce competent contributors to the Jewish State. Years later, prominent citizens would declare that this stern, even annihilating educator had stiffened their backbone and laid the grounds for careers in education, technology, and especially the military.[12]

A MWOA Showcase

Visitors to *Kfar Yeladim Ra'annanah* inevitably commented on its extraordinary cobbler. "*Yoḥanan Ha-sandlar*" (John the shoemaker) was a red bearded Polish Jew, a character out of Sholom Aleichem. Ever cheerful, he taught boys his craft and they, in turn, made shoes for the entire community. Every visitor was taken to his workshop to see shoes stacked neatly on shelves lined with newspaper scalloped at the edges, Yoḥanan, however, was no colorful peasant but a learned Jew. In the evening he taught selections from the *Gemarah* to students who exhibited interest.[13]

The large children's farm village inaugurated during Israel's bitter and protracted struggle for independence became the showcase of Mizrachi Women. In time, its innovative educational program, magnificent synagogue, trim lawns, productive fields, and well-tended gardens attracted visitors from home and abroad. Visiting tourists happily purchased products of its workshops. Wisely, Gotsfeld encouraged the weaving shop to fashion prayer shawls, women's scarves, and tablecloths, then ship them to MWOA chapters abroad. Thus did the village play a small role in compensating the parent body for time and treasure surrendered on its behalf.

Kfar Batya

The Children's Village's homelike atmosphere and enlightened teaching methods bore the imprint of Enoch's pedagogy, but everyone knew that without Gotsfeld's nine year effort, it would not have come into being. For that reason in January, 1948 she received a signal honor. Assuming her Hebrew name, *Kfar Yeladim Ra'anannah* became Kfar Batya; to visitors from abroad it was known as The Bessie Gotsfeld Children's Village. The new designation yielded surprise and embarrassment, especially in light of her statement, repeated endlessly with slight variations, "reward comes of itself in the satisfaction of seeing the fulfillment of an ideal blossoming into reality."[14] To celebrate MWOA's most ambitious project to date and the village's new name, the New York and New Jersey Region tendered a sumptuous banquet at New York's Waldorf Astoria Hotel. Shalom Secunda conducted his orchestra and a large audience heard two speakers. One was Rabbi Meir Berlin (now Bar Ilan), the man responsible for the large JNF land donation. In line with the widespread practice of sanctioning Jewish activity with a gentile imprimatur, the second speaker was Jorge Gracia Granados, Guatemala's Ambassador to the United States. The dinner invitation hailed him as "staunch supporter of the UN's vote on the establishment of the Jewish State."[15]

Mendel's Death

Events closer to home, however, marred whatever happiness the distant tribute could deliver. Mendel was dying. For two years spiraling pain had wracked his body. Eliezer took a leave of absence from the kibbutz and stayed with Bessie and Mendel during the uncle's final bedridden year. The end of Mendel's life brings to mind the O. Henry story "The Gift of the Magi," in which a husband and wife relinquish their most precious possessions in order to secure a gift for the other. Bessie was Mendel's principal concern. To Leona Goldstein he confided that he tried to conceal the pain and took as little medicine as he could bear to ease emotional and financial burdens on his wife. Bessie, in turn, nearly force-fed the pills and kept the clinical reports to herself for fear that emotional distress would compound his physical suffering.

Mendel finally succumbed on March 10, 1948. That Bessie did not totally surrender to grief owes much to the support of family and community. Her physician forced her to eat and injected life-saving insulin. He remained with her during eulogies delivered at BZM Tel Aviv (and attended by many local citizens and representatives of Orthodox institutions). After that he drove her to the cemetery and then home. Eliezer, retaining the role of son, slept in her apartment all week. Niece Leona, scheduled to return to the United States that very day, extended her stay for another month. In April Belle Goldstein, flew to Palestine for a short visit of consolation. Students, staff, and alumni joined the mourning and the comforting.

Graduates purchased black-bordered newspaper ads addressed "to our grieving mother." Students vied for the honor of reciting the *kaddish* [memorial blessing] for childless Mendel. Bessie selected three boys who had studied informally with her husband; they recited the prayer daily for the requisite eleven months. [16]

But the most sustaining factor was work. On the morning after the conclusion of *shiv'a* (the seven-day mourning period) Bessie rose and dressed early. To Leona's queries she responded, "I'm going to Beth Zeiroth, of course. I've been out for a week and have to go back to work. "There is so much to do" [17]

Not that it was easy to concentrate. To a South American Mizrachi leader she confided the personal sorrow, then straightaway used the opportunity to tout accomplishment under austere conditions.

> Hard for me to write you after my great personal loss. I ask *Hashem* for strength to continue my work for our poor people and our suffering homeless children. We must not let any consideration prevent us from this holy work and hope your org. will undertake the project we discussed. Have asked New York office to send you a film about life in Eretz Yisrael, which should help in your work.
>
> As we wrote you in a previous letter, we have opened a vocational school where the children learn key making, weaving, and ceramics. Hope to increase the curriculum in time. Our chicken house in Raanana develops well and is not only educational but we have our own eggs for the children and can give each one three eggs a week. Considering the Eretz Yisrael economy, this is very pleasing. Have also cultivated 25 more dunams of land, enabling us to raise vegetables; also planted 150 dunams with watermelons on the 500 dunams the KKl [Jewish National Fund] has given us to work.[18]

Meshek Yeladim Motza

There was indeed much to do as the date of Israel's birth approached. The War of Independence affected every child and adolescent under Bessie's care but posed a special danger to one group. As Mendel lay dying, the staff and children of the Motza Children's Home prepared to leave their beautiful home in the Judean hills near the Arab villages of Kolonia and Castel. For months the teachers stood guard every night. Haganah officers inspected their defenses and recommended that they slept in two thick-walled inner classrooms. They complied, hoping to remain in their mountain retreat, but that proved impossible. Sitting beside her husband's sickbed, Gotsfeld realized the encroaching danger to these children, already uprooted by one war and about to be displaced by another. Observers told her how the little ones stubbornly tended the garden and planted two trees on the Fifteenth of Shevat, (the Jewish Arbor Day) while the staff packed up the furniture.

With deep reluctance, on February 9, 1948 all boarded a bus headed for Jerusalem. By that time the road had become so dangerous that the teachers carried

Sten guns. The children settled temporarily in a large house in the Montefiore Quarter of Jerusalem, but this was not the end of their troubles. On April 8, 1948 they could hear sounds of battle from Motza. News that their mountain haven was destroyed threw them into visible consternation, for hope of return had sustained them. Conditions in Jerusalem during the siege compounded the distress. Food was scarce, replenished only when a convoy survived the perilous journey from Tel Aviv. There was little water, no kerosene, and infrequent electricity. To stave off thirst, children trudged to a distant well; to fill their bellies they gleaned wood for cooking beans, at times the sole staple. Food finally arrived via what was known as "the Burma Road," an alternative route constructed after Arab attackers cut off the Jerusalem—Tel-Aviv highway.

In June the children had to move again, this time to the *Talbiah* district of Jerusalem. For compensation they were given a fine house, the very one in which the Peel Commission had lodged a decade before. Even better than the improved accommodations was the discovery of an underground well on the property. The children emerged unscathed until the first truce, but when it ended, three mortars fell on the building, lightly injuring a few of them. By September, they were able to resume their studies, but since so many of their teachers were in the army they attended classes with other Jerusalem children. (The Motza Children's Home would remain in the Talbiah building until the early 1980s, when it would move to Gilo, a new Jerusalem suburb, and assume the name *Bet Hayeled* or Childhaven.) [19]

The children in *Mosad Aliyah* also had to be evacuated to Tel Aviv. BZM in Tel Aviv remained open, but at great peril. When Tel Aviv was bombed in June, 1948, two bombs fell close to the building. No one was injured, but the force of the bombs broke doors and shattered windows.[20]

Two Striking Honors

For Bessie Gotsfeld, spring and autumn, 1948 were bookmarks bracketing special honors for herself and her organization. Because Tel Aviv, unlike Jerusalem, was not subject to siege or dislocation, it was the locus of state-forming ceremonies. In April, The Zionist Actions Committee of the World Zionist Organization (*Va'ad Hapoel Hazionu*) scheduled an important meeting. Gotsfeld invited the group to gather at the BZM building and put all facilities at their disposal. There the Actions Committee voted to declare the State of Israel on the day after the British withdrawal.[21] On May 14, 1948 (5 *Iyar* 5708), when David Ben-Gurion declared Israel's independence at the Tel Aviv Museum, Gotsfeld was one of the invited guests. The following poignant words began her eyewitness report to the MWOA membership.

> It is with mixed feeling that we are writing to you these words.
> At last, after years of suffering, after periods in which millions of our
> people were exterminated, after so much blood and tears were shed,

our hearts are full of gratitude and prayer that a page of hope and heroism is added to our history. Words cannot express our feeling of thankfulness that we were privileged to have the *z'chus* [merit] to witness the beginning of our independence, of our statehood. And if our independence came in our day, then we must be, in the words of Herzl "worthy of it." It is up to us now to continue our battle so that all our brethren who died for *Kiddush HaShem* [to sanctify God's name], in the concentration camps, on the land and in the seas, and on the hills and valleys of Erez Yisrael have not fallen in vain.

The entire Yishuv, on the day of our independence felt the significance of Friday. Every heart was beating rapidly with anticipation and hope. At four o'clock in the afternoon, the temporary Jewish Government was assembled in the Museum of Tel Aviv. I too was privileged to participate at the Declaration of our Independence. The ceremony was very dignified and impressive, and there wasn't a person present, neither on the dais nor in the audience, whose eyes didn't shed tears of joy. It was quite a small assembly; most of the people from Jerusalem could not be present. But each one present represented not himself alone, not his party, but the entire Jewish people – its wishes, its aspirations, and its strivings of the past two thousand years. As we descended from the balcony, the throngs of people outside the Museum greeted the assemblage with joyous songs and with determination to do their best to achieve the aims which had just been proclaimed by our leaders. [22]

That the formal decision to acclaim statehood took place in the Tel Aviv BZM building seems poetic compensation for humiliation suffered during World War II when British officers appropriated it. In 1942 the facility had been saved by the good graces of Bella Gesundheit, who sheltered the school in her large home. Six years later BZM returned the kindness, not to the donor but to refugees from another war. During the struggle for independence, Arab civilian irregulars as well as units of the Arab Legion attacked the *Etzyon* Bloc. In the Bloc or *Gush* were four small HaPoel Hamizrachi settlements — *Kfar Etzyon, Ein Tzurim*, and *Massu'ot Yizhak*. With a total population of 450, they were located on hilly terrain near the Bethlehem-Hebron road, Just before the Declaration of Independence, residents joined units of the Haganah, in an attempt to save the settlements for the nascent State. All fought bravely, but numbers and materièl were insufficient to repulse the enemy amour. Many lost their lives. Those who surrendered suffered deep degradation. Though the bloc was lost to the Jews for two decades, their resistance helped Jerusalem's defenders consolidate their positions.[23]

Some Etzion women managed to flee; others were incarcerated under terrible circumstances. Gotsfeld, upon learning that young women from *Massu'ot Yitzhak* were released from a Trans-Jordan prison, volunteered to shelter them. Of the eighty-six refugees, fifty found a temporary home in BZM Tel Aviv. When they arrived at midnight, bruised, disheveled, and frightened, staff and students pampered them with hot showers and warm food. The refugees remained in place until they found permanent shelter and useful work. Other women and children from the "Gush" also found a haven in BZM and waited there for incarcerated husbands. With great joy Gotsfeld, alongside the staff and students, witnessed family reunions.[24]

Bessie's sixtieth birthday was the second bookmark of an unforgettable year. She sailed to the United States a month after her birthday, in November 1948; nine years had passed since her last visit. At MWOA's 23rd National Convention she delivered a highly emotional speech that detailed the current adversity, for Orthodox women the equivalent of Golda Meir's oratory before the wider Jewish community. Her address culminated in a plea for help.

> We have to build despite a war; in spite of the fact that we have no materials; that it is hard to find instructors or teachers because they are all mobilized, all fighting the war; in spite of everything, we have to go on. We have to find ways and means of how to carry on our constructive work in Palestine, in Israel...
>
> Help us! Do not think that you have already done the job because we have achieved Statehood! This is just a beginning. It is now that we have to fulfill a promise. We need everything in Israel, my dear friends. Everything! And we can only do it by your help, by your having complete faith in us to do it and by your helping us to do it.[25]

"Everything" was beyond the women's capacity, but they honored Gotsfeld with a gala luncheon at the Waldorf Astoria. From Dvorah Rabinowitz, now National President, she received a *bon voyage* gift of $250,000 earmarked for special projects.[26] Smaller boons included letters from child and adult admirers in Israel and gimmicks such as a box of flowers from Kfar Batya and a cake baked by students at BZM Tel Aviv.

Internal Tensions

Midst the excitement, one problem continued to bedevil Gotsfeld, stormy relations with the other female constituencies of Mizrachi. During the 1946 World Zionist Conference, while she was recuperating from her aborted journey, representatives of *Omen*, Hapoel Hamizrachi Women, and MWOA had discussed merger. Fearful of the consequences, the MWOA put off final disposition but did sign on to the loose confederation, "Central Mizrachi Women's Organization in Eretz-Israel." Sarah Herzog, wife of the Chief Rabbi, became president. Vice presidents represented the three groups. In that capacity Gotsfeld agreed to supply clearly specified funds to projects of the other two.[27]

It was bad enough when female Mizrachi groups in Israel challenged MWOA's autonomy and made a bid for its hard-won assets. But the distress resulting from their machinations was minor in comparison with the pain produced by a challenge on this side of the Atlantic. It was many years since MWOA had settled the dispute with the Boston Hapoel Hamizrachi. Now Gotsfeld again confronted a challenge to MWOA's exclusive right to organize religious Zionist women in North America. The challenge came from an Israeli woman named Tova Sanhedrai. Sanhedrai had long admired Gotsfeld's accomplishments,[28] but she was even more invested in Hapoel Hamizrachi, which she hoped to play a significant role in the incipient State. Only American Jewry, she was convinced, possessed the means to advance causes dear to Hapoel Hamizrachi, among them facilities for religious women workers who, for want of funds, were turning to the Histadrut.[29] Sanhedrai traveled to the United States in the winter of 1948 and remained for many months. At the time, Rabbi Berlin was still trying to amalgamate all the religious women's organizations under the *Mercaz Olami* umbrella. Both MWOA and *Moeze t Hapoalot* refused to surrender their independence, but consensus between them was limited to that issue. As previous discussions with Moshe Shapiro had indicated, the Hapoel Hamizrachi had long railed against what it considered MWOA's excessive parsimoniousness. The only remedy, its leaders concluded, was to bypass MWOA and form a separate American woman's organization.

Other challenges to MWOA's hegemony had failed, but this one succeeded, for a variety of reasons. Mizrachi was losing its hold even in America. Old timers such as Kirshblum and Gellman were no match for Dr. Raphael Gold (Ze'ev Gold's brother, a psychologist and Mizrachi ideologue)[30] and Yankel Greenberg, both articulate spokesmen for Hapoel Hamizrachi. Gellman's reminder that a Mizrachi convention had once proclaimed MWOA the only legitimate women's organization within Mizrachi made little impression. His arguments were far outweighed by the needs of the hour and the attraction of a new female leader.

In Tova Sanhedrai of *Moezet Hapoalot* Gotsfeld met her match in intelligence, discipline, and sense of personal rectitude. During the convulsive struggle for Israel's independence, Sanhedrai criss-crossed the United States and Canada. Radiating the appeal of an emissary from the beleaguered Yishuv, she pleaded for a new instrument to sustain workingwomen and children of the religious kibbutzim. Deeply touched, members of MWOA contributed to her cause. Some even helped found the new organization, Hapoel Hamizrachi Women. For Gotsfeld this was no more palatable than other members' dual membership in MWOA and Hadassah.

In June Belle Goldstein wrote that Sanhedrai's intention was to "invade" the Canadian Mizrachi Women, but this failed because of Dvorah Rabinowitz's and Mollie Golubs's intervention. Still, Bessie added in a letter to Goldstein:

> She did succeed in getting them to pledge $60,000 for a Bet
> Chaluzot in Tel Aviv. When Dvorah and myself saw this was a "fait
> accompli," they insisted that the moneys would go through you, and
> that you would have to be on the committee. They did this as a strategic
> means to keep the Canadian Women within the organization and to

acknowledge you as their representative.[31]

In an effort to iron out their difficulties, Gotsfeld and Sanhedrai scheduled several meetings. Sanhedrai had previously claimed that ideology rather than financial need dictated her American operation, but when she approached Gotsfeld, money was her first request. In Gotsfeld's eyes she was Moshe Shapiro in a skirt. Concealing her fury, Gotsfeld addressed her opponent quietly but responded in the negative. Sanhedrai departed, disappointed but hardly surprised.[32]

Relations with Omen were no better. Omen focused on Europe rather than America, even enlisting Bessie's old friend and supporter Anita Müller-Cohen. Once again Sarah Herzog pleaded with Gotsfeld to consider a merger, again to no avail.

Gotsfeld, at sixty, had lived a full life. She would carry on for another thirteen years, but no period in her life could rival the disappointments and accomplishments, the despair and the triumphs of 1947 - 1948.

12

Final Years

The see-saw year 1948 brought on substantial lifestyle changes. Gotsfeld learned that Mendel's heroic efforts to save money by ordering as few painkillers as possible had a realistic financial basis. Buildings inherited from his father had lost value. As Tel Aviv spread northward, the neighborhood of the Gotsfeld properties, south of the fashionable hub, was deemed "the wrong side of Allenby [Road]". Middle class occupants moved north, and the value of the property plummeted, forcing Mendel to dispose of them. At the time of his death, he owned only the building in which he and Bessie resided. The paltry rental income from the other apartments could not sustain her. She had always lived modestly but had never suffered privation. With poverty tapping at her door, she swallowed pride and principle and requested a salary. MWOA hastily complied, but accepting the money undoubtedly inflicted considerable pain.

Nor could she sustain the punishing daily routine of previous years. Dvorah Rabinowitz realized it during her time in Palestine, and she convinced her friend to slow down. Together they worked out a plan. It would take at least three people to perform the tasks that Gotsfeld had executed when the projects were fewer, the institutions were smaller, and she was younger and stronger. To MWOA's National Board Rabinowitz recommended a budget for an administrator, a secretary, and a bookkeeper. Americans who assumed these positions on a temporary basis would return to America and, bright with the aura of insiders, champion MWOA's work before members, prospective members, and the wider public.[1]

Gotsfeld retained her title, appropriately modified to "Israeli Representative of MWOA," but the additional designation of "Honorary President of MWOA" was actually a gentle push upstairs. So was the name by which children in MWOA institutions knew her. The "*Doda*" (aunt) or, if the client was very young, "*Imma*" (mother) of pre-state years became "*Savta*" (grandmother).[2] As time passed and her visits to the sites tapered off, however, most students knew her by reputation rather than daily contact.[3] (At the end of her life the aging Szold, by contrast, did not retire from Youth Aliyah, but others, especially Hans Beyth handled day-to-day affairs. Still, like Gotsfeld, she had kept abreast of organizational affairs until felled by her final illness in February, 1945.)

If Gotsfeld surrendered micromanagement, she held on to macro-supervision, at the same time reiterating that decisions were the prerogative of the central office in New York.[4] She remained active on MWOA's Israel Committee. Before any major undertaking, organizational leaders still sought her opinion about what was possible and what was not. Predictably, she continued to insist on fiscal responsibility. She still considered it her duty to call attention to costs. In 1952 she wrote:

> The[re] have been delays, shortages of materials, construction problems and rising building costs. Today in Israel, there is another factor which must be considered gravely by this convention. Along with the required expansion of facilities there is a rise in the cost of operation and maintenance of existing institutions and projects. Salaries have continued to rise. The prices of materials and commodities have also risen. [5]

In "retirement" Gotsfeld demonstrated flexibility uncommon in organizational founders. To save money, she advised dropping *Tel Ra'annan* and *Bet Halutzot*; in her estimation, they had outlived their usefulness. A few months later she reconsidered the first recommendation because of its "propaganda" value.[6] In other respects as well, she was willing to stray from original plans. MWOA had set its sights on BZMs in Israel's three main cities. It never built one in Haifa; instead it lent the name to a small facility supported by the Mizrachi Woman's Organization in England. When changing needs dictated a different type of institution in that city, she went along.

She also welcomed educational innovation in the first BZM's, where the course of study expanded from two to three years and a commercial course was added. Students who elected a career in education studied an additional year and then enrolled in a one-year course for kindergartners or specialized training in food preparation, soil chemistry, crafts, etc. Some stayed on to teach.[7] In the course of time, the name Bet Zeirot Mizrachi would disappear, as the BZMs became comprehensive high schools.[8]

The Bar-Ilan Memorial School and Memorial Center

The MWOA adolescent educational program that attracted the most public attention was Kfar Batya's high school. Gotsfeld and her staff decided to name it after Rabbi Meir Bar Ilan, the name assumed by Rabbi Berlin a year before his death in 1949. Although Berlin had been Gotsfeld's first mentor in religious Zionism and her support in the early years, the two had not always been in accord. Still, when he secured the large tract of JNF land for Kfar Batya, the slights that Gotsfeld had previously suffered at his hand seemed trivial. She remembered only his encouragement of female education and rejoiced in his genuine ardor for the new institution. She must have realized, moreover, that his address at Kfar Batya's opening, delivered shortly before his final illness, must have strained his diminishing energy.

Bar Ilan's death following so soon after Mendel's and the loss of fully one percent of Israel's Jewish population during the War of Independence was enough to disorient a younger and more robust woman than Bessie Gotsfeld. Still she pressed on. The Israeli Orthodox community was shaken by the rabbi's death, and its deep regard for the man who had led it so vigorously certainly inspired the naming of Israel's second university, which rose under their auspices. But MWOA got there first. On August 7, 1949 ground breaking of The Bar-Ilan Memorial School and Memorial Center at Kfar Batya took place. In her report to the members, Gotsfeld mentioned the impassioned eulogy tendered by Rabbi Bezalel Cohen, chairman of the Religious Youth Aliyah. Furthermore, in an effort to arouse their self-esteem she enumerated the other celebrities who attended. Those duties dispatched, she highlighted the aesthetic, psychological, and spiritual impact of the ceremony.

> The Village looked very beautiful. The stage for the guest speakers was decorated with flags, the children dressed in their holiday clothes...A holiday spirit prevailed. The Succah served as the canteen where very delicious cakes and cold drinks were at the disposal of the public... It was a touching moment when Tuvya Bar-Ilan, son of our great and sainted leader, Rabbi Meir Bar-Ilan, signed the Megillah, which was placed in the ground at the end of the ceremonies...The audience was so inspired and spiritually elated that it is really impossible to relate in words exactly what transpired. [9]

New facilities, experimental education in a rural milieu, co-education, and a broader curriculum were not the only advances during the late 1940s and early fifties; another was the ethnic makeup of the student body. On this matter, there was a return to original principles. It will be remembered that Gotsfeld's first reconnoiter of the Yishuv had summoned the imperative to educate daughters of religious Jewish emigrants from Arab lands and poor local girls. Historical events during its construction dictated modification of the original plan. The school had opened in 1933, the first year of the Nazi regime. It was soon evident that German and, later, East European girls were even more disadvantaged than native-born girls, in this case by lethal prejudice rather than poverty and class. Through the thirties, European refugees predominated in the BZM population. When the British ban on immigration reduced their number, Gotsfeld again planned to accept local young women. The dramatic arrival of the Children of Teheran in 1943, however, placed that plan on hold. During the next five years, European survivors dominated the news and their sorry state sparked the resolution to assist them. Child refugees from Nazi tyranny constituted the population of MWOA's various farm schools; the first seventy children in the Raananah village, for example, had been Europeans released from internment on Cyprus.

But that state of affairs would not continue. After the War of Independence and the subsequent European influx, most Jews who immigrated to Israel hailed from Arab countries. Children born in Morocco and Yemen, (and also Rumania) joined resident Polish and Hungarian youth in Kfar Batya as well as the other Israeli farm villages and urban schools. A single room could house a child from Hungary, another from Morocco, and third from Iraq. By 1950 over 3000 children were educated in MWOA–sponsored urban institutions and children's villages, and thousands more benefited from its social service programs. Still, there was never enough money to settle and educate all the religious children who languished in *maabarot* (transit camps). To a Sephardi man who supported the Mizrachi Organization in Mexico, Gotsfeld expressed her fears and solicited aid. Estimating the percentage of children from religious homes in this migration as 90%, she wrote:

> Since [there are] not enough religious places, some [Sephardi and Yemenite] children stay for months in these camps. There is a danger from irreligious parties in the Yishuv; the *Hashomer HaZayir* [left-wing socialist party] does everything possible to absorb these children in their institutions with the pretext that they will be supplied with kosher food. Our spiritual values and heritage are in danger to be forgotton, *has ve'halila* [Heaven forbid.]... We appeal to you to ally with us in this holy work and give a helping had to Mizrachi Women of Mexico who participate actively in the rescue of these children."[10]

The aid was forthcoming; the new Mexican group pledged a tidy sum for a new building in Kfar Batya.[11]

Not all new residents were orphans. Among the enrollees were Israeli children whose mothers and fathers could not afford to maintain them, much less educate them. Gotsfeld determined to preserve family bonds, even when parents could not spare money or time to travel. She dedicated a line in the budget for parcels to be sent home under a child's signature and encouraged staff and students to accommodate parents who arranged a quick visit. [12]

In the urban schools, Gotsfeld took care to assimilate girls from third - world countries to the mores of modern Israel. She directed the BZM staff to maintain neatness and order. Students wore either uniforms or white shirts. Curtains graced every dormitory window, intended to cultivate a sense of privacy in girls raised in homes where there was no concept of personal space.[13]

Social service programming expanded to a significant degree during Gotsfeld's last years. In the 1950s and thereafter, MWOA maintained vocational training centers, settlement houses, kindergartens, day centers and after-school clubs in large cities and small villages.

The Kraushaar Synagogue

It had always been Gotsfeld's mission to recover bodies, minds, and souls, in the process developing religiously faithful and useful citizens of a Jewish polity. Midst all the excitement surrounding the opening of Kfar Batya, she announced an intention to construct a synagogue as soon as possible: "For, if the Children's Village is to assume the form of a young religious community, it cannot exist without a Synagogue at its center." [14]

The proposed synagogue would fulfill one of three objectives previously encapsulated as "rescue, rehabilitation, and religious training." [15] In line with the Mishnaic saying that Torah cannot flourish among people with empty stomachs, it was appropriate to prioritize the first two, but religious fealty, a prime objective of every MWOA installation, found expression both in the classroom and a makeshift worship service. It was a chore to dismantle the dining room every Friday and convert the space into a synagogue, but staff and students did so without complaint. For Gotsfeld, this was insufficient. To erect a synagogue, moreover, was to pursue objectives beyond religion. It was also a matter of aesthetics and symbolism, and not incidentally, a means of attracting publicity. These considerations had governed her directive to village planner Ben Ury to place the synagogue in a prominent place. Like a medieval cathedral, it was to stand on a hill, commanding the village. [16]

Gotsfeld's aspiration for a handsome building reached fulfillment when the Goldie Kraushaar Synagogue was completed in 1953. It was the first house of worship in an Israeli children's farm village. Three years after her death came the transformation of its interior. Dr. Nathan Dasberg, a Dutch rabbi, was at the time Director of Kfar Batya. He arranged for the transfer of the interior fittings, furnishings, and ritual vessels of a synagogue from the devastated Jewish community of Leewarden, Holland to the Kraushaar Synagogue. [17] The handsome building became a posthumous homage to Bessie Gotsfeld's spirituality, aesthetic sensibility, and dedication to Jewish renewal. She did live to see the dedication of the Joseph Zev and Miriam Bracha Schreiber Synagogue in Mosad Aliyah in 1958.

A Productive Old Age

The last decade of Gotsfeld's active life had two faces. Life without Mendel was not easy and mounting physical ailments compounded the distress. Hearing aids were no longer of much use, nor were eyeglasses. Diabetes continued to demand its due. Her body was racked with rheumatism and she developed a heart condition. [18] She looked older than her years. Yet at the same time her mind remained sharp and she was able to enjoy the honors bestowed upon her.

She returned to the United States in 1950 to celebrate MWOA's Silver Jubilee Year and remained there for several months. By that time the organization was sponsoring fifty facilities, wholly or in part. Gotsfeld commended the women for their donations, and at the same time urged them to expand their fund raising efforts to care for children from Arab countries then streaming into Israel. Along with the pleas on humanitarian grounds came a warning that, in the absence of new religiously oriented facilities, the children would succumb to secular forces.[19]

Having departed at the end of November, she was unwilling to return in 1951, when the Woman's International Exposition honored her for distinguished service. Her friend Mollie Golub, MWOA national president at the time, accepted the award from Harold Stassen, Chancellor of the University of Pennsylvania (and perpetual U.S. presidential aspirant). Other awardees were a nun, a social worker, the educator Maria Montessori, Mrs. Douglas Macarthur, and Georgia Neese Clark, the first woman appointed U.S. Treasurer.[20]

The following year Gotsfeld gathered the energy to travel to the United States, where she was needed to kindle interest in MWOA's new projects. At the National Convention that convened in Atlantic City in November, she delivered her best-remembered address.[21]

Soon there was a new honor. For many years MWOA had set aside funds for the Jewish National Fund. Acknowledgment came in 1955 with the dedication of The Bessie Gotsfeld Forest in the Jerusalem Corridor.

In the same year Kfar Batya welcomed ten adolescent boys and two girls from Ethiopia, the first African Jews to arrive in Israel. A second group followed in 1956, raising the number to twenty-seven. After a two-year teacher-training course under Youth Aliyah sponsorship, the young people returned, reluctantly, to their native land as Jewish teachers, later to witness the school that they built destroyed by arsonists. When Ethiopian Jews migrated en masse to Israel in the mid -1980s ("Operation Moses"), the Kfar Batya alumni provided invaluable assistance to the newcomers. By 1996 twenty-four of the original twenty-seven had settled in Israel.[22]

Separatism Reconfirmed

In 1956 the *Mercaz Olami* attempted to merge all Mizrachi organizations into two single-sex entities: male Mizrachi and *Hapoel Hamizrachi*, and female *Omen*, Hapoel Hamizrchi Women, and MWOA. To achieve that objective, Gotsfeld's old antagonist Moshe Shapiro, representing the National Religious Coalition and a Cabinet member in the Israel government, submitted a twelve-point proposal for an "indivisible" woman's organization. Sarah Herzog also pleaded with Gotsfeld to bring MWOA into the fold. It was the notion of indivisibility that gave the American women pause. True, Shapiro offered a sop to MWOA by granting them exclusive control over their own projects. Since they already had that, it was hardly an incentive. Nor was his proposal to base the union in Israel, the seat of the other two organizations. The heart of the matter, however, was Point #10:

> Where the Women's Mizrachi Organization of America shall
> desire to establish new institutions, they shall do so after prior

consultation with the *Mercaz Olami* of the Women's Mizrachi and
Hapoel Hamizrachi and in coordination with the general policy of the
Mercaz Olami shel Hamizrachi-Hapoel Hamizrachi. "[23]

From the beginning Gotsfeld had promoted three principles: organizational
sovereignty, fiscal discipline, and exclusivity. It seemed to her that the proposed
amalgamation would effectively demolish them all. Were MWOA to surrender its
independence, it would lose the right to formulate policy and choose new projects
without interference from other groups. Still worse, the women would have to support
institutions with expenditures that they did not overseer. All along, MWOA had
willingly joined hands with the other two organizations in social service, always
carefully stipulating the extent of its commitments, but it would brook no interference
with its signature institutions, the technical schools and the children's farm villages.
Furthermore, the proposed merger would reimpose submission to male Mizrachi in
the guise of the *Mercaz Olami.* This logic and these traditions had governed
Gotsfeld's negative response to Berlin and Shapiro's petitions through the years.

In 1959 the various Israeli Orthodox groups created a united political
front. Mizrachi and Hapoel Hamizrachi became the National Religious Party. The
Orthodox female groups in Israel fused and assumed the name The National
Religious Women's Organization.[24] In America, however, MWOA and Emunah
Women of America, the organization established by Tova Sanhedrai, did not
combine, and to date (2006) remain separate, a legacy of Bessie Gotsfeld.

If Gotsfeld's resolution to maintain organizational integrity and exclusivity
was unflinching, Szold's responses to outside pressures were more nuanced. In
1918, when the ZOA was founded, Hadassah, like the FAZ and the other mainstream
Zionist organizations, was, on paper at least, dissolved, Szold went along, and
agreed to serve as head of its Department of Education. That didn't mean much, as
Hadassah chapters continued to meet and support its own programs, with her silent
consent. Her response was much more forceful when women challenged Hadassah's
exclusivity. In 1923, when Emma Gottheil and Eva Leon, original Hadassah
members, formed a woman's auxiliary to the new Keren Hayesod, she lashed out at
them, insisting, like Gotsfeld, that there was room for only one broad-based American
female Zionist organization. In regard to financial matters, the two women demanded
fiscal restraint in equal measure. [25]

Active to the End

Gotsfeld's final voyage to the United States took place in October, 1959,
when a MWOA National Convention honored her, belatedly, at a seventieth birthday
celebration. After responding graciously to the tributes, she set forth her lifelong
principles and explained the raison d'etre of the organization. It was a heartening
moment for the general membership but a sad one for old friends who detected
undeniable physical deterioration. That Gotsfeld was aware of her perilous condition

is indicated in two sentences near the end of her talk: "I do not know how soon I shall see you again. I hope it will be soon and that I may have the joy of greeting each one of you in *Eretz Israel.*" [26]

That wish was granted, at least in part, when tourists visited Israel. Through the 1950s, whenever her strength permitted, Gotsfeld courted visiting MWOA members or prospectives. Letters from America sent in advance indicated where the women (and some husbands) had booked rooms. When the tourists arrived, they found her at the hotel. She greeted them warmly and arranged to take them to schools, farm villages, and social service centers under MWOA sponsorship. There she found an attractive student or *madrikh* to show off the best features. Together, they viewed the up-to-date equipment while she encouraged contact with the children and staff. On the ride home, she did not solicit funds overtly; instead, she informed her primed listeners of the high cost of maintaining the equipment and programs that they admired.

Continuing the not-so-subtle persuasion, she invited visitors to her Tel Aviv home. Students from BZM served tea and sweets at her dining room table, while discussion centered on MWOA accomplishments and plans for the future. After members returned home, the bus trips and receptions at 29 Yonah Hanavi Street became an occasion for boasting. Women gained prestige in their individual chapters for having warmed themselves in the charisma of Bessie Gotsfeld. [27]

Some people who came for a short time remained in the country. Grace Hollander, a very active MWOA leader, and her husband Herman arrived in 1947. While war raged, Grace took charge of food distribution in the urban schools. Herman, on leave from his prosperous family business, became an advisor on trade and industry during the transition from mandatory rule to an independent state. At the end of the war. they decided to settle in Israel with their three small children. Herman served as Israel's trade representative in several foreign countries and Grace devoted her efforts to MWOA's Israel Committee. [28]

New friends, some young, others less so, continued to come into Gotsfeld's life. Ill at ease with spoken Hebrew, she was most comfortable with English speakers. Judy Kallman, a Czech refugee orphaned in the war, had studied in England. Her charm, beauty, and mastery of the language made her an appropriate guide for the tourists that Gotsfeld accompanied to Kfar Batya. When Eleanor Roosevelt visited the farm village in 1955, Gotsfeld chose her to present the customary bouquet. When the girl expressed preference for a commercial course over an agricultural one, Gotsfeld arranged the transfer to BZM in Tel Aviv, though it was filled beyond capacity.[29] She also took a under her wing an English student named Sophie. When Sophie married Jacob Szobel, Gotsfeld invited him to join the staff. Eventually he became the Executive Director of MWOA in Israel. The couple became like family and their son called her *savta*. Towards the Szobels Gotsfeld displayed an attitude that was alternately gracious and patronizing. Perhaps because of their personal and professional closeness, perhaps because physical distress was taking its toll, she could be merciless in her criticism. It was indeed tough love.[30]

New Yorker Dinah Dyckman, MWOA president from 1957 to 1959, was a frequent visitor. On one occasion, she and Gotsfeld escaped the Tel Aviv heat for a pension in *Bet Hakerem*, near Jerusalem. Dyckman expected a relaxing vacation, but found, to her surprise, that Gotsfeld, the ailing septuagenarian, had mapped out activities for every waking hour. Even as her friend's body suffered new insults, Dinah marveled, her controlling spirit still prevailed.[31]

In her final years, Gotsfeld's closest associate outside of the family was Mollie Golub, lawyer, former MWOA president, and treasured friend. According to Herman Hollander, Golub's most prominent character traits were a warm personality and a marked analytic ability.[32] Without doubt, these shared qualities smoothed progress of the friendship. Golub did not settle in Israel, but she traveled there frequently to check on the organization's income and expenditures. After her return to the United States, the two remained in constant contact. Golub's steadfast support at the end of Gotsfeld's career evokes memories of Fraidelle Haskell's loyal partnership at the beginning.

To bridge the geographic gap between herself and her comrade, Golub became Gotsfeld's epistolary confidante. Bessie's letters recorded frequent consultation with physicians and hospitalizations, though she spared her the most perturbing details. She did indicate a painful swelling in the legs that followed several heart attacks. Still, most of this correspondence, like the one with Belle Goldstein, indicates ongoing surveillance of organizational affairs. Many discussed the progress of a new Bet Zeirot in Beersheba, from planning, to financing, to construction. Of especial interest was the composition of the staff. The habit of criticism, mild in her earlier days, sharpened at this time. Many evaluations of personnel were downright unkind. She complained about inefficient and incompetent administrators and bookkeepers. She examined every application for a post in the major institutions and did not hesitate to pass judgment. Considering an applicant for educational director of Kfar Batya who brought positive references from several Orthodox rabbis, she registered two objections. First, "His approach to the problems is more that of a Rabbi than of an Educator." More crucial, from her point of view, was the claim that he was "a [Jewish Theological] Seminary man and occupied a Conservative pulpit. She feared that his selection "might lead to all sorts of controversies. This is not a matter of a majority decision but a matter of principle."[33] Fidelity to Orthodoxy, then, continued to override democratic consensus or any other values. She knew that Mizrachi luminaries such as Rabbis Meir Bar Ilan and Leo Jung claimed that Conservative Judaism abandoned "the unalloyed word of God".[34] How, then, she queried, could MWOA clients be allowed access to anyone sullied by contact with that movement?

Equal to her obsession with fiscal responsibility and passion for religious Orthodoxy was her unwavering zeal for organizational independence. It was so powerful that she even harbored misgivings about organizations that participated in joint efforts with MWOA. During World War II a Canadian group had started a BZM in Kfar Etzion; it disappeared, of course when the Arabs occupied the Etzion

Block. During the late '50s and early '60s MWOA joined hands with the Mizrachi Women of Canada to open a community center in Haifa and a vocational high school in Beersheba.[35] Predictably, Gotsfeld entertained reservations about joint ventures. She knew that she no longer could dictate policy, but a confidential letter to Golub expressed her lurking fears.

> I was astounded to see this week that the letterhead of the Canadian Org. read Mizrachi and Hapoel Hamizrachi Women... We consummated the partnership with the Mizrachi Women of Canada. Now that this organization merged with another organization, how does that affect the partnership? Already Mrs. L. is sending invitations to the office in the names of this merged organization. Under such circumstances the Canadian organization, who [sic] is not very organization-conscious may do things which might cause great embarrassment to us.

Because she doubted the Canadians' loyalty, she advised denying them parity in the conduct of their joint ventures:

> Perhaps the partnership must be subject to an agreement containing some circumscribed clause. Referring to the correspondence of our office with Canada, I would suggest that same should be limited to reports, accounts, and minutes, and not involve anything that might be interpreted [as] organizational matters. Of the suggestions or decision or advisability of adding the 2 issues they should learn from the minutes or through the discussions which have taken place at your Board. ...Are they entering the partnership as of the school year 1961-2? The outlay this year is going to be considerable, as well as the maintenance. Up till now they did not participate at all. We alone were and are the bearers of all preliminaries and running the school, and they share neither the expenditure nor the responsibility.[36]

In truth and despite Gotsfeld's fears and suspicions, joint efforts facilitated MWOA's penetration into two important centers of Jewish population.

It wasn't only women's organizations that challenged Gotsfeld's independent stand. In the voting for elective office, she certainly cast her vote for the National Religious Party list. Nevertheless pictures of the Tel Aviv BZM featured in the party's pre-election publicity upset her. By her lights, they contradicted her longstanding principle that MWOA remain apolitical.[37]

Last Year of Life

In 1961 Bessie Gotsfeld's life took a fatal turn. At age 73, she contracted an abdominal malignancy and cancer coursed through her body. At first she tried to keep her condition a secret. The correspondence with Golub contained only veiled references to the disease that would kill her: "On a personal note there are always the old problems, with some new ones always being added."[38] In January 1962, the Beersheba school that she had long anticipated was finally becoming a reality, but she was too ill to attend the groundbreaking ceremony. A headline in *The Mizrachi Woman*, "Ground Breaking for New School Center in Beersheva," added a note of regret for "the absence of "Bessie Gotsfeld, MWOA's honorary president, the inspiration and impetus behind all the work of Mizrachi Women, who, unfortunately, was not well enough to make the trip to Beersheba."[39]

Withal her mind remained active and her will indomitable to the end. With unremitting conscientiousness, she continued to examine minutiae and offer detailed recommendations, as the following excerpt from a letter to Mollie Golub, dated February 24, 1962, indicates.

> When conditions reach a point the way they have in our setup, things need personal attention, as I have already indicated on many occasions. More so now, in view of the changed monetary situation. ... Indeed all requests dealing with expenditures must definitely be curbed until a definite policy, which I hope will be established this time. With reference to finances, we must find a way to clear all debts and do business on a 30 day cash basis controlled from the main office or else any number of controllers and supervisors will not help us. The savings on purchases alone would be at least 8%. We also must establish a principle if we want to work with loans. How unwholesome a condition this creates when absentee management is concerned, as is in our case I need not explain. I am these days under great tension and it is difficult for me to write without upsetting myself emotionally. I hope that if somebody will come and I repeat it, not too late, so that not only budget but also the future program of every *Mosad* [institution] will be determined and administrative functions set up; maybe this will result in more satisfaction and happiness for those at the helm on the American scene as well. Maybe we will have to share responsibilities and control over *Mosdot* with government or municipal agencies, but this can only be decided on the spot, not on an impulse, but after careful and thorough consideration and reflection of every phase involved. If you are planning to have somebody come here very soon, the office here should be advised since it would be advisable to consider together all requests and proposed innovations in view of U.S. Board's perspective.

Even at this late date, she retained an eagerness to benefit from the experience of others: "Enclosed I am sending you the four year plan adopted at the WIZO convention. Sometimes it is interesting to know the approach (of) other organizations active in similar fields as ours."

During her final months of life, Gotsfeld's body was racked with pain. On several occasions she was hospitalized at the Assuta Hospital in Tel Aviv, where Mendel had taken his last breath. She had once considered giving up the apartment but, after a long talk with financial expert Herman Hollander, had decided against it.[40] Since 1959 someone had slept in her home, usually a BZM student; now she required full-time supervision. Belle Goldstein came from the United States and maintained a deathwatch along with the Rauchwergers and Eliezer Goldman.[41] On July 25th Gotsfeld sank into a coma and died four days later, surrounded by family members. The death certificate attributed her demise to carcinoma and diabetes.

With full knowledge that the end was near, Gotsfeld kept MWOA in mind. Her will bequeathed her house to two relatives and to Mizrachi Women of America. (The parties sold the house and split the proceeds.) [42]

Momenti Mori

That her legacy was far grander than a house and a few modest furnishings was indicated by the reaction to her passing. The funeral service, conducted on July 26, 1962 at the Tel Aviv BZM, attracted members from the entire Orthodox community. Students, social workers, educators, counselors, alumni and former staff members from all MWOA institutions filled the hall. Cabinet ministers Joseph Burg, Zerah Warhaftig, and even Moshe Shapiro read flattering eulogies.[43] The response to her death in America was even more striking. At the end of the traditional period of thirty days of deep mourning, MWOA sponsored a mass memorial meeting in the West Side Young Israel Synagogue. Twenty-two thousand women from the greater New York area (out of a national membership of 50,000) received invitations. They didn't all come, of course, but the large hall was jam-packed. Attendees heard representatives of Youth Aliyah, the Religious Zionists of America, and other organizations. The Israeli Consul spoke, as did the director of the Haifa Community Center, representing the scores of institutions that Gotsfeld had founded. Since that time, Amit leaders in both Israel and America have frequently summoned her ghost as an incentive to action. [44]

No one's fate is predictable at birth, but Bessie Goldstein Gotsfeld undoubtedly exceeded the expectations that even her loving parents could have entertained for their oldest child. Her accomplishments are all the more remarkable because of the many obstacles that she surmounted. And there are so many "what ifs." Had the family of Leibush Goldstein remained in Przemsyl, she might not have survived the Great War, when the area was a battleground. A diabetic, she certainly would have perished in the next European conflict for want of insulin. Had she contracted that condition a year or two before its onset, she would not have reached age thirty-five. Had Rabbi Berlin not visited her home, she might have become a lukewarm supporter of Hadassah or a smaller Zionist organization. Had her father not met Mendel's father in distant California, she might have married a man with no physical connection to the Holy Land, preventing or at least postponing settlement there and impeding her ambitious program. The life that she did lead, with all of its twists and turns, facilitated a matchless career that continues to inspire

Zionist women. In the words of her niece Leona Goldfeld, Bessie Goldstein Gotsfeld "lit a torch and its flame still burns, illuminating the path she walked and the road she carved ahead for others to tread." [45]

13

Personality and Principles

"Sabra," a prickly pear that grows in the Negev is a common designation for native-born Israelis. Conventional wisdom has it that while these people, like the fruit, are spiky on the outside, they are tender and malleable on the inside. Bessie Gotsfeld, born in Europe and tutored in America, but long settled in Israel, epitomized these qualities. In transactions that challenged her principles and procedures, she was as tough as they come. She held her ground against equally opinionated Henrietta Szold. Her steely self was evident when she encountered opposition within Mizrachi circles. She imposed her strong will upon MWOA members who considered joining forces with other organizations, whether American or Israeli. Nor would she accede to the demands of Hapoel Hamizrachi figures, whether male or female. Though a staunch partisan of Orthodox Judaism, she nevertheless refused to be cowed by rabbinical authority. MWOA began when she stood up to Rabbi Fishman. She deeply respected Rabbi Berlin and regarded him as her Zionist mentor, but when he rejected her proposals for augmenting her agenda, she created programs on her own. In dealings with architects, school administrators, businessmen, local politicians, and Zionist notables outside of Mizrachi, she was equally decisive.

But she exhibited a softer side as well. Her behavior towards the young people entrusted to her care was especially kind and loving. In the early years she knew every teenager in the BZMs by name, background, and interest. She was equally concerned with young working women, both immigrants and locals, who lived in the *Batei Haluzot* (hostels) while they looked for work, supporting them with a line on the MWOA budget. She visited them often and in private conversations helped them clarify problems, thereby stiffening their resolve to settle comfortably into religious Zionist society. Children especially were welcome in her home, where she received them with hugs and smiles, juice and cookies.

Furthermore she inclined a sympathetic ear to adults in need and reserved small sums to tide them over. She first met Yoel Shiftan, the future director of Mosad Aliyah, when the young man asked for a small sum to purchase a farm implement for a tottering religious farm colony. She quickly complied with the request, at the same time keeping him in mind as a potential project director.[1] On visits to America she was a master of diplomacy and sociability, two personal qualities associated with female leadership. Once, when she was on a speaking tour in the U.S, a woman brought along her elderly and ailing mother, a longtime member. When the two women approached, Gotsfeld was conversing with a potentially large donor. Wishing neither to interrupt the conversation nor to snub the aged veteran, she extended her arm to the older woman and caressed her, without interrupting the discussion.[2]

Illustrating the nexus of her strong will and tender heart is her behavior during the curfew that followed the bombing of the King David Hotel in 1946. Disregarding official directives to stay off the street, she found her way to the Motza Children's Home, comforted the frightened little war refugees and supplied them with provisions.

Everyone acquainted with Gotsfeld recognized her high standards of efficiency and fiscal responsibility, one of the characteristics that Stogdill finds in true leaders.[3] Those who knew her best, however, were quick to mention her willingness to display flexibility when confronted with unexpected situations. Though parsimonious in most matters, Gotsfeld would expand the budget for special needs. "There is always money if a thing *must* be done" was her response when presented with a particularly pressing need, especially for children rescued from the hell of 1940s Europe. When a six-year-old "Teheran" child could not function in an institutional setting, she found a family willing to care for him and the funds to support him.[4] When the reception center at Mosad Aliyah was full, she nevertheless found a way to accommodate needy applicants.[5] When teen-aged refugees requested permission to pursue an academic program on their own, she allowed them to remain in Kfar Batya. Finally (though this does not exhaust the list), in response to a growing demand for Nehama Leibowitz's Torah lessons, she managed to finance their distribution, though the project was not in the budget.[6]

A Personal Code: Faith and Nationalism

Honorable leadership inevitably rests upon heartfelt conviction, and in its service Gotsfeld summoned intellectual and moral toughness from the core of her being. Addresses delivered in American speaking tours as well as personal letters clarified the principles that prompted her behavior. Long before they achieved their final formulation, they were adumbrated in a letter written from Europe at the time of the 1929 Hebron Yeshiva massacre: "All this human life sanctified on the altar of our faith and nationalism."[7] Faith and nationalism were the twin pillars of her belief structure. Thirty years later she summarized her "nationalism," her personal Zionism, in a terse sentence. "We have conceived of our work not as an isolated, humanitarian endeavor, but as an integral contribution to the growth of Israel."[8] In private correspondence she railed against people who degraded Zionism from a Jewish renaissance to a Jewish charity, who, as she put it, "don't realize that we are a Zionist setup, and not a philanthropic organization."[9] Though she courted prospective donors with sentimental accounts of ragged and unlettered children, rebuilding the Jewish homeland and regenerating the Jewish religion and culture remained her principal objectives. In 1939, while on a fund raising tour of American cities, Gotsfeld alerted her husband to this phenomenon:

> I received letters from Mrs. Herzog and Gesundheit asking no less of an appropriation for Children Relief than £1200 per month. Mrs. Gesundheit cabled up to adopt the orphanage as a project. You see, dear, the approach of these people is philanthropic. If it is not too much money, they are prepared to drop a piece of work and take up another. They lose sight of the fact that we are a Zionist setup. We have so much trouble in getting Palestine — why not take up another territory? This whole thing is absurd.[10]

Henrietta Szold harbored equal disdain for women who were willing to support public health and welfare in the Yishuv even though they rejected Zionism's central doctrines of national return and a restored Hebrew culture. "Unless, we insist upon the Zionist coloring," she wrote, " the result will be degeneration into flabby philanthropism."[11]

Gotsfeld's Philosophy

In major addresses delivered before MWOA conventions in 1952 and 1959, Gotsfeld clarified her ideological position. [12] She recounted the sacrifices to which Israelis willingly submitted in order to absorb and rehabilitate hundreds of thousands of refugees from Europe and the Middle East, "flying from terror and persecution – the homeless, the penniless, the unprepared." What, she inquired rhetorically, was the purpose of all that work? Why did Israelis accept a punishing austerity? Was it merely "to create a small nation?" The answer, of course, was no; Israel's very existence serves the purpose of "recreat(ing) a tradition."[13]

"Tradition" in 1952 was the equivalent of "faith" in 1929. The latter word had been appropriate in the context of the massacre of young Torah scholars. Belief in God, however, was not a common subject of conversation in Jewish religious circles; it was, rather, deemed axiomatic. This practical woman, at any rate, was more comfortable discussing the instrumental benefits of religious practice than the theology in which it was grounded.

Three functions that she ascribed to religious Judaism in Israel were safeguarding morality, integrating the population, and legitimating the Jewish state. Unlike the liberal rabbis of her generation, she felt no need to summon the Hebrew Bible to support a claim of Jewish moral superiority; she knew that for her audience it was self-evident. The 1952 address mentioned morality five times but never spelled it out. It concluded with an uncharacteristically universalistic vision of a religiously observant population "conscious of the contribution they are making towards a world of peace and justice, of individual freedom and morality."

A second instrumental function of halakhic Judaism was integration. For the immigrant child, Gotsfeld observed, Jewish rituals are a sustaining comfort in a strange new land, a link between the ancestral home and the new environment. In service of the nation, religious rituals integrate Jews from various countries of origin around a common past, a common condition, and a common destiny. They promote group identity, communal harmony, and national unity. In sum, integration on a religious basis encompasses time and space, cementing bonds between generations and centering the nation on a common ideal.

For Gotsfeld religious observance accomplished a third objective, legitimating Jewish settlement in the Holy Land. A 1939 speech had asserted that only Torah "gave the Jew an eternal deed to Eretz Israel."[14] Aware of the charge that Jews were stealing land from the indigenous Arabs, her argument implied that, in the absence of Torah, Zionists would have no justifiable claim to the land, that they would be interlopers and colonialists. If Torah alone validates the Jewish control of Palestine, then it follows that people who observe the ritual as well as the moral Law are the best guarantors of national sovereignty.

To carry the argument forward she emphasized the educational value of the religious tradition. Because Jewish tradition is deeply moored in the Bible, she asserted, every planting and harvesting turns the Biblical heritage into a present reality while ritual performance confirms and strengthens that identification. "Today, when a child in Israel enters the Sukkah, he gives thanks for the harvest in the field which he himself has planted."[15]

In Gotsfeld's vision, then, Jewish religious observance collapses time. This formulation accepted a premise of mainstream Zionism and at the same time challenged one of its implications. Like David Ben-Gurion and other secular Israelis, Gotsfeld made the leap from Scripture to modern Israel, ignoring, for the sake of argument, all that transpired in between. Secular Zionism minimized the importance of religious law, since it that was codified only after the destruction of the Second Temple. Gotsfeld's notion of Bible-based laws as tools of national integration and legitimation, on the other hand, implied the superiority of religious Zionism to secular Zionism.

Because religious Zionism is the most genuine Zionism, she told her followers, it imposes a special obligation upon them. Their personal bond with MOWA institutions was the moral equivalent of the identification of Israeli children with their Biblical ancestors. It followed that members were not mere onlookers and donors but partners in the Zionist reconstruction in which she was engaged. To emphasize the connection, she called them "co-workers, borrowing the very term by which she designated staff in the institutions that they funded."[16]

Schools under MWOA sponsorship especially, Gotsfeld assured her audience in 1959, justified this line of reasoning. In a young country with a youthful population, the best means of conferring material and spiritual benefits upon the individual, the society, and the state was education. MWOA-sponsored schools, she boasted, had become a model that all Israel should emulate. Instruction in language, science and technology helped develop the fledgling Jewish state. Religious studies contributed to its spiritual well being and fostered morality, integration and legitimation. All this she summarized as "thoughtful education, directed education, specific education, and education in an atmosphere which will insure the continuity of the tradition of our people."[17]

Still, contemporary conditions called for amelioration. Implicit in Gotsfeld's analysis was the Mizrachi principle that Israel was an imperfect state and would remain so as long as secular Jews called the tunes. This incentive to further action forced her into an awkward position. She had always preached that education rather than politics was the decisive Zionist act and had resolved never to participate in the electoral process within the Yishuv or the State. She never deviated from this posture, even though her basic motive remained clear. The 1959 lecture masks what may have been unconscious embarrassment in a double negative: "Religious issues cannot be fought out in the corridors of the Knesset if we have not got a consciously religious youth." By that logic, education was indeed politics in another form.

"The Bridge"

Gotsfeld's Zionist code then hewed to the classical Mizrachi position — "The Land of Israel for the People of Israel in accordance with the Torah of Israel,"[18]— idiosyncratically spelling out its implications for the new state. Her most frequently quoted statement, however, extended beyond the position of her Mizrachi mentors. To formulate her position for an American constituency, she constructed the following metaphor.

> Mizrachi Women's work is a great bridge which extends from America to Israel... the traffic goes in both directions... What goes across that bridge from America to Israel is material aid, moral assistance, technical and industrial information and the best in America's democratic faith. What comes across the bridge from Israel to America is the rebirth of a tradition – the cultural and spiritual stability which can reinforce American Jewry's sense of security, of pride, and of faith... No one who does not understand that the traffic goes in both directions has not fully grasped the significance of the establishment of Israel as a whole.

In light of the fact that American Jews, non-Zionists as well as Zionists, had been providing material and technical aid for several decades, there was nothing new about that part of the metaphor. Two additional "transports" from west to east, however, are noteworthy. "Moral assistance" implied that modern Israel, beleaguered on all sides, required a voice among the nations. This is noteworthy because it invested a diaspora community with a legitimately Zionist function.

Even more inventive was her declaration of an additional advantage gained through contact with the United States. From the time that Orthodox Zionists created an independent faction within the movement, Mizrachi leaders had drawn a distinction between the spiritual and the material. Though disposed to working alongside secular Zionists in the process of "upbuilding" the land, they defined culture in purely Jewish terms. To endorse extraneous standards, many believed, was to stray from Jewish tradition. Gotsfeld did not accept this line of reasoning. By her lights, Israel could benefit from "the best of America's democratic faith." To qualify the statement with the words "the best" may have implied that some American values were not applicable to Israel, for example the separation of church and state, which all branches of Mizrachi considered unsuitable for a Jewish commonwealth. Yet the testimonial as a whole made the point that Zionism was not a one-way street. All good did not flow from east to west, from ancient to modern times. American democracy, she alleged, was a model that Israel could well emulate.

To portray America as a source of good for Jews was to challenge a central tenet of classical Zionism, the dismissal of life outside of Palestine as deficient and even destructive of Jewish values. Traditional Jews, in fact, could not dispense with the Diaspora, as the rabbinic law that they followed devolved from the Babylonian Talmud and commentaries from many parts of the world. Over and above this, Gotsfeld indicated approval of American values shared by many Jews after the trauma of the Holocaust.

The second part of the "bridge" metaphor, enumerating Israel's gifts to American Jewry, was a prophecy for the future rather than an exposition on the present. With the benefit of hindsight, we can marvel at Gotsfeld's prescience; through the years Israel's triumphs and troubles have galvanized American Jewish activism and kept many Jews within the fold. The assertion that the connection to the Jewish state stimulated the rebirth of traditional Judaism in the United States, however, is yet to be tested.

Echoes of the applause that greeted Bessie Gotsfeld after her American lectures resounded through the decades. The name Mizrachi Women of America would eventually become a distant memory, as the organization chose new names, first American Mizrachi Women, then, in 1982, Amit. Bessie Gotsfeld's addresses can thus be seen as MWOA's finest hour, when its aging founder set forth the principles that had sustained it in the past and would continue to do so in the future.

14

Female Leadership and Empowerment

Bessie Gotsfeld's organizational leadership deviated from patterns traced in the social – psychological literature. Studies of the male and female managerial style indicate that the typical male is autocratic and directive while the female prototype is participative and democratic.[1] Bessie Gotsfeld's leadership included elements of both. First, the "male" characteristics and the reaction to them. From a distance of 8000 miles she monitored the day-to-day workings of MWOA, in the early years suggesting slates of officers and continuing through her life to let her will be known on important matters. So strong was her personality and prestige within the organization that even women who disagreed with her did not dare to challenge her in public.[2]

For the male Mizrachi establishment, Gotsfeld's insistence on a MWOA agenda formulated and executed in accordance with her priorities rather than theirs was presumptuous. She was often at loggerheads with World Mizrachi Central (*Mercaz Olami*), usually over monetary matters. Rabbi Fishman and Moshe Shapiro would have gladly wished her away. Rabbi Berlin facilitated some of her endeavors, but he proved invariably hostile to her suggestions for programs that deviated from his concerns. Unashamedly Herman Hollander expressed male resentment when he maintained that Gotsfeld was "no team-worker, but rather "a benevolent dictator."[3] Another critic was Joel Shiftan, director of Mosad Aliyah. Gotsfeld, outwardly amiable and convivial, he recalled twelve years after her death, would verbally encourage collegiality, soliciting the opinions of people she called her "co-workers."[4] As they offered suggestions, she would listen carefully, reflect for a time, and then, more often than not, reject them, usually claiming strain on the budget. [5] In private he let on that he was one of few directors of MWOA institutions granted a written contract.[6] All the men respected Gotsfeld's accomplishments, yet this small and pleasant woman who controlled her world by means of an outsized "masculine" style made some of them uneasy.

The Feminine Side

Before discussing the feminine aspects of Gotsfeld's leadership, it should be noted that the term feminist in contemporary parlance does not apply to Gotsfeld. She was comfortable with Jewish religious patriarchy and concepts such as female marginality and the commodification of women's sexuality and reproductive capacity[7] were neither in her vocabulary nor in her inmost heart. To the contrary, her language and some of her objectives seemed to relegate women to their traditional place in Jewish society. She valorized traditional family and religious values and a stated objective of her first efforts was to train future mothers who would bolster religious Zionism in the Yishuv.

Nevertheless, she strongly rejected the assumption that leadership and autonomy are male prerogatives, for many years an entrenched attitude in mainstream Judaism in general and Orthodox society in particular. Some of her reports indicate contempt for men who considered the MWOA programs a threat to culturally defined gender roles. Her statements can be read as assurances that rather than a threat to Orthodoxy, they actually strengthened it, that they helped women feel at home in traditional society. Beyond that, she went so far as to imply the equality, even the superiority of the female to the male in Jewish life. The fact that a man was an ordained rabbi or Mizrachi leader did not preclude judgments impugning his intelligence or common sense.[8] To impress staff at MWOA institutions with the significance of their work, she declared that a teacher of boys educates a man, while a teacher of girls educates an entire family.[9] Her choice of one analogy advances that position. When Youth Aliyah sent her a contingent of boys rather than girls, she compared herself to a woman anticipating the birth of a girl who graciously accepts a boy. This statement suggests that the reception was grudging, that boys are second choices, and that the new mother (and the analogous mother institution) preferred girls.[10] This was hardly a common sentiment in Orthodox circles, where men thank God daily for their masculinity. That cautious comment, however, was her most feminist statement on record.

If Gotsfeld's profile matched neither that of a contemporary feminist nor of the traditional woman of her generation, it certainly was a gendered response to her Orthodox milieu, and a model for her followers. After she left America, the organization of which she was a mere "representative" continued to follow the course she had laid out. From her calm but firm refusal to accede to Rabbi Fishman's demand for the fruits of their fundraising efforts in 1924, MWOA members learned to manipulate gender to their advantage. Gotsfeld's gesture set a precedent for their exploitation of Dvorah Rabinowitz's pregnancy to prevent the 1934 Mizrachi national convention from squelching their bid for recognition as an independent body. By their lights, recognition was already ten years overdue. A decade after that they would not accept directives from World Mizrachi demanding amalgamation with other Mizrachi women's groups.[11]

Without exception, Gotsfeld's educational efforts helped advance the position of Jewish women within the Orthodox community and even beyond. Whenever the opportunity arose, she expressed unfaltering trust in female spirituality, mental capability, and aptitude for prestigious positions, including national leadership.

Her central mission was to actualize female potential in a community that conventionally regarded females as less deserving of communal resources than males. To satisfy adolescent girls' spiritual (and social) requirements, she established synagogues at every school. Classes at the BZMs encouraged students to stretch their minds while preparing for useful work. Distriibuting Nehama Leibowitz's circulars among kibbutz women pursued the same objective. So did the decision that allowed girls as well as boys resident in Kfar Batya to prepare for the university. Whenever she could, Gotsfeld found talented women to administrate educational programs and to manage the BZMs. Nearly as inspired as the choice of Nehamah Leibowitz to head BZM's Judaica department was the engagement of Dr. Jenny Thaustein, director of the Jerusalem BZM from 1940 to 1948. (Thaustein would later join Israel's Health Ministry and administer its Mother and Child Care Service.) When planning new facilities, Gotsfeld found places for women; a female architect, for example, designed an important Kfar Batya building.

Public addresses before the American membership called attention to the new roles of women in the Yishuv.

> We cannot speak nor write about Palestine of today without devoting a proper place to women's activities and the role the woman is playing in the upbuilding process of modern Palestine. Whether it is in the country participating in agriculture, industry, commerce, culture, civil service, social service. Women in kibbutzim, women on guard and women in politics.[12]

A letter to Chilean women affirmed female potential at a time when the population of MWOA institutions was overwhelmingly female.

> The contribution of the Mizrachi Women's Organization of America is indeed a vital factor in the development of the Yishuv in Eretz Yisroel, for through its institutions, nursery and children's homes and vocational schools in Eretz Yisroel, opportunity is given to thousands of refugee and Palestinian children to enable them to take the proper place in the economic and cultural life of the Yishuv. With the added factor of spiritual guidance, which is always included in our curriculum, these children are being given inner strength, which prepares them for the leadership of our people.[13]

Empowering Orthodox Women in America

MWOA's 1928 charter, which Gotsfeld helped fashion, attributed the organization's animating impulse to "the desire of self-expression and self- assertion in her work for Palestine." Regardless of Gotsfeld's "masculine" style top-down directives, her ultimate objective was to energize her followers, thereby conforming to the "feminine" style analyzed by the sociologists. Pursuing this goal among the American membership required removing herself from the limelight, leaving space for new people to flourish. She never accepted the title of president, not in Seattle, where she organized women who supported religious Zionism, nor in New York, when she bypassed the older women's hidebound *Achios Mizrachi* and cultivated the talents of the younger women. Until her retirement her own position remained the humdrum "Palestinian representative." This accomplished two purposes. First, her absence from the American scene encouraged new leadership. Second, it offered the opportunity to transmit what social psychologist Alfred Bandura calls "empowering information," i.e. words of encouragement, positive emotional support, positive persuasion, and the experience of successfully mastering tasks.[14] Letters from the Jerusalem office published in the various organizational bulletins offered concrete information and inspired the resolution to raise more funds to carry out the ambitious programs.

Before she left the United States, she recruited talented women—among them Jrina Shapiro, Dvorah Rabinowitz and Belle Goldstein. Through the years, these women retained close contact with her. From their posts In the United States they learned to cope with the demands of the hour and delegate authority to up-and-coming new members who would eventually take over. On visits to the United States during the 1930s and 1940s, Gotsfeld looked for younger women with a potential for leadership. A talented few among them agreed to stay in Israel for a year or two and balance the books. Mollie Golub was the final bookkeeper and confidante. After her return to New York, she corresponded with her mentor and apprised her of organizational matters. For the older woman they became an opportunity to unburden herself of problems resulting from her dangerously declining health, though the bulk of the correspondence, till the very end, concerned MWOA affairs of the moment.

Gotsfeld and Szold

A blend of masculine and feminine qualities also characterized Henrietta Szold's leadership. Like Gotsfeld, she cultivated loyal assistants, notably talented upper class educated women with no previous interest in Judaism. She sent Alice Seligsberg to Palestine after the Great War to administer the American Zionist Medical Unit. Jessie Sampter and Irma Lindheim, secular women redeemed for Zion through her efforts, settled in the Land of Israel, (though both eventually abandoned Hadassah for Labor Zionism.) As Hadassah leaders, all four waged battles for recognition from the General Zionists who first tried to dissolve the woman's organization, and when that proved unsuccessful, to belittle its accomplishments. Long after Szold discarded official ties to Hadassah to participate in the Mandate's Jewish shadow government, she kept in touch with the next generation of Hadassah officers. Her words persuaded Rose Gell Jacobs and Tamar de Sola Pool not only to fund Youth Aliyah but even to cover the building costs of Kfar Noar Dati.

Szold and Gotsfeld shared personal qualities that distinguished them as leaders of women. One was the ability to think out of the box. In the nineteenth century the only important American Jewish women's organization was the National Council of Jewish Women. Its objective was vague and non-ideological; the founding charter pledged "to further the best and highest interests of Judaism and humanity."[15] In the early twentieth century, women excited by the promise of a restored Jewish homeland shunned the existing men's organizations and struck out on their own. Founding an organization that championed a principle required the determination to stand up to men who mocked such "unfeminine" action. To accomplish anything necessitated a critical mass of women with sole control over the money that they raised. We have seen how Gotsfeld held the line, enduring the slurs of Mizrachi and Hapoel Mizrachi spokesmen as well as women in other Zionist groups who wanted to harness MWOA's funds to their own programs. This is parallel to Szold's reactions to similar affronts on the part of ZOA leaders and the women who started Keren Hayesod Women.

Flexibility also marked these two leaders. Both managed to rise above their own principles when confronted by new situations, Szold when she accepted underage children in Youth Aliyah, Gotsfeld when she closed institutions that no longer served their purpose.

These qualities are not exclusively feminine, but they do indelibly mark Hadassah and MWOA. In the annals of American Zionism the achievements of the two founders helps explain why both organizations have been more successful in every sense— monetary contributions, numbers, and endurance— than their masculine counterparts.

The Gotsfeld Legacy

With few exceptions, founders of American Jewish women's organizations were either unmarried or childless. It would be unprofitable, however, to speculate as to whether Gotsfeld's pioneering endeavors would have reaped such fruit had a brood of children occupied much of her time. What can be ascertained are the innovations that she initiated in religious Zionism. In sum: they valorized Orthodox women in Israel and America. In the United States The Mizrachi Women of America secured organizational and personal independence from male domination and cultivated members' latent talents. In the Yishuv, urban Batei Zeirot Mizrachi set new occupational standards for Orthodox women and unlocked sacred and secular wisdom for girls heretofore ignorant of both. The rural children's villages of the 1940s, '50s and beyond encouraged girls (and boys) uprooted by war and politics to look to the future rather than lick their wounds.

This then is the substance of Bessie Gotsfeld's message and the measure of her personality: unbending insistence on personal, institutional, and religious prerogatives; an ongoing battle for organizational sovereignty within the larger Mizrachi world; and an unwavering respect for feminine competence.

Appendix
Two Important Speeches

Bessie Gotsfeld, Address at the Keynote Session, 27th Annual MWOA
National Convention, November 9, 1952.[1]

I greet you not only for myself, but warmly as the representative of our administrative board and of our institutions in Israel. There is no member of our staff who does not feel keenly, as the day by day tasks are carried forward in Israel, that behind her stands the great, organized body of American Mizrachi Women.

Each of us is an agent for your conscience and your love. The hand which feeds a child, or clothes a child, or trains a child – is not only the hand of the *madrich* or teacher. It is your hand as well. For your contribution to the welfare of our children and to Israel itself is a direct contribution – a practical contribution— a tangible and immediate contribution.

We in Israel know this. We know that we are partners in this work. We know that Mizrachi's work is a great bridge which extends from America to Israel. I would like to talk tonight about that bridge – not in the form of a report on our accomplishments in Israel, but covering certain aspects of our work which are important to an understanding of the relationship which exists between you, as Mizrachi women in the United States, and those of us who represent you and carry forward the actual work in Israel.

I have said that our work is a bridge. I must add that on this bridge the traffic goes in both directions. No one who does not understand that the traffic goes in both directions has fully grasped the significance of the establishment of Israel as a whole, and the role Mizrachi Women play in it. What goes across that bridge from America to Israel is material aid, moral assistance, technical and industrial information and the best in America's democratic faith. What comes across the bridge from Israel to America is the rebirth of a tradition – the cultural and spiritual stability which can reinforce American Jewry's sense of security, of pride, and of faith.

But the extent to which Israel can contribute a new morality to the modern world- as it did to the ancient world — rests heavily on the people of Israel as a whole, and on the religious-Zionist movement in particular.

The young state is trying to fight its way through a moral as well as economic crisis. In five years of Medinat Israel we have made great strides. We have produced more food that we dreamed of producing. We have made the Negev, for example, yield 50% above its expectations. In this connection you will be interested to know, I am sure, that 1500 dunams of land in the Negev have been allotted to our Children's Village. This tract will be cultivated, not only as a productive experience, but as an educational experience by teams of twenty children at a time going to the Negev. It is a dramatic example of the interrelation between our educational work and the productive requirements of Israel.

But of we have made strides in the production of food and goods – if we have borne austerity cheerfully – if we have brought in almost a million newcomers – it has not been only to create a small nation. It has been to recreate a tradition. This is the meaning of the tremendous practical strides which have been made in Medinat Israel during the first five years.

This is the meaning of the great accomplishments of Mizrachi Women during the years since the establishment of Israel. And, my friends, it is possible for me to report to you that the spiritual rebirth for which we hope and pray is, in fact, taking place at this moment. It is taking place naturally, as part of the day-to-day life of our institutions. You cannot fully grasp the vitality of Jewish observance in the reborn State of Israel. Always, in the past, it was necessary to refer back 2000 years – to conditions as they were 2000 years ago. But today, when a child in Israel enters the Sukkah, he gives thanks for the harvest in the field which he himself has planted. The prayer for rain is real and meaningful; rain is needed to fructify the land itself. Today in Israel we perform these *mitzvot* naturally – without even being conscious of them as religious observances. They are woven deeply into the fabric of our lives. The achievements in Israel invigorate and refresh every Jewish soul. It is only as a nation living in our land that we can understand our predecessors who labored and fought, suffered and sang and prophesied in this same land.[2]

And yet, my friends, despite these hopeful aspects, there are grave spiritual, religious, and cultural problems which must be solved. In their solution, the voice of the Mizrachi Women's Organization of America must be heard – clearly, firmly, practically. Great is the danger for religious values in Israel, especially where youth and children are concerned. To combat this danger is the immediate task of the Mizrachi Women.

There is another aspect of Israel's life which must be viewed clearly and gravely if we are to proceed in the correct direction. And this aspect is to provide a common ground for the immigrants from Europe and the new *olim* from North Africa and the Middle East. East and West must be brought together in Israel, and the most effective common ground educationally is the common denominator of our religious traditions. With our institutions as the instruments, we must take our place in the forefront in this struggle. These children and youth of the late immigration arrive, for the most part, illiterate, uneducated, totally without knowledge of modern living. They must be brought up to a level with the children of Western origin- and this is no easy or simple task. And from this level, all of these children must be carried still higher and further so that they can contribute to Israel's productive and spiritual life.

Most of the new emigrant youth are largely maladjusted to the life in Israel. There are groups which have been subject to difficult economic conditions and an unhealthy social environment. More important, there exists a tension between the mentality and scale of values which animate the effort of New Israel. This youth comes mostly from religious homes. The proper method is constructively to utilize the traditional background of this youth in guiding them to constructive life in the land.[3]

I have not dwelled on the actual work of the Mizrachi Women's Organization of America because this work will be covered in detail during the four days of this convention. But it is the meaning of this work which must be in our minds and in our hearts at every moment if we are to understand clearly what we are doing- what we must do. The services in Israel which your devotion has made possible have saved thousands of children in Israel for traditional Judaism. Thousands more must be trained vocationally, trained for life on the land, and above all, trained in the ways of our fathers.

A new problem in child welfare has now arisen in Israel – Jewish children in mission schools. These are children of under-privileged and broken homes, of the new *olim* who came to Israel with their parents. The missions hold out great benefits to the parents as well as to the children. These children must also become our major concern, and we must gear our work in that direction as well.[4]

The second fact which I wish to stress is that the Mizrachi Women's Organization of America has never gone forward to build projects purely for the sake of building them. Each and every project we have ever undertaken has been a response to a burning need of Israel. Out of the groundswell of events, as the years pass, the needs are forced clearly to the surface. And when these needs have been clear and urgent, we have never failed in the past to meet them. In the continuation and expansion of our work, we have had many difficulties. They have been delays, shortages of materials, construction problems and rising building costs. Today in Israel, there is another factor which must be considered gravely by this convention. Along with the required expansion of facilities there is a rise in the cost of operation and maintenance of existing institutions and projects. Salaries have continued to rise. The prices of materials and commodities have also risen. All this means that we shall have to reckon with an expanding budget.

Yet, my friends, we cannot be confined in our thinking, only to the financial aspects of our work. Our efforts must include a profound interest in the treasures of the human spirit. For it is these treasures that we are safeguarding in the hearts of our children, by the great deeds which Mizrachi Women perform.

No one can question today that for religious Jewry the burning need is for great educational effort aimed at inculcating the timeless value of the Torah and propagating its way of life in Israel. This effort we are making, and shall continue to make. We shall make it while the state of Israel grows to two million, to three million, yes to four million Jewish citizens. And we shall make it with your help.

With your help and faith the traffic shall go both ways on the bridge between us, and Israel shall reach its full potential as a cultural center and a center of man's faith.

The experience of our work during the years preceding the State – decades of many hardships, dangers, strain, achievement and success, gives us the assurance that we shall be equal to the burden resting on our generation if we do our duty faithfully and constantly.[5]

With your help, the Jews of all the world shall walk proudly and with dignity, in the ways of their fathers, conscious of the contribution they are making towards a world of peace and justice, of individual freedom and morality.

May G-d bless you and help you. And may the spirit of Torah burn brightly in your deeds in the coming year.

Bessie Gotsfeld, Address at the 33ᴿᴰ National Convention of MWOA, Philadelphia, October 26 – 29, 1959 [6]

Deeply moved, I wish to express to all the members, officers and friends my grateful appreciation for the many good wishes and recognition, as well as for the personal confidence reposed in me and expressed at all times. This 33rd Annual Convention crowns a successful service of a third of a century in the growth of Religious Zionism. Such anniversaries are more than symbols. They serve as reminders of the pace of human achievement and by marking that pace, they also indicate the quality of the achievement.

One of the great values of the work which the Mizrachi Women's Organization has performed in the past third of a century is that we have conceived of our work not as an isolated, humanitarian endeavor, but as an integral contribution to the growth of Israel. Today, as we stand on the threshold of a new era, it is important once again for each Mizrachi Women to understand what the larger outlines of Israel's future may be. Only (by) understand(ing) the major trends in Israel's development can we make our maximum contribution to that development.

In the first decade of Statehood, Jewish distress has been the principal factor in mass immigration. To our gates have come those flying from terror and persecution – the homeless, the penniless, the unprepared. In the years to come, Israel's greatest internal problems will also be to set a pattern of life and a social structure which will express the culture and habits of the people of Israel. It is in these fields that we, as a religious-Zionist movement, will bear the greatest responsibilities. It is in these tasks that we must begin now to make greater contributions to Israel's life and growth.

Today we have to cope with a newcomer to Israel of a different kind. The immigrant who comes from Eastern Europe has been completely deprived of his Jewish heritage, deprived of his Jewish consciousness. We are now about two million in Israel. We have begun to bring in the third million. Where will the newcomer come from? What will its characteristics be? How will that new immigration be integrated? What will the channel of communication be with those who have already settled in the Land, those who come from such differing backgrounds and cultures? These are the questions of today and of tomorrow. They are not only questions of economic self-sufficiency. They are questions which point to the heart of survival of the Jewish tradition, of Jewish religion. And it is these questions towards which our work must direct itself.

The great problem in Israel is education and the use of education to create a wholesome, integrated, enriched, growing pattern of life, within a sound social structure in which the culture of a people can flourish and continue to make its unique contribution to the world. This means not just any education. It means thoughtful education, directed education, specific education and education in an atmosphere which will insure the continuity of the tradition of our people.

We are already dealing with children who come from homes in which illiteracy is the rule. And we are dealing also, with children who have experienced the dignity and freedom of Jewish nationhood. We have already enrolled in our schools the children of those who themselves have benefited from an education in Mizrachi Women's institutions. These two types of children together must build side by side the future of Israel. These children are symbols of the educational problem Israel faces. Unless these children can be brought together within a common framework of education, there will be a breakdown in the process of upbuilding Israel.

Religious issues cannot be fought out in the corridors of the Knesset if we have not got a consciously religious youth. And, my friends, it is the sad truth, that for the most part, there are grave shortcomings in Israel's educational capacity for this all-important task. The Government itself has recognized the most important of these shortcomings by recently introducing into the curriculum a course in Jewish consciousness. My friends, Jewish consciousness is not a subject to be taught in school on certain days at certain hours. Jewish consciousness is a way of life. And it is the way of life of every child who comes under our wing. The common bond which can hold together the diverse elements of our population is the common bond of our religion. It is our tradition which has been the mainspring of Jewish survival for thousands of years. It is our tradition which is Israel's hope of integration.

What is needed then, is what we, as an Organization, for a third of a century have provided in our network of projects – a progressive orthodoxy which brings together the age-old truths of our fathers and the most modern techniques of education and individual development.

The problems of integration in Israel will not lessen in the years to come. They will grow, unless some starting point to deal with these problems is created, and unless the resources to deal with these problems keep pace with the problems themselves.

This is the challenge we face. We are dealing not only with individual children. We are dealing not only with schools and villages and centers. We are dealing not only with the practical difficulties of maintaining and expanding our institutions. We are dealing with the life of a nation. We cannot stop halfway.

Thirty-three years ago a handful of women dreamed of erecting a new force for religious Zionism – a new force that would strive towards the erection of a Jewish State based on the principles of Torah. Now there is need for a revitalization of this vision – a vision that will bring this Organization to increased effectiveness in building Israel AL PI TORAH.[7]

I pray that you will reach out to find the willing hands of thousands more of American Jewish women. I pray that you will work together, in strength and unity, sharing, as you have shared for a third of a century the rewarding experience of service to our people and the highest ideals of our faith. As partners in the historic adventure of building a country and fashioning a people, you have given of your time, energy and resources. The tangible achievements of your devoted labors are to be found in the education, rehabilitation, and social welfare services of Mizrachi Women's institutions – your villages, schools, vocational training centers, settlement houses, kindergartens, day centers and after-school clubs.

Many of you have visited Israel. You have seen for yourselves the impressive results of the fruit of your labor. You have seen the country and the people. You have seen the fulfillment and you have also been able to experience the problems at first hand. Great tasks have been accomplished. Much still remains to be done. You must strengthen your will and purpose for the future of Israel. I am certain you will return home from this Convention inspired by what you have heard, heartened by your share in the practical achievements – stimulated to resume your work with refreshed zeal. With your help the Medina will enhance its creative effort and advance the welfare of its people.

I do not know how soon I shall see you again. I hope it will be soon and that I may have the joy of greeting each one of you in Eretz Israel. Until that time, I carry in my heart, the warm image of your love which I treasure as one of the great spiritual possessions of my life.

May you go from strength to strength. And be blessed in your efforts for a religious Israel. AMEN.

Abbreviations

AABI	—	Amit Archives, Bar Ilan University
AANY	—	Amit Archives, New York City
AJA	—	The American Jewish Archives Journal
AJH	—	American Jewish History (Journal)
AJHS	—	American Jewish Historical Society, New York
CZA	—	Central Jewish Archives, Jerusalem
HA	—	Hadassah Archives, New York
Hagler	—	Hagler Archives, Mosad Harav Kook, Jerusalem
MJV	—	Mizrachi Jubilee Volume, ed. Pinchus Churgin and Leon Gellman (Mizrachi Organization of America, New York, 1936)
MWOA	—	Mizrachi Women's Organization of America

Notes

Notes to Introduction

[1] See Michael Brown, "The American Element in the Rise of Golda Meir, 1906 - 1929," Jewish History 6:1), pp. 35 -50 and Alon Gal, "Henrietta Szold and the American Jewish Political Tradition," in *An Inventory of Promises, Essays on American Jewish History In Honor of Moses Rischin*, ed. Jeffrey S. Gurock and Mark Lee Raphael (Brooklyn, NY, 1995), pp 89-114.
[2] Donald H. Miller, "A History of Hadassah 1912 -1935" (New York University, Ph.D. diss., 1968), and Carol Kutcher, The Early Years of Hadassah, 1912- 1921 (Brandeis University dissertation, 1976).

[3] For further discussion of educational issues in the Yishuv see Shne'ur Zalman Abramov, Perpetual Dilemma: Jewish Religion in the Jewish State. Cranbury, N.J.: Associated University Presses, 1976, pp. 113 -115 , and Ehud Luz, *Parallels Meet: Religion and Nationalism in the Early Zionist Movement (1882 - 1904)* (Philadelphia, J.P.S., 1988), pp. 246 -250.

[4] Stogdill, R. M. (1948). "Personal factors associated with leadership: A survey of the literature." *Journal of Psychology* 25 (1948): 35-71.

[5] Stogdill, R. M. *Handbook of Leadership: A Survey Of Theory And Research.* (New York: Free Press, 1974.).

[6] H.A. Michener, J.D. DeLamater, and S.H. Schwartz, *Social Psychology* (2nd ed.) Orlando, FL: Harcourt Brace Iovanovich, 1990.

[7] H. Astin and C. Leland, *Women of Influence, Women Of Vision. A Cross-Generational Study Of Leaders And Social Change.* San Francisco: Jossey-Bass, 1991 and Jay A. Conger, "Leadership: The Art of Empowering Others," *The Academy of Management Executive* (1989) 3:1, 17 – 24.

[8] See F.E. Fiedler, "The Effect of Leadership and Cultural Heterogeneity on Group Performances: A Test of the Contingency Model," *Journal of Experimental Social Psychology* 2: 237 – 264, 1968.

Notes to Chapter 1

[1] "Przemysl," in *Encyclopedia Judaica* (Jerusalem, The Macmillan Co., 1971), 13: 1298. For a survey of the city under Austrian rule (1772 – 1918), see Arie Menczer, ed., *Przemysl Memorial Book* (Israel: *Irgun Yotzei Przemysl*, 1964), pp. 69 – 154.

[2] i.e. David Moses Friedman (1828 - 1900), the son of Israel Ruzhyn, who was a great-grandson of Dov Baer, the Maggid of Mesirech. Dr. Joseph Burg, who met Gotsfeld in Berlin when he was a student, qualified the identity of her father's rabbi by saying "I believe her father was a Hassid of the Rabbi of Czorkow, who had a strong tendency towards both Eretz Yisrael and to general world culture." (See Joseph Burg, 'A Most Important Chapter,' in *As I Remember Her*, (compilation of reminiscences of Gotsfeld by prominent Israelis) 1972, p.2, AABI and AANY. For the details of the Ruzhin dynasty, see *Encyclopedia Judaica* 14: 526-531. (Abraham Joshua Heschel, the Polish-born Jewish philosopher who settled in New York in 1945, was a scion of that dynasty.)

[3] See Henrietta Szold's article on traditional literature for women "What our Grandmothers Read," *The Hebrew Standard* (April 5, 1907): 1-2.

[4] See Hannah Stein, "Bessie Gotsfeld," p.9. undated essay in Bessie Gotsfeld, Life, AANY (hereafter BG Life).

[5] Jacob (Jacob) Goldman, son of Bessie's sister Sarah, interviewed in Westport, Connecticut on June 20, 2002, told me that he didn't realize that Adela Goldstein was not his biological grandmother until after her death.

[6] Ibid; Sarah Goldman, "Memories of Bessie of an Entire Period," 1940, B G Life.

[7] Eliezer Goldman (Sarah's older son), letter to author, June 22, 2002.

[8] Eliezer Goldman, telephone interviews by author, Ramat Gan, May 22 and 23, 2000.

[9] Friendship with the Genauer family extended to the next generation. Sylvia Genauer and her daughter Blu Greenberg, interviews by author, Riverdale, New York, January 23, 2002.

[10] See Wolf Gold, "First Days," in *MJV,* Hebrew Section, p. 42. Leona M. Goldfeld claims that Rabbi Meir Berlin's tour took him to Seattle, and that he set up a Mizrachi chapter

sitting around the Gotsfeld table ("Bessie," published by Amit, n.d. p. 8). The published correspondence from his American journeys during the time that the Gotsfelds resided there, however, does not mention that city, as it does so many others. See Rabbi Meir Bar Ilan, *Letters,* ed. Nathaniel Katzburg. Ramat Gan: Bar-Ilan University, 1976, vol. I.

[11] "Seattle Savors Its Memories," AANY.

[12] Quoted in Goldfeld, "Bessie," p. 8.

[13] Ibid, p. 13.

[14] See Deborah Dash Moore, *At Home in America: Second Generation New York Jews* (New York: Columbia University Press, 1981) Chapter 2.

[15] Most of the personal material was gathered from interviews by the author with Gotsfeld's nephews Eliezer and Jacob (Jack) Goldman; niece Leona Goldfeld, telephone interviews, Israel, May 22- 23, 2000 and New York, May 15, 2003; and niece Raizel Rauchwerger and her husband Leon, Ramat Gan, May 22, 2000. See also Goldfeld, "Bessie," passim.

[16] See Boris D. Bogen, *Born a Jew* (NY: The Macmillan Co, 1917) pp. 216 - 219. Bogen sets the opening of the Clara de Hirsch School in 1905. The correct date was 1897. Recent studies of the two schools include Nancy B. Sincoff, "Educating for 'Proper' Jewish Womanhood: A Case Study in Domesticity and Vocational Training, 1897 - 1926, in *American Jewish History* 77:4 (June, 1988): 572 – 599; and Melissa Klapper, "Jewish Women and Vocational Education in New York City, 1885 - 1925," *AJA* 53 (2001): 113 -146.

[17] This is what Gotsfeld told Nehama Leibowitz, as reported in "As I Remember Her, " p. 14.

[18] Leona Goldfeld's loving rendition of her aunt's life's story published years after her death, maintains that Rabbi Berlin visited her Seattle home and stimulated her interest in Zionism. See "Bessie," p. 8. But Bessie's personal memoir, "History of the Mizrachi Women's Organization as Told by Bessie Gotsfeld",p.1 (B G Life) places their meeting in New York shortly after her return from Seattle in 1919.

[19] Sylvia Genauer interview, 23 January 2002.

[20] Paula Hyman, "Immigrant Women and Consumer Protest: The New York City Kosher Meat Boycott of 1902," *American Jewish History 70* (September 1980), pp. 91 - 105.

[21] Gotsfeld, "History of the Mizrachi Women's Organization of America as told by Bessie Gotsfeld," p.2, B G Life.

[22] Fishman, "The First Days," p. 43.

[23] See Introduction.

[24] Ibid.

[25] Sheila Rothman, *Woman's Proper Place: A History of Changing Ideas and Practices, 1870 to the Present* (New York, 1978), cited in William Toll, "A Quiet Revolution: Jewish Women's Clubs and the Widening Female Sphere, 1870 - 1920," *AJA* (Spring, Summer, 1989): 8-9.

[26] I found benevolent societies in virtually every Jewish community in still-rural Westchester County, New York before World War I. See Baila R. Shargel and Harold Drimmer, *The Jews of Westchester, a Social History* (Fleishmanns, N.Y.: Purple Mountain Press, 1994), pp. 95 –97.

[27] Eliezer Goldman, interview. He thought that early on Gotsfeld was a member of the Women's League for Palestine, formed to aid the Yishuv on a non-Zionist basis.

[28] A thumbnail sketch of Gold's life can be found in Leo Jung, *Men of the Spirit* (New York: Kymson Publishing Co., 1964), pp. 181 -193).

[29] Paraphrase of the Hebrew quoted by Geula Bat Yehuda in the biography of her father, *Harav Maimon B'dorotav* (Jerusalem: Mossad Harav Kook, 1979), p. 223. An earlier and

shorter biography by the same author is *These Are the Generations of Rabbi Judah Leib Ha-Cohen Maimon* (also in Hebrew), (Jerusalem: Mosad Harav Kook, 1964).
[30] For Rabbi Berlin's life before his settlement in Palestine, see his *MiVolozhin ad Yerushalayim*, eds. Y. Bernstein and I. Tirosh, (Tel Aviv, 1971). For a summary of all his activities, see M. Krone, *Harav Meir Bar-Ilan* (1954).
[31] See Gotsfeld, "History of the Mizrachi Women's Organization," pp. 3-4, B G Life; Goldfeld, "Bessie," p. 11.
[32] The quotations come from an untitled article, probably by Belle Goldstein, published in *The American Mizrachi Woman* 47:2 (December, 1975) 7.
[33] Sylvia Genauer, interview.
[34] Belle J. Goldstein, "In the Beginning," *The American Mizrachi Woman* 48:1 (September - October, 1975): 4.
[35] Florence L Denmark, "Women, Leadership, and Empowerment," *Psychology of Women Quarterly 17* (1993) 343- 356.
[36] Yoel Shiftan, interview by author, May 18, 2000.
[37] Eliezer Goldman, interview; Kerstein, "Origins," p. 244.
[38] Devorah Weissman, "Religious Girls' Education in Jerusalem during the Period of British Rule: 5 Educational Ideologies" (Hebrew) (PhD Disseration, Hebrew University, 1994), p. xiii.
[39] See Israel Kolatt, "Religious, Society, State in the National Home Period," in Shmuel Almog, Jehuda Reinharz, and Anita Shapira, eds. *Zionism and Religion* (Hanover and London: University Press of New England, 1998), p. 280.
[40] This was the experience of both my mother and my mother-in-law.
[41] See Carol Bell Ford, *The Girls, Jewish Women of Brownsville, Brooklyn, 1940 - 1995* (S.U.N.Y. Press, 1999).
[42] quoted in *New York Times* Magazine, July 2, 2000, p. 29.
[43] Papers, AANY. Since there is seldom a "1" without a "2", the text is obviously incomplete.

Notes to Chapter 2

[1] Howard M. Sachar, *A History of Israel from the Rise of Zionism to our Time* (N.Y.: Alfred A. Knopf, 1976), p. 174.
[2] Franzensbad is now known by its Czech name, Frantiskovy-Lazane. It is in the Sudetenland, near Carlsbad. Franz Kafka's *Letter to His Father*, written in 1919, mentions his father's frequent patronage of that spa (and the son's refusal to join him) (New York: Schocken Books, 1966) p.9.
[3] Gotsfeld's letters to Belle Goldstein and Mollie Golub are located in AANY.
[4] Actually Moshe would gain a hero's reputation. According to one report he and two fellow students had physically prevented access to a howling mob storming the yeshiva. Leo Jung, who visited Palestine in 1929, claims that he convinced the American Consulate to send an armed convoy to bring Moshe and other Americans who landed in jail to Jerusalem. When the Americans refused to leave without their non-American friends and the Torah Scrolls, he maintains, he persuaded the consul to transfer them as well. Jung, *Men of the Spirit* (New York: Kymson Publishing Co, 1964, p. 188-9.
[5] *Congress Zeitung*, August 1, 1929, p. 39, lists the ten Mizrachi representatives. At this Congress, the World Zionist Organization established the Jewish Agency.

[6] I found no record of the second person on the Committee.

[7] Kolatt, "Religion, Society, State," p. 292.

[8] Yeshaya Bernstein, "Hapoel Hamizrachi b'Eretz Yisrael," in *MJV*, Hebrew Section, pp. 88 - 97; Moshe Krone, "From Rodges to Yavneh," London: Bahad, 1945.

[9] See below, chap. 11.

[10] In AANY. The extant document ends abruptly; a second page is unavailable. Also curious is the attempt to scratch out the 2 paragraphs beginning with "Mrs. Lippa."

[11] The only record of this transaction available to me is by Gotsfeld in her "History of the MWOA," pp. 5 -6. Whether the land was leased to the women or sold to them is unclear. Perhaps it accounts for the site of the children's home in MWOA's care during the 1940s. See below, ch.10.

[12] Ibid. pp. 5-6.

[13] See Norman Bentwich, *Ben-Shemen, A Children's Village in Israel, Jerusalem*: The Jewish Agency, n.d.

[14] Goldfeld, "Bessie," p. 21.

[15] Eliezer Goldman, letter to author.

[16] Eliezer Goldman and Raizel and Leon Rauchsweger, author interviews.

[17] "From A Letter of Mrs. Gotsfeld ," in the The Bulletin of the MWOA, January, 1933, indicates that Bessie had resided in Palestine for fifteen months.

[18] Bessie Gotsfeld to Belle Goldstein (hereafter Gotsfeld to Goldstein), September 3, 1929, AANY.

[19] See file marked "1931" in, folder "Papers and Reports." AANY.

[20] Gotsfeld to Goldstein, passim. Letters to her sister Sarah, were, unfortunately, later discarded. Jack Goldman, interview.

[21] Telephone interview with Leona Goldfeld, Israel, May 22, 2000.

[22] Joseph Burg, "A Most Important Chapter," in *As I Remember Her*, (3 part collection), p. 1, AA BI and AANY.

[23] See the handwritten note on the back of a 2-page paper, entitled "The Mizrachi Women's Organization of America, Its Aim and Project" (1931-3), BG Histories AANY.

[24] See Shulamit Levanon's review of the past, delivered before the Second World Mizrachi Women's Conference, August 1, 1955, entitled "The World Mizrachi Women's Organization - the Past and the Future," blue file, AANY.

[25] Goldfeld, "Bessie," p. 20.

[26] Ibid; Nehama Leibowitz, "As I Remember Her," in *As I Remember Her*. p. 13; Yaffa Eliach, interview with author, October 1, 1998; Israel Friedman's speech at a Memorial for Bessie Gotsfeld, AANY.

[27] Gotsfeld to Goldstein, August 2, 1936.

[28] Goldfeld, "Bessie," p. 21.

[29] Leibowitz "As I Remember Her," p.13.

[30] Weissman, "Religious Girls' Education in Jerusalem during the Period of British Rule," p. xiii.

[31] Melissa Klapper, "Jewish Women and Vocational Education," pp. 113 - 146. See also Jenna Weissman Joselit, "Saving Souls: The Vocational Training of American Jewish Women, 1880 - 1926," in Jeffrey S. Gurock and Marc Lee Raphael, eds., *An Inventory of Promise: Essays in Honor of Moses Rischin* (Brooklyn, Carlson, 1995): 151 - 169.

[32] Klapper, "Jewish Women and Vocational Education," p. 117.

[33] "The Mizrachi Women Organization of America, 1932," (Yiddish) Mercaz Olami, 3n. Hagler.
[34] Gotsfeld to Goldstein, July 19, 1932.
[35] Gotsfeld to Goldstein, December 20, 1932.
[36] Alice H. Eagly and Blair T. Johnson, "Gender and Leadership Style," Psychological Bulletin 3:2 (1990) 233–256.
[37] Alice H. Egly, Steven J. Karrau, and Mona G. Makhijani, "Gender and the Effectiveness of Leaders: A Meta-Analysis (*Psychological Bulletin of The American Psychological Association, Inc.*, 1995), 117: 1, p. 126.
[38] according to studies summarized in Alice H. Egly, Steven J. Karrau, and Mona G. Makhijani, "Gender and the Effectiveness of Leaders: A Meta-Analysis (*Psychological Bulletin of The American Psychological Association, Inc.*, 1995), Vol.117, No.1, pp 126.
[39] Leibowitz, "As I Remember Her," p. 13.
[40] Gotsfeld to Goldstein, letters of 1932 and 1933, passim.

Notes to Chapter 3

[1] See Tova Sanhedrai, "As I Remember Her," in *As I Remember Her*, p.10.
[2] Norman Bentwich, *Jewish Youth Comes Home, the Story of Youth Aliyah, 1933 - 1943* (London: Victor Gollancz Ltd, 1944), p. 31.
[3] See David S. Wyman, *Paper Walls :America and the Refugee Crisis, 1938 – 1941* (University of Massachusetts Press, 1968), pp. 155 – 183.
[4] Norman Bentwich, *Fulfilment in the Promised Land*, 1917 – 1937 (London, The Soncino Press, 1938), p. 105.
[5] "Letter from Mrs. Haskell," *The Bulletin of the Mizrachi Women's Organization of America*, 1:2 (January, 1933):1
[6] Fradelle Haskell, "Our Achievement in Palestine," *The Bulletin of the Mizrachi Women's Organization of America* 1:6 (September, 1933) :1.
[7] See Levanon, "World Mizrachi Women's Organization," AANY p. 1.
[8] Luz. *Parallels Meet*, p. 114.
[9] Bessie Gotsfeld, "The Mizrachi Vocational Institution," *MJP*, English Section, pp. 77–82; Leona Goldfeld interview.
[10] See Anne Mendelson, *Stand Facing the Stove; the Story of the Women Who Gave America The Joy of Cooking* (New York: Henry Holt & Co, 1996), p.117.
[11] "Hennery" is apparently Gotsfeld's translation of the Hebrew word *lul*.
[12] Hannah Armon, "Bet Zeiroth Mizrachi" pamphlet, p. 16, CZA , S75\12
[13] See Bessie Gotsfeld, "The Mizrachi Vocational Institution," Part III.
[14] The undated fragment probably comes from a letter of 1935.
[15] See "Bet Zeirot file," CZA, S75\12.
[16] "Report of Meeting of Sept. 24th, 1936," ; "Summary of Article by Dr. Nehama Liebowitz on the Immigrant Girl in the Beth Zeiroth Mizrachi in Jerusalem," Papers and Reports, Historic, AANY; *The Mizrachi Woman* (May 1948): 19.
[17] See "Bet Zeirot Mizrachi," AABI.
[18] Gotsfeld to Goldstein, December 20, 1932 and n.d. (probably October, 1933).

Notes to Chapter 4

[1] Norman Bentwich, *Jewish Youth Comes Home, The Story of Youth Aliyah,* (London: Victor Gollancz Ltd, 1944), p. 35.

[2] Ibid, p. 50; Marlin Levin, *Balm in Gilead, The Story of Hadassah* (New Schoken Books, 1992) pp. 112 - 119; Chasya Pincus, *Come From the Four Winds; the Story of Youth Aliyah* (New York: Herzl Press, 1970), pp. 17 -18.

[3] See Marian G. Greenberg, "Joyful Mother of Children, Youth Aliyah Under Henrietta Szold," pp. 1-2, in RG1, Box 44, HA; and *There is Hope for Your Children: Youth Aliyah, Henrietta Szold and Hadassah* (New York: Hadassah, 1986), pp. 7 - 10.

[4] MZOA would take over some of the property for a new youth village, Mosad Aliyah. See below, chap. 9.

[5] Greenberg, *There is Hope for your Children*, p.12; Norman Bentwich, *Jewish Youth Comes Home*, pp. 51 - 52; Moshe Krone, "From Rotges to Yavneh," London: Bahad: September, 1945.

[6] See Henrietta Szold to Ella Blau, December 13, 1933, A125/112, CZA; Szold to Anita Müller-Cohen, December 19, 1933, 125/18, CZA; and Cohen to Szold, December 24, 1933, S75/12, CZA. (n.b. When I conducted my research in 2000, there were plans to reorganize these papers.)

[7] Mark A. Raider, *The Emergence of American Zionism* (New York: New York University Press, 1998.)

[8] The full text of Gold's speech is in the file "Religious Zionists of America," MS-NAT R35, Box 2, CZA.

[9] On the tactics employed by Mizrachi to force the decision, see Samuel Rosenblatt, "Mizrachi's Role after the Last Zionist Congress," in *MJV*, English Section, pp. 17 - 24. For Gotsfeld's pleased response, see her letter to Belle Goldstein, dated September 10, 1935.

[10] David Eliach, interview by author, October 1, 1998.

[11] See Szold to Anita Müller-Cohen, December 19, 1934, A125\18, CZA.

[12] Szold feared exploitation of the children in places with no outside supervision. See "Minutes of the Meeting Held with the *Jüdische Jugendhilfe* in Berlin on Tuesday, September 24, 1935", A125/112, CZA.

[13] Szold to Dr. J.L. Magnes, n.d., A125/112, CZA.

[14] Council for Preparing German Youth to Szold, December 24, 1933; Memo from Representatives of German Religious Youth (undated, in 1934 folder); Rabbi Dr. Isak Unna of Manheim to Dr. Chaim Weizmann, February 2, 1934. in S75/12, CZA.

[15] See Szold to Gotsfeld, February 8, 1934 and February 28, 1934, A125/112, CZA.

[16] Szold to Rose Jacobs, 9 March 1936, A125/112; Szold to Eva Stern, CZA, July 27, 1936, p. 1, 125/912, CZA; Szold to Jacobs, April 12, 1936, RG1/BOX 1/F66, HA.

[17] Gotsfeld to Goldstein, December 20, 1932.

[18] Devorah Rabinowitz Masovetsky, interview by author, Jerusalem, May 2, 2000. See also "Amit Chronology, Our Formative Years and the Holocaust," *Amit Magazine*, 1995.

[19] See files of "Mercaz Olami" 10/6, Hagler. (Files in this collection are not clearly delineted.) Other memos from the war years in the same archive register complaints that BZM was not receiving funding.

[20] Gotsfeld's underlined message, Gotsfeld to Goldstein, n.d. (1929.)

[21] Gotsfeld to Goldstein February 6, 1935.

²² Ibid.
²³ Gotsfeld, "The Mizrachi Vocational Institution," in *MJP*, English section, p. 77.
²⁴ Ibid, p. 82.

Notes to Chapter 5

¹ Izzie Troubin, Memoirs, misc., AANY.
² Gotsfeld to Goldstein, March 2, 1935. Dr. Judith Berlin was married to the renowned Talmud scholar and professor Saul Lieberman. In Jerusalem she taught at the Mizrachi Teachers' Training School. After settling in New York she became principal of the Shulamith School an Orthodox Girls' Yeshiva in Brooklyn.
³ Capital letters in text, Reports, AANY.
⁴ See Henrietta Szold to *Jüdische Jugendhilfe*, August 13, 1935, S75\62, CZA; "Minutes of the Meeting Held with the JJ in Berlin on Tuesday, September 24, 1935, A125\112, CZA; letters exchanged between Bessie Gotsfeld, Henrietta Szold and the *Jüdische Jugendhilfe* in S75\62, passim, CZA.
⁵ Jenny Thaustein, "As I Remember Her," p. 3.
⁶ Gotsfeld to Goldstein, September 10, 1935.
⁷ Goldfeld, "Bessie," p. 30.
⁸ Gotsfeld to Goldstein, April 14, 1936; June 15, 1936.
⁹ See long letter from Henrietta Szold to Olga Epstein, March 8, 1966, RG1\Box1\F66, HA; and Norman Bentwich, *Ben Shemen, A Children's Village in Israel* (Jerusalem: Jerusalem Post Press, n.d.).
¹⁰ See recapitulations of the charges in Szold to Rose Jacobs, March 1, 1936, RGI/Box 13/F66, HA; and a memo of March 9, 1936, A125/112, CZA; S.Z. Shragai to Ilsa Warburg, April 26, 1936, RGI/Box 13/F66, HA. The Hertz paraphrase is from Szold's letter to Jacobs, April 21, 1936 (response to March 3, 1936 letter) RGI/Box 13/F66, HA.
¹¹ Reiterated in several of Szold's letters. See RGI/Box 13/F66, HA.
¹² Shragai to Szold and Szold to Rose Jacobs, April 21, 1936, RGI/Box 13/F66, HA. "Kfar Hanoar Hadati" Mercaz Olami Progress Report, Bulletin #8, March, 1944, p. 11, Hagler.
¹³ Szold to Jacobs, April 21, 1936 (response to letter of March 27), RGI/Box 13/F66, HA.
¹⁴ See Szold to Eva Stern of the *Arbeitsgemeinschaft*, A125/912 July 27, 1936, CZA.
¹⁵ Szold to Olga Epstein, March 8, 1936, op. cit.
¹⁶ Henrietta Szold to Olga Epstein, March 8, 1936, RGI/Box 13/F66 HA.
¹⁷ "Hadassah Votes $15,000 to House Orthodox Youth," Hadassah News Release, May 11, 1936; Arbeitsausschuss für religioese Jugend-Aliyah to the Hadassah Organization, May 26, 1936; "Investments in Kfar Hanoar Hadati from 1937 - 1940," all in RGI/Box 13/F66, HA.
¹⁸ reported by Szold to the *Jüdische Jugendhilfe*, August 13, 1935, S75/62, CZA.
¹⁹ e.g. Meyer Berlin' to Mrs. Moses P. Epstein, July 3, 1936, , RG1/B1/F1 HA; Szold to *Jüdische Jugendhilfe*, May 15, 1933, S75/61, CZA.
²⁰ Szold to Jacobs, April 21, 1936. (response to letter of March 6.)
²¹ Gotsfeld to Goldstein December 1, 1935.
²² Gotsfeld to Goldstein, November 17, 1936.
²³ See Hadassah National Board Minutes, March 11, 1936, RG1\B13\f6, HA; and apologetic letter from Professor Ernst Simon to Sir Robert Waley Cohen, August 9, 1936 (copy), A125/912, CZA.

[24] Szold to Müller-Cohen, June 23, 1935, S75\61 CZA; Fishel is discussed in Jacobs to Szold, March 3, 1935 and Szold to Jacobs, March 1, 1936, both in RGI/Box 13/F66, HA.

[25] Szold to Eva Stern, July 27, 1936. Fishel is discussed in Szold's letter to Rose Jacobs, March 9, 1936. Both in RGI/Box 13/F66, HA.

[26] Hannah Armon learned horticulture from Eli Feuchtunger and joined Kibbutz Amunim. See her essay in a pamphlet commemorating a reunion of 1939 BZM Jerusalem graduates, n.d. "Bet Zeirot Mizrachi," S75/ CZA.

[27] This was Rose Jacobs' paraphrase of the argument responding to a MWOA representative, Mrs. L.V. Freudberg of Washington, D.C., February 18, 1936, RGI/Box 13/F66 HA.

[28] "Mizrachi-Hadassah Relations re Youth Aliyah," from Hadassah Board Minutes, March 11, 1936, HA\f66; See also Meir Berlin to Henrietta Szold, 25 Sivan, 1935 S75/160, CZA,.

[29] Rose Jacobs to Mrs. L.V. Freudberg, February 18, 1936; Rose Jacobs to Mrs. Abraham Shapiro, May 14, 1936; "Mizrachi-Hadassah Relations re Youth Aliyah in Hadassah National Board Meeting, March 11, 1936, all in RGI/Box 13/F66, HA.

[30] Rose Gell Jacobs to Henrietta Szold, March 3, 1936, RGI/Box 13/F66, HA.

[31] Szold to Jacobs, April 21, 1936 (response to March 6th letter.)

[32] Szold to Jacobs, April 21, 1936 (response to letter of March 3, 1936).

[33] Ibid.

[34] Gotsfeld to Goldstein, July 9, 1936.

[35] For the origins of the Meier Shfeyah Children and Youth Village, see Bentwich, *Jewish Youth Comes Home*, p. 33 and Levin, *Balm in Gilead*, p. 131. The village, founded in 1920, became a Junior Hadassah project during the 1930s.

[36] A letter from Szold to Judith Epstein, Acting President of Hadassah, discusses a meeting with Rabbi Berlin. He urged increased accommodation for religious children. RGI/Box 13/ F66, 4 pp, HA. Szold tried to see the rabbi many times, but rarely succeeded. For her opinion of his philosophy and methods, see Szold to Jacobson April 21, 1936 (response to March 3, 1936 letter).

[37] Jehuda Reinharz, "Zionism and Orthodoxy, A Marriage of Convenience" in *Zionism and Religion*, p. 130.

[38] Gotsfeld to Goldstein, June 15, 1936.

[39] I discussed contacts between Gotsfeld and Szold in "American Jewish Women in Palestine: Bessie Gotsfeld, Henrietta Szold, and the Zionist Enterprise," *AJH* 90:2 (June 2002) 141 – 160.

Notes to Chapter 6

[1] Gotsfeld to Goldstein, August 25, 1936.

[2] Masovetsky interview, May 29, 2000.

[3] On the Peel Commission, see Sachar, *A History of Israel* pp. 204-208.

4 Herman Hollander, *My Life and What I Did with It* (Jerusalem: Koren Publishers Jerusalem Ltd., 1979), p.58. For short biographies of Shragai and Shapiro, see Alfassi, Yitzhak, ed. *Torah V'Avodah, Vision and Deed: The History of Hapoel Hamizrachi, its Founders and their Performance, 5682 - 5692* (Hebrew) (Tel Aviv: Rosemarin 1985): 111, 191-2.

[5] Shlomo Zalman Shragai, *Tehumim* (Jerusalem: Mosad Ha-Rav Kuk) 1951. On Shragai's repuation as a Marxist, see Herman Hollander, *My Life*, pp. 58-9.

[6] See Meir Bar Ilan, "Achievements and Aspirations" in Yosef Tirosh, ed., *Religious Zionism, an Anthology* (Jerusalem: World Zionist Organization, 1975), p.108.

[7] See the pronouncements of annual Hapoel Hamizrachi conferences, in Yitzhak Alfassi,ed., *Torah V'Avodah,Vision and Deed: The History of Hapoel Hamizrachi, its Founders and their Performance* (Tel Aviv: Hapoel Hamizrachi, 1955), passim.

[8] Geula Bat-Yehudah, *Harav Maimon*, p. 320.

[9] Two family members interviewed by the author had different opinions of Gotsfeld's motives. The first summarized above, was the opinion of Leon Rauchwerger, husband of Bessie's niece Raizel, the second of her nephew Eliezer Goldman.

[10] See Melvin I. Urofsky, *American Zionism from Herzl to the Holocaust* (Lincoln: University of Nebraska Press, 1972), pp. 270-298.

[11] Gotsfeld to Goldstein, August 21, 1936.

[12] Gotsfeld to Goldstein, May 13, 1937.

[13] Ibid.

[14] Betty Gafni, "Bessie Gotsfeld , z"l ," *The American Mizrachi Woman* (1980): 8.

[15] This was Mira Bramson's personal experience. This whole section owes much to Mira Bramson and Judith Kallman, double interview by author, New Rochelle, New York, February 2, 1999.

Notes to Chapter 7

[1] Jacob was 17 or 18 years old at the time. The adventuresome lad set his heart on being the first in the family to greet Aunt Bessie. Jacob (known as Jack) was on his school's newspaper staff. With the aid of questionable press credentials from the school and innate huzpa, he managed to board the pilot boat sent to meet large ships entering the port of New York. J. Goldman, interview; B. Gotsfeld to Mendel Gotsfeld, June 25, 1939, AANY.

[2] Ibid. "Tillie …just breaks my heart. A beautiful flower downtrodden by a scoundrel." According to family members, Ben Shahan found another woman at the very time that he was becoming famous. After the divorce, Tillie, who supported their two children, became Executive Director of the Institute for Pacific Relations. She was to lose the position when it disbanded after investigation by the House Unamerican Committee. She was the only sibling who predeceased Bessie. (Leona Goldfeld and Jack Goldman inteviews).

[3] Sarah Shane, interview by author, Jerusalem, May 22, 2000.

[4] Jack Goldman, interview. Eliezer Goldman died on October 27, 2002.

[5] Sachar, *A History of Israel*, p. 226.

[6] from a one page excerpt from a letter in Misc, AANY.

[7] "Seattle Savors Its Memories," Misc., AANY.

[8] *Mosad L'Aliyah Bet*, founded in 1938 by the Histadrut, was the center for illegal Jewish immigration to Palestine.

[9] All quotations in this section are from Notes and Speeches, 1939, in AANY (The one with statistics must have been written in 1940.)

[10] Ibid.

[11] See "Hakibbutz Hadati," in *Encyclopedia of Zionism and Israel* (New York: Herzl Press/ McGraw-Hill, 1971), 1:452.

[12] "Mrs. Gotsfeld Addresses Her Co-workers," *Mizrachi Women's News* 8:3 (Pesach, 1941): 1.

[13] Ibid.

[14] Burg, "As I Remember Her," pp. 2 -3.

[15] Leibowitz, "As I Remember Her," p. 13.

[16] *Studies in the Weekly Sidra, 5721*, translated and adapted by Aryeh Newman. Jerusalem: Yehuda Press, 1961.

[17] I attended one of her Jerusalem courses during the academic year 1957–58, as did my daughter Rebecca in 1988-89.

[18] Burg, "As I Remember Her, " p. 2.

[19] See Katz's favorable assessment of Bessie Gotsfeld, entitled "Like a Jewish Mother Choosing a Chatan," in *As I Remember Her*, pp. 8-9.

Notes to Chapter 8

[1] File labeled "1942," AANY.

[2] Partial treatment of the Children of Teheran is found in Marlin Levin, *Balm in Gilead*, pp. 179 - 180 and Chasya Pincus, *Come from the Four Winds, the Story of Youth Aliyah* (New York, Herzl Press, 1970), chap. 2. Two studies devoted wholly to the subject are Devora Omer, *The Teheran Operation, The Rescue of Jewish Children from the Nazis* (Washington, D.C. : B'nai B'rith Books, 1991) and Ada Schein, *The Teheran Children Affair* [Hebrew] (Jerusalem: Hebrew University diss., 1991).

[3] Pincus, *Come from the Four Winds*, p. 70; Omer, *The Teheran Operation*, Chap. 12.

[4] Ibid, p. 85.

[5] See Laumberg's report, n.d. and Szold's report, "Child Refugees at Teheran," November 15, 1942, both in RG1/Box 2/F8, HA.

[6] In recent years Ben-Gurion has received criticism for lukewarm efforts to rescue European Jewry during World War II. In response to that calumny, Shabtai Teveth invokes the Teheran Children predicament. He points out that, having ascertained the murder of two million East European Jews, Ben Gurion asked Stanislaw Kot, who represented the Polish government-in-exile in the Middle East, for permission to outfit the Teheran teenagers and their leaders in Polish uniforms, thereby facilitating egress to Palestine through Iraq. Permission was denied. See *Ben-Gurion and the Holocaust* (New York: Harcourt Brace & Co., 1996), p.41.

[7] For details about the temporary children's camp or "Children's Home" near Teheran and Zipporah Sharett's role in it, see Schein, *The Teheran Children Affair*, chap.3, and Omer, *The Teheran Operation*, pp. 157 -214.

[8] The most complete English language account of the Teheran Children's Home and the journey to Palestine is found in Omer, The Teheran Operation. The book is based on recollections of the young director, David Laor (previously Laumberg, later Lt. Colonel Laor) and, to some extent, also his wife, Rachel Drexler Laor, who became an Israeli educator.

[9] Szold, "Child Refugees at Teheran," December 18, 1942, p. 1.

[10] (Loosely translated from the Hebrew.) "The Children of Teheran," Hanoar Hadati, Religious Youth Division, World Center, Mizrachi, Jerusalem, March, 1943. Y/T 2/8/1238, Hagler.

[11] See Szold, "Child Refugees at Teheran."

[12] An example of continuing anger in Orthodox circles over placement of the Teheran Children is Joseph Friedenson, *Dateline Istanbul*, (New York: ArtScroll, 1993) pp. 99 – 105.

[13] Correspondence between Szold and J. Alexander of Johannesburg (January 31, 1943); Chief Rabbi Herzog (February 1, 1943); Hadassah National President Tamar de Sola Pool (February 4, 1943), all in RG1/Box 2/F 13, HA.

[14] On contacts with the Polish government-in-exile, see Schein, *The Teheran Children Affair*, p. 88.

[15] See below, note 20.

[16] Bramson interview. (Mira Bramson, one of the Teheran refugees, ten years old in 1943, has a clear memory of the episode.)

[17] See Szold to Gisela Warburg, January 26, 1943, RG1/Box 2/F8, HA.

[18] Bramson interview.

[19] In the letter to Mr. J. Alexander of the South African Zionist Federation, January 31, 1943, RG1/Box 2/F8, HA.

[20] Isaac Halevi Herzog and Ben-Zion Meir Hai Uziel to David Ben-Gurion, 28 Sivan, 1943, YT 41/3, Hagler.

[21] The Aguda excoriated Mizrachi for its backsliding, calling its stand on the Children of Teheran "two-faced." *The Children of Teheran Accuse*, (Jerusalem: Agudat Israel, 1953), chap. 5. Y/T, Hagler.

[22] See "The Children of Teheran" report from Hanoar Hadati, March, 1943; 2/8/1238, Y/T, Hagler.

[23] This was never the position of Chief Rabbi Isaac Herzog, who argued that since Hitler destroyed the European yeshivas, it was up to the Jews of Palestine to reconstruct them. Herzog to Szold, February 1, 1943, RG1/Box 2/F8, HA. While the children were en route to Palestine, Rabbi Meyer Berlin sent a cable to Johannesburg Mizrachi objecting to Youth Aliyah's plans to place children in left- wing settlements and institutions rather than "spiritual education under auspices of Chief Rabbi Herzog." As head of Mizrachi, however, he accepted Youth Aliyah's recommendations after an additional Mizrachi member was added to Youth Aliyah's Central Committee in February 1943. Szold quoted the cable, dated December 20, 1942 in a letter to Tamar de Sola Pool, February 4, 1943), RG1/Box 2/F8, HA.

[24] See B.B. to Rabbis Meir Berlin and Ze'ev Gold, May 24, 1943, YT/ 48, Hagler.

[25] Szold to Mr. J. Alexander (Johannesburg), January 31, 1943, RG1/Box 2/F8, HA; Szold's acknowledgment of the receipt of the prayer books in a letter to the Mizrachi, dated 9 March, 1943. Y/T 48/3, Hagler.

[26] See Y.H. Farbstein (Mizrachi) and I.M. Levin (Agudat Israel) to Szold, 1 March 1, 1943, Y/T 48/1/949, Hagler.

[27] Out of a total of 70 madrikhim and child care workers, 25 came from Mizrachi and eight were from Agudat Israel. See "The Children of Teheran," report of Hanoar Hadati, op. cit.

[28] See *The Children of Teheran Accuse*, chap. 3. The entire correspondence that Agudat Israel carried on with rabbis and Youth Aliyah is included in this chapter.

[29] Months before the children arrived, Youth Aliyah determined to examine all aspects of their lives, including the religious affiliation of their parents. See Szold to J. Alexander of Johannesburg, January 31, 1943, p. 2. RG1/Box 2/F8, HA.

[30] Bramson interview; Schein, *The Teheran Children Affair*, chap. 3.

[31] See A. M. Gankhovsy to Mizrachi Central Committee, 18 Adar 1, 5703, Y/T, Hagler.

[32] That this was a precedent already in effect before the Children of Teheran's arrival is indicated in Szold's letter to Herzog, dated February 2, 1943, RG1/Box 2/F8, HA. She agreed to send two Hungarian boys who "declared their adherence to the Agudat Yisrael movement" to Agudah settlements, with prospects of their transferal to yeshivot.

[33] See Alexandra Lee Levin, ed., *Henrietta Szold and Youth Aliyah: Family Letters, 1934 - 1944* (NY: Herzl Press, 1986), pp. 64 – 68.

[34] See letter from "B.B." addressed to Rabbis Meir Berlin and Ze'ev Gold, 19 Iyar, 5703 (May 24, 1943), 48/1/1693, 1943, Hagler.

[35] Schein, *The Teheran Children Affair*, p. 85.
[36] B.B. addressed to Rabbis Meir Berlin and Ze'ev Gold, 19 Iyar, 5703 (May 24, 1943), 1943, 48/1/1693., 1943, Hagler.
[37] *The Children of Teheran Accuse*, chap. 5.
[38] Schein, *Teheran Children Affair*, pp. 111 - 122.
[39] Gotsfeld to Goldstein, July 2, 1936.
[40] Bessie Gotsfeld, "Palestine Committee Report," from "Proceedings of the 18th Annual Convention of the Mizrachi Women's Organization of America", November 8 – 10, 1943, p.49, AANY.
[41] Ibid. pp. 48-49. Italics in the text.
[42] Thaustein, "As I Remember Her," p. 6.
[43] Gotsfeld, "Palestine Committee Report," p. 50.
[44] Ibid, p. 49.
[45] Ibid. The capitals are in the text.
[46] See "Beit Zeriot Mizrachi, Jerusalem - 30 Years," AABI.
[47] e.g. M. Zaidel to Moshe Shapiro, 26 Tishrei 5704 (October 13,1943); Bessie Gotsfeld to Mercaz Olami (October 15, 1942), both in f. 42/43, Hagler.

Notes to Chapter 9

[1] Thaustein, "As I Remember Her". P 4 is missing, but its contents can be surmised by what follows on p. 5 and the other sources); "From Bessie Gotsfed z"l, a Letter written in 1943, Mizrachi Women's Program Plannning, 1973" 10:1, pp. 17–19; ; Joseph Nelson, "Recovering Beit Zeirot, Tel Aviv," in *Amit 72:3*,75th Anniversary Issue (Summer 2000): 14 - 15.
[2] "From Bessie Gotsfeld z"l, a Letter Written in 1943," reprinted in *Mizrachi Women Program Planning* X, (Sept-Oct., 1973): 1, AANY.
[3] Bessie Gotsfeld, "Palestine Committee Report," *Proceedings of the Eighteenth Annual Convention of the MWOA*, November 8 – 10, 1943, p. 54, Board Letters, AANY.
[4] See Sachar, *A History of Israel*, p. 230 and reports in *Davar* and *Mizrachi Women's News* (Pesach, 1941) :2.
[5] Gotsfeld to C. Gottlieb, October 17, 1945, AABI.
[6] See Gotsfeld's summary of Mizrachi Women's war work in her article "Rosh Hashonoh 5706, " *Mizrachi Woman* (September, 1945): 1.
[7] See "Establishment of Children's Village and Farm School Urged by Bessie Gotsfeld, Palestine Representative," in *News Bulletin* 2 [of MWOA] (March-April, 1944): 3-4.
[8] Sarah Herzog, "Rabbanit Sarah Herzog, Personal Recollections," unpublished mss. translated by Shoshanah-Dolgin Be'er, AABI.
[9] David Eliach, interview.
[10] David and Yaffa Eliach, double interview. On later re-emergence of Holocaust memories, see Pincus, *Come From the Four Winds*, especially the chapter entitled "Not One Child Cried," pp. 129 - 151.
[11] S. Deborah Ebin, "The Story of the Meshek Yeladim. The Children's Village & Farm School," n.d., Records, AANY.
[12] See Dvorah Rabinowitz, "Description of Projects of the Mizrachi Women Established and Maintained in Palestine," p. 5, Reports, AABI.
[13] Interview with Yoel Shiftan, Jerusalem, May 18, 2000.
[14] The original name was soon shortened to *Mosad Aliyah*. Years after Gotsfeld's death. It

was changed to *Kfar Hanoar Aliyah.*

[15] See "Activities in Israel of the Mizrachi Women's Organization of America, 5708 (1947-1948)" in AMR, p.6, AANY.

[16] Shiftan, interview.

[17] Ibid; notes from Shiftan sent to me via Shoshana Dolgin-Be'er, September, 2000.

[18] "Activities in Israel, 5608", p.6; Yaffa Eliach, interview. Eliach learned embroidery there and made a tablecloth for Gotsfeld.

[19] See "Palestine Diary," *The Mizrachi Woman*, Autumn 1946, p. 16.

[20] See Gotsfeld, "Too Many of Israel Have Perished," *Mizrachi Woman*, March 1945.

[21] Bessie Gotsfeld, "Analysis of Mizrachi Women's Projects in Palestine, 1945": New York, February 5, 1945, p.2, AMR, AANY.

[22] Mrs. Bessie Landau (National Secretary of MWOA) to Mr. B. Mindel, General Secretary of Mizrachi Federation of Great Britain and Ireland, May 4, 1946, AABI.

[23] Marlin Levin, *Balm in Gilead*, p. 135.

[24] See "Convention Call," in *Mizrachi Women's Bulletin* 11:1 (October 1949) p 1.

[25] See "Rabbanit Sarah Herzog."

[26] *Ha-Rabbanit,* (Emunah, National Religious Woman's Organization, Israel (Tel Aviv, Arieli Press, n.d.) p. 103; see letters in AABI.

[27] my emphasis.

[28] Unfortunately, I could not find the source of the statement.

[29] Joseph Burg to Meir Berlin, February 9, 1944, Hagler, 43\44.

[30] Judah Warshaver, "The Fruitful Work of Mizrachi Women in the Land of Israel;" Bessie Gotsfeld interview, *Der Mizrachi Weg* (Yiddish), December, 1945, pp. 2-3; (nameless) periodicals, Hagler.

[31] Gotsfeld to Berlin, July 3, 1944,10/6/1709, Hagler.

Notes to Chapter 10

[1] Letter from Eliezer Goldman, June 22, 2002.

[2] All the above quotes are from "Verbatim Report of Administrative Board Meeting with Mr. Moshe Shapiro, June 28, 1946," in Board Letters on Zionism, AANY.

[3] "Mrs. Rabinowitz' Report," Part II, July 1947. Reports, AANY.

[4] Gotsfeld to C. Gottlieb, October 17, 1945, AABI.

[5] Miram Chinowitz of Montevideo to Gotsfeld, August 8, 1946, AABI.

[6] Gotsfeld to Chinowitz, September 29, 1946, Idem.

[7] Ibid.

[8] Dvorah Rabinowitz, "Palestine Diary," July 2, 1946 in *The Mizrachi Woman* (Autumn, 1946): 18.

[9] Belle Goldstein, "A Rare Human Being," 1964, Records, AANY.

[10] Interviews with Dvorah Rabinowitz Masovesky, Teaneck, N.J., June 7, 1999 and Jerusalem, May 20, 2000; Esther Lopata retold the anecdote in "Vignettes from Besançon to Basel," *Amit* (Winter, 2000) : 33 -35.

[11] Dvorah Rabinowitz, "My Year in Erez Yisroel," *The Mizrachi Woman*, (Autumn, 1947): 10.

[12] "The Palestine Activities of the Mizrachi Women's Organization of America, Post-war Development," n.d., Reports, AANY.

[13] Ibid.

[14] Both quotations are from Gotsfeld, "'The Mizrachi Vocational Institution," in *MJV*, p. 77.

[15] See above, Chap. 3.

[16] Norman Bentwich, Ben-Shemen, a *Children's Village in Israel* (UNESCO, Études Pedagogiques #7, n.d.) pp. 29 - 30.

[17] A. L. Gellman, "A Noble Jewish Soul, " Bio., AANY.

[18] For the sake of clarity, I inserted quotation marks and bracketed words and changed incorrect orthography. Bessie Gotsfeld Memorial Meeting and Remembrance, BG Life, AANY.

[19] M. Ben Ury, "Memorandum concerning the plan for the "Children's Village in Raanana of MWOA," appended to Gotsfeld's letter to the MWOA's National Office in New York, February 18, 1945, AANY.

[20] Dvorah Rabinowitz, "My Year in Erez Yisroel," *The Mizrachi Woman* (Autumn, 1947): 11.

[20] Letter from Eliezer Goldman, June 22, 2002.

[20] All quotes are from "Verbatim Report of Administrative Board Meeting with Mr. Moshe Shapiro, June 28, 1946," in Board Letters on Zionism, AANY.

[20] Dvorah Rabinowitz, "My Year in Erez Yisroel," p. 11.

Notes to Chapter 11

[1] Dvorah Rabinowitz, "My Year in Eretz Yisroel," p. 10; "Children's Modern Village," *Palestine Post*, November 21, 1947, reprinted in *The Mizrachi Woman* 20:3 (January-February, 1948): 16-17. A report on the dedication ceremony is found on pp. 14 - 16.

[2] Ibid.

[3] Hollander, *My Life*, p. 181.

[4] When questioned about her choice of the cottage system, Gotsfeld had replied that some things take precedence over cost.

[4] See S. Deborah Ebin, "The Story of the Meshek Yeladim; the Children's Village & Farm School," in Reports, BZM, pp. 8-10, AANY; David Eliach interview; Rauchwerger double interview.

[5] *The Mizrachi Woman* (January-February, 1948): 16.

[6] M. Ben Ury, "Memorandum concerning the plan for the "Children's Village in Raanana." AABI.

[7] Rauchwerger double interview.

[8] See "The Bessie Gotsfeld Children's Village and Farm School, an Experiment in Democratic Living," n.d., in Gotsfeld Memorial Meeting and Remembrances, AANY; "Cornerstone Laying at the Bar Ilan School in Kfar Batya, Raananah," (one of the few Hebrew language articles in *Die Mizrachi Frau* xx:i (Autumn, 1949). For a later description, see Nathan Dasberg, "Twenty- Five Years of Religious Youth Aliyah." Jewish Agency: Youth Aliyah Department, Jerusalem, 1960, Hagler.

[9] This is what Yaffa Eliah told me. For a slight discrepancy, see the next note.

[10] David and Yaffa Eliach interview. Ben G. Frank, "A Graduate of Kfar Batya – Today a Scholar and Writer," *The American Mizrachi Woman*, May, 1975; Sarah Bronson," The Journey of Professor Jacob Klein," *Amit* 78:3 (Summer, 2006) 11-13. Yaffa Eliach (who prepared a stunning photograph exhibit of her Polish town for the Holocaust Museum in Washington) claims that she approached Gotsfeld with the proposal and six were admitted

while Klein recalls that the academic program was Enoch's idea and that he selected five.

[11] David Eliach interview.

[12] David and Yaffa Eliach interviews; Daniel Ventura "In Memory of our Teacher H. Z. Enoch," 1997, and "Hayim Tzvi Enoch," unsigned typescripts (Hebrew), AA BI.

[13] This section is based upon MWOA reports, 1947 - 8 in AANY and AABI; and interviews with David and Yaffa Eliach, Raizel and Leon Rauchwerger, Leona Goldfeld, Judith Kallman, Mira Bramson, and Jacob Goldman.

[14] See Belle Goldstein, "Bessie Gotsfeld - A Profile," in *The Mizrachi Woman*, (January - February, 1948) : 8.

[15] See idem, p. 23 for a copy of the invitation to the dedication dinner.

[16] Goldfeld interview.

[17] Leona Goldfeld and Eliezer Goldman, interviews; Goldfeld; "Bessie," pp. 35 – 38. (The quote is from p. 38).

[18] Gotsfeld to Fanny Meyer of Montevideo, March 22, 1948 , AABI,.

[19] Fritz Goldschmidt (director of Motza Children's Home), "Motza Diary," *The Mizrachi Woman* (August 1949): 4-5, 24-26; Goldfeld, "Bessie," p. 44.

[20] Gotsfeld to Meyer of Montevideo, June 6, 1948, AABI.

[21] In a letter dated April 6, 1948, Gotsfeld informed Meyer that deliberations were scheduled to began that day.

[22] Bessie Gotsfeld, "Palestine Diary," *The Mizrachi Woman* 20:5 (June-July, 1948): 4.

[23] See Knohl, Dov, ed. *Siege in the Hills of Hebron, the Battle of the Etzion Bloc* (New York and London; Thomas Yoseloff, 1958.) Especially enlightening is a "Postscript" written by Yigael Yadin, pp. 365 – 37. Yadin was Chief of Operations in the General Staff during the War of Independence. Israelis, some with personal connections to the original settlers, returned to rebuild the area after the 1967 war.

[24] Excerpt from Gotsfeld's address at the Mizrachi Women's 1948 National Convention, transcribed in *The Mizrachi Woman* 20 (December, 1948): 10; Gotsfeld to Fanny Meyer, supra, n. 17.

[25] *The Mizrachi Woman* 21 (January 1949): 17.

[26] *The Mizrachi Woman* 20 December, 1948): 10

[27] In letter to Hava Cohen, national president of MWOA, dated January 5, 1948, Sarah Herzog complained that MWOA had not supplied promised funds, probably due to Mendel Gotsfeld's illness. The letterhead included Bessie Gotsfeld in the trio of vice-presidents, AABI.

[28] Sanhedrai, "As I Remember Her," pp.10 – 11.

[29] This was the argument advanced by Miriam Eliash, Sanhedrai's lieutenant. See "Report of Negotiations with Mercaz, Re: *Hamoezet Hapoalot* and MWOA, Given by Mrs. Lionel Golub at Meeting of Administrative Board, September 29th, 1948," p. 2, Board Letters on Zionism, AANY.

[30] See Dr. H. Raphael Gold, "The Religious Psychology of Zionism," *MJP*, English Section: 67-69.

[31] Goldstein to Gotsfeld, June 5, 1948, AANY.

[32] "Report of Negotiations," p. 3; "Memorandum on Relationship, pp. 1-2; Masovetsky interview.

Notes to Chapter 12

[1] See "Mrs. Rabinowitz' Reports," Parts 1 and 2, July, 1947, Papers and Reports, Historical, AANY.

[2] Goldfeld, "Bessie," p. 38.

[3] Bramson interview. Mira Bramson, who lived, studied, and worked in BZM Tel Aviv during the early 50s, never saw Bessie Gotsfeld in person.

[4] e.g. Gotsfeld to Mollie Golub, February 14, 1960, AANY.

[5] From a Mizrachi circular "Yours to Quote," PRH, AANY.

[6] Gotsfeld to Golub, December 12, 1959 and February 14, 1960

[7] Bramson interview.

[8] Bramson and Kallman interviews. The expansion and renaming of the Jerusalem school as "The Esther and David Shapiro High School" took place in 1952. BZM Tel Aviv was transferred to the Wolf and Julia Eisenberg Comprehensive High School in 1975, thirteen years after Gotsfeld's death. Today the name "Bet Zeirot" is confined to Amit's social service institutions for girls. In 1981 Amit was declared an official Reshet (network) of Israel's religious, technical secondary education.

[9] *Mizrachi Womam* 22:1 (Autumn, '49): 1.

[10] Gotsfeld to Ben Monte Sinai, February 9, 1950, AABI.

[11] Gotsfeld to Betty Hanan and Esther Aron , April 20, 1950, AABI.

[12] Yoel Shiftan's address at "Bessie Gotsfeld Memorial Meeting in Israel," July 19, 1974, BG Passing, AANY.

[13] as Gotsfeld told Blu Genauer (later Greenberg, interviewed by author, January 23, 2002), during her student visit to Israel during the 1955 – 56 academic year.

[14] *The Mizrachi Woman* 20:1 (Autumn, 1947): 2.

[15] See "Analysis of Mizrachi Women's Projects in Palestine, " probably 1944, AMW, AANY.

[16] See Ethel K. Lipshitz, "Palestine Diary," *The Mizrachi Woman*, Jan-Feb., 1948.

[17] See Susan Gopstein, "The Faith of Leeuwarden," *The Jerusalem Post*, October, 1990. Ilan Ramon, the Israeli astronaut who perished in the Columbia Shuttle disaster of January 2003, carried a miniature Torah scroll that Rabbi Dasberg, Natan's father, had given Yoachim Yosef on the occasion of his secret bar mitzvah ceremony in Bergen-Belsen. Rabbi Dasberg, Sr. died two months later. Yoachim Yosef survived the war and become a physicist in Tel Aviv. Before Ramon's departure, he handed the treasured scroll to the astronaut. Sadly, it suffered the same fate as its original owners.

[18] Bessie Gotsfeld To Mollie Golub, passim,1958 – 1962, AANY.

[19] Bessie Gotsfeld, Address to National Board, November 21, 1950; Letter to MWOA, November 28, 1950, BG Life AANY.

[20] Harry Truman appointed Mrs. Clark in 1949 to that position, where she would remain until 1953. Notice of the award was sent to Molly Golub at the MWOA office. PRH, AANY.

[21] For the text of Gotsfeld's keynote address at the 27th National Convention, held on November 9, 195; see the Appendix.

[22] Shmuel Abraham, "Remembering the Ethiopian Jews of Kfar Batya, 1986, AABI; Sarah M. Averick, "A Miracle Revisited," *Amit* 69:2 (Winter, 1996): 12 –16, 38 – 40.

[23] Moshe Shapiro to Rabbanit Cohen, Jerusalem, April 30, 1956, Board Letters on Zionism, AANY.

[24] Dolgin-Be'er, "The Rabbanit", pp. 103, 107.

[25] See my article "American Jewish Women in Palestine", passim.

[26] For text of the 1959 address, see the Appendix.

[27] Ilka Bestoff, telephone interview by author, Jerusalem, May 25, 2000.

[28] Hollander, *My Life*, pp. 145 – 172.

[29] Kallman interview.

[30] Dinah Dyckman, interview by author, New York City, April 21, 2002.

[31] Ibid.

[32] Hollander, *My Life*, p. 180.

[33] Gotsfeld to Golub, n.d., 1959. She calls the man Rabbi Passau. In 1983 the Jewish Theological Seminary of America published a list of graduates of all its schools to that date ("The Seminary Register, Part II.) No Rabbi Passau appears on the list. He may have been one of a number of rabbis ordained in Orthodox institutions who served Conservative congregations.

[34] See Leo Jung, "Modern Trends in Judaism," in *MJP*, English Section, p. 38.

[35] Mrs. Samuel Goldstein to Mrs. Miram Mainz, October 22, 1945, AABI; Goldfeld, Bessie, "Selective Chronology" in "Bessie."

[36] Gotsfeld to Golub, July 23, 1961.

[37] Ibid.

[38] Idem, Aug. 4, 1961.

[39] *The Mizrachi Woman* (January, 1961): 5.

[40] Gotsfeld to Golub, July 5, 1961.

[41] Belle Goldstein survived her friend for many years. She made news in 1998 when, at age 100 she immigrated to Israel with her daughter Leona Goldfeld. (As noted above, her daughter Raisel Rauchwerger was long resident there). She died on September 10, 2001 and was buried on the fateful day now known as 9\11.

[42] Letter from Eliezer Goldman.

[43] Ibid; Goldfeld, "Bessie," p. 39.

[44] papers in BG Life, AANY.

[45] Golfeld, "Bessie", p. 40.

Notes to Chapter 13

[1] Jernny Thaustein "As I Remember Her;" p. 3; Genauer, interview; Shiftan, interview.

[2] related to me by an Amit member in the Jerusalem Amit Office, May 21, 2000.

[3] Stogdill, , R. M. (1948), pp. 35-71.

[4] Thaustein, pp. 6 – 7.

[5] Shiftan, Interview.

[6] Thaustein, "As I Remember Her", pp. 6 – 7.

[7] Gotsfeld to Goldstein, September 3, 1929.

[8] 1959 Address.

[9] Gotsfeld to Goldstein, November 20, 1939.

[10] Bessie Gotsfeld to Mendel Gotsfeld, November 22, 1939 AANY.

[11] Henrietta Szold to Mrs. Brodie, April 10, 1913, Henrietta Szold Papers, Box I, f29, Jewish Historical Society of Maryland.

[12] See Appendix.

[13] 1952 Address.

[14] Notes from a 1939 speech, From Notes and Speeches, Gotsfeld Speeches, AANY.
[15] 1952 Address .
[16] See Bessie Gotsfeld, "Rosh Hashonoh, 5706," in *The Mizrachi Woman* (September, 1945): 21; Shiftan, interview.
[17] 1959 Address.
[18] This is S. Zalman Abramov's translation of Rabbi Meir Berlin's slogan in *Perpetual Dilemma*, p. 68.

Notes to Chapter 14

[1] Eagly, Karau, and Makhijani, "Gender and the Effectiveness of Leaders: A Meta-Analysis," pp. 125 –145.
[2] Masovetsky, interview, June, 2000.
[3] Herman Hollander, *My Life* , p. 182. Hollander's friendship with Moshe Shapiro probably influenced his perception of Gotsfeld.
[4] Shiftan, "Gotsfeld Memorial Meeting," AABI.
[5] Gotsfeld Passing, AANY; Shiftan interview.
[6] Shftan, interview
[7] See Gerda Lerner, *The Creation of Patriarchy* (New York: Oxford University Press, 1986) pp. 212- 213.
[8] Gotsfeld to Goldstein, passim.
[9] Shiftan, "Gotsfeld Memorial Meeting."
[10] Naomi Greenberg Cohen, "Verbatim Report," MWOA National Board Meeting, June 24, 1947, AABI.
[11] See cablegrams in AABI.
[12] From a 1939 speech, Notes and Speeches, AANY.
[13] Gotsfeld to Madam Huskin, Secretary, Santiago Organizacion Mizraji Femenina, July 20, 1947, AABI.
[14] Alfred Bandura, " Self-Efficiency: Toward a Unifying Theory of Behavioral Change," *Psychological Review* 84:2 (1977): 191-215.
[15] Faith Rogow, "National Council of Jewish Women," in *Jewish Women in America, an Historical Encyclopedia (*New York, 1997): II:968.

Notes to Appendix

[1] in PRH, AANY.
[2] This sentence, not in the original typescript, was added later.
[3] This paragraph was also added later.
[4] In material for publicity, there follows a list of accomplishments and new needs to accommodate the expanding schools and children's farms. It was at this point that BZM Jerusalem was transformed into the Esther Shapiro Vocational High School for Girls.
[5] This sentence was also added.
[6] in PRH, AANY
[7] Capital letters in the text.

Index

About the Author

Baila Round Shargel is a native of Baltimore, Maryland, and a graduate of Goucher College and the Baltimore Hebrew College. In 1982 she received a doctorate in Jewish history at the Jewish Theological Seminary. She teaches at Manhattanville College.

A social and cultural historian with a concentration in American Jewish history and Zionism, she has written dozens of essays, among them the seminal "Evolution of the Masada Myth." Her previous books are *Practical Dreamer: Israel Friedlaender and the Shaping of American Judaism (1985)*; *The Jews of Westchester, a Social History(1994)*; and *Lost Love: the Untold Story of Henrietta Szold (1997)*.

Marvin Fox
*Collected Essays on Philosophy and on Judaism, Volume One:
Greek Philosophy, Maimonides*, 2003.

*Collected Essays on Philosophy and on Judaism, Volume Two:
Some Philosophers*, 2003.

*Collected Essays on Philosophy and on Judaism, Volume Three:
Ethics, Reflections*, 2003.

Zev Garber
Methodology in the Academic Teaching of Judaism, 1986.

Zev Garber, Alan L. Berger, and Richard Libowitz
Methodology in the Academic Teaching of the Holocaust, 1988.

Abraham Gross
*Spirituality and Law: Courting Martyrdom in Christianity and
Judaism*, 2005.

Harold S. Himmelfarb and Sergio DellaPergola
Jewish Education Worldwide: Cross-Cultural Perspectives, 1989.

William Kluback
*The Idea of Humanity: Hermann Cohen's Legacy to Philosophy
and Theology*, 1987.

Samuel Morell
Studies in the Judicial Methodology of Rabbi David ibn Abi Zimra,
2004.

Jacob Neusner
Amos in Talmud and Midrash, 2006.

*Ancient Israel, Judaism, and Christianity in Contemporary
Perspective*, 2006.

The Aggadic Role in Halakhic Discourses: Volume I, 2001.

The Aggadic Role in Halakhic Discourses: Volume II, 2001.

The Aggadic Role in Halakhic Discourses: Volume III, 2001.

Analysis and Argumentation in Rabbinic Judaism, 2003.

Analytical Templates of the Bavli, 2006.

Ancient Judaism and Modern Category-Formation: "Judaism," "Midrash," "Messianism," and Canon in the Past Quarter Century, 1986.

Canon and Connection: Intertextuality in Judaism, 1987.

Chapters in the Formative History of Judaism. 2006

Dual Discourse, Single Judaism, 2001.

The Emergence of Judaism: Jewish Religion in Response to the Critical Issues of the First Six Centuries, 2000.

First Principles of Systemic Analysis: The Case of Judaism within the History of Religion, 1988.

The Halakhah and the Aggadah, 2001.

Halakhic Hermeneutics, 2003.

Halakhic Theology: A Sourcebook, 2006.

The Hermeneutics of Rabbinic Category Formations, 2001.

Hosea in Talmud and Midrash, 2006.

How Important Was the Destruction of the Second Temple in the Formation of Rabbinic Judaism? 2006.

How Not to Study Judaism, Examples and Counter-Examples, Volume One: Parables, Rabbinic Narratives, Rabbis' Biographies, Rabbis' Disputes, 2004.

How Not to Study Judaism, Examples and Counter-Examples, Volume Two: Ethnicity and Identity versus Culture and Religion, How Not to Write a Book on Judaism, Point and Counterpoint, 2004.

How the Halakhah Unfolds: Moed Qatan in the Mishnah, ToseftaYerushalmi and Bavli, 2006.

How the Halakhah Unfolds: II. Nazir in the Mishnah, Tosefta, Yerushalmi, and Bavli. Part A. Mishnah Tractate Nazir. Tosefta Tractate Nazir. Yerushalmi Tractate Nazir, 2006.

How the Halakhah Unfolds: II. Nazir in the Mishnah, Tosefta, Yerushalmi, and Bavli. Part B. Bavli Tractate Nazir. Yerushalmi-Bavli Nazir Systematically Compared. Nazir Viewed Whole, 2006.

How the Halakhah Unfolds: III. Abodah Zarah in the Mishnah, Tosefta, Yerushalmi, and Bavli. Part A. Mishnah Tractate Abodah Zarah. Tosefta Tractate Abodah Zarah. Yerushalmi Tractate Abodah Zarah, 2006.

How the Halakhah Unfolds: III. Abodah Zarah in the Mishnah, Tosefta, Yerushalmi, and Bavli. Part B. Bavli Tractate Abodah Zarah. Yerushalmi-Bavli Abodah Zarah Systematically Compared. Abodah Zarah Viewed Whole, 2006.

The Implicit Norms of Rabbinic Judaism. 2006.

Intellectual Templates of the Law of Judaism, 2006.

Is Scripture the Origin of the Halakhah? 2005.

Israel and Iran in Talmudic Times: A Political History, 1986.

Israel's Politics in Sasanian Iran: Self-Government in Talmudic Times, 1986.

Jeremiah in Talmud and Midrash: A Source Book, 2006.

Judaism in Monologue and Dialogue, 2005.

Major Trends in Formative Judaism, Fourth Series, 2002.

Major Trends in Formative Judaism, Fifth Series, 2002.

Messiah in Context: Israel's History and Destiny in Formative Judaism, 1988.

Micah and Joel in Talmud and Midrash, 2006.

The Native Category - Formations of the Aggadah: The Later Midrash-Compilations - Volume I, 2000.

The Native Category - Formations of the Aggadah: The Earlier Midrash-Compilations - Volume II, 2000.

Paradigms in Passage: Patterns of Change in the Contemporary Study of Judaism, 1988.

Parsing the Torah, 2005.

Praxis and Parable: The Divergent Discourses of Rabbinic Judaism, 2006.

Rabbi Jeremiah, 2006.

Reading Scripture with the Rabbis: The Five Books of Moses, 2006.

The Religious Study of Judaism: Description, Analysis and Interpretation, Volume 1, 1986.

The Religious Study of Judaism: Description, Analysis, Interpretation, Volume 2, 1986.

The Religious Study of Judaism: Context, Text, Circumstance, Volume 3, 1987.

The Religious Study of Judaism: Description, Analysis, Interpretation, Volume 4: Ideas of History, Ethics, Ontology, and Religion in Formative Judaism, 1988.

Struggle for the Jewish Mind: Debates and Disputes on Judaism Then and Now, 1988.

The Talmud Law, Theology, Narrative: A Sourcebook, 2005.

Talmud Torah: Ways to God's Presence through Learning: An Exercise in Practical Theology, 2002.

Texts Without Boundaries: Protocols of Non-Documentary Writing in the Rabbinic Canon: Volume I: The Mishnah, Tractate Abot, and the Tosefta, 2002.

Texts Without Boundaries: Protocols of Non-Documentary Writing in the Rabbinic Canon: Volume II: Sifra and Sifré to Numbers, 2002.

Texts Without Boundaries: Protocols of Non-Documentary Writing in the Rabbinic Canon: Volume III: Sifré to Deuteronomy and Mekhilta Attributed to Rabbi Ishmael, 2002.

Texts Without Boundaries: Protocols of Non-Documentary Writing in the Rabbinic Canon: Volume IV: Leviticus Rabbah, 2002.

A Theological Commentary to the Midrash - Volume I: Pesiqta deRab Kahana, 2001.

A Theological Commentary to the Midrash - Volume II: Genesis Raba, 2001.

A Theological Commentary to the Midrash - Volume III: Song of Songs Rabbah, 2001.

A Theological Commentary to the Midrash - Volume IV: Leviticus Rabbah, 2001.

A Theological Commentary to the Midrash - Volume V: Lamentations Rabbati, 2001.

A Theological Commentary to the Midrash - Volume VI: Ruth Rabbah and Esther Rabbah, 2001.

A Theological Commentary to the Midrash - Volume VII: Sifra, 2001.

A Theological Commentary to the Midrash - Volume VIII: Sifré to Numbers and Sifré to Deuteronomy, 2001.

A Theological Commentary to the Midrash - Volume IX: Mekhilta Attributed to Rabbi Ishmael, 2001.

Theological Dictionary of Rabbinic Judaism: Part One: Principal Theological Categories, 2005.

Theological Dictionary of Rabbinic Judaism: Part Two: Making Connections and Building Constructions, 2005.
Theological Dictionary of Rabbinic Judaism: Part Three: Models of Analysis, Explanation, and Anticipation, 2005.

The Theological Foundations of Rabbinic Midrash, 2006.

Theology of Normative Judaism: A Source Book, 2005.

Theology in Action: How the Rabbis of the Talmud Present Theology (Aggadah) in the Medium of the Law (Halakhah). An Anthology, 2006

The Torah and the Halakhah: The Four Relationships, 2003.

The Unity of Rabbinic Discourse: Volume I: Aggadah in the Halakhah, 2001.

The Unity of Rabbinic Discourse: Volume II: Halakhah in the Aggadah, 2001.

The Unity of Rabbinic Discourse: Volume III: Halakhah and Aggadah in Concert, 2001.

The Vitality of Rabbinic Imagination: The Mishnah Against the Bible and Qumran, 2005.

Who, Where and What is "Israel?": Zionist Perspectives on Israeli and American Judaism, 1989.

The Wonder-Working Lawyers of Talmudic Babylonia: The Theory and Practice of Judaism in its Formative Age, 1987.

Jacob Neusner and Ernest S. Frerichs
New Perspectives on Ancient Judaism, Volume 2: Judaic and Christian Interpretation of Texts: Contents and Contexts, 1987.

New Perspectives on Ancient Judaism, Volume 3: Judaic and Christian Interpretation of Texts: Contents and Contexts, 1987.

Jacob Neusner and James F. Strange
Religious Texts and Material Contexts, 2001.

David Novak and Norbert M. Samuelson
Creation and the End of Days: Judaism and Scientific Cosmology, 1986.
Proceedings of the Academy for Jewish Philosophy, 1990.

Risto Nurmela
The Mouth of the Lord Has Spoken: Inner-Biblical Allusions in Second and Third Isaiah, 2006.

Aaron D. Panken
The Rhetoric of Innovation: Self-Conscious Legal Change in Rabbinic Literature, 2005.

Norbert M. Samuelson
Studies in Jewish Philosophy: Collected Essays of the Academy for Jewish Philosophy, 1980-1985, 1987.

Benjamin Edidin Scolnic
Alcimus, Enemy of the Maccabees, 2004.

If the Egyptians Drowned in the Red Sea Where are Pharaoh's Chariots?: Exploring the Historical Dimension of the Bible, 2005.

Baila Shargel
Female Leadership in the American Jewish Community, 2007.

Rivka Ulmer
Pesiqta Rabbati: A Synoptic Edition of Pesiqta Rabbati Based upon all Extant Manuscripts and the Editio Princeps, Volume III, 2002.

Manfred H. Vogel
A Quest for a Theology of Judaism: The Divine, the Human and the Ethical Dimensions in the Structure-of-Faith of Judaism Essays in Constructive, 1987.

Anita Weiner
Renewal: Reconnecting Soviet Jewry to the Soviet People: A Decade of American Jewish Joint Distribution Committee (AJJDC) Activities in the Former Soviet Union 1988-1998, 2003.

Eugene Weiner and Anita Weiner
Israel-A Precarious Sanctuary: War, Death and the Jewish People, 1989.

The Martyr's Conviction: A Sociological Analysis, 2002.

Leslie S. Wilson
The Serpent Symbol in the Ancient Near East: Nahash and Asherah: Death, Life, and Healing, 2001.